Philosophy as a Humanistic Discipline

Philosophy as a Humanistic Discipline

Bernard Williams

Selected, edited, and with an introduction
by A. W. Moore

PRINCETON UNIVERSITY PRESS
PRINCETON AND OXFORD

Library of Congress Cataloging-in-Publication Data

Williams, Bernard Arthur Owen.
Philosophy as a humanistic discipline / Bernard Williams ; selected,
edited, and with an introduction by A.W. Moore.
p. cm.
Includes bibliographical references.
ISBN-13: 978-0-691-12426-1 (alk. paper)
ISBN-10: 0-691-12426-4 (alk. paper)
1. Philosophy. I. Moore, A.W., 1956– II. Title.
B29.W493 2006
101–dc22   2005043029

British Library Cataloging-in-Publication Data is available.

This book has been composed in Sabon

Printed on acid-free paper. ∞

pup.princeton.edu

Printed in the United States of America

10   9   8   7   6   5   4   3   2   1

Contents

Preface

Patricia Williams

It is sad, but appropriate, that my final, practical gesture of appreciation and love for Bernard should be to help with the publication of the last three collections of his philosophical writings. *The Sense of the Past: Essays in the History of Philosophy*, *Philosophy as a Humanistic Discipline*, and *In the Beginning Was the Deed: Realism and Moralism in Political Argument* will be published by the Princeton University Press three years after his death in June 2003. Bernard helped and encouraged me in countless ways in my publishing career, bearing out my conviction that editors in university presses should be judged by their choice of advisers as well as by the authors they publish.

Like many who knew him, I thought Bernard was indestructible—and so, I think, did he! But when he was recovering from the drastic effects of his first bout of treatment for cancer in 1999, we talked for the first, and almost the only, time about what should happen to his papers if he could not finish *Truth and Truthfulness*. Thankfully, he published it in 2002, although he would have expanded it in several ways if time had not seemed so pressing. What I learned from this conversation was that Bernard had no faith in his, or any philosopher's, ability to predict whose work would be of any lasting interest to their successors. That was for the future to decide. So, although he was totally against what he called posthumous "laundry lists," he refused to express any other opinion about what should be published after his death. Fortunately for me, he did specify that, although I should handle the practicalities of publishing as I thought fit, he would ask "a young philosopher of gritty integrity and severity of judgement who understood the sorts of things he had been trying to do in philosophy" to keep me on the philosophical straight and narrow. That was Adrian Moore. I am deeply grateful to him for the careful consideration he has given to the complicated, general issues of publication and re-publication, and for his friendship. He is the sole architect of this particular volume.

My heartfelt thanks, also, to Walter Lippincott, the Director of the Princeton University Press, and his staff in Princeton and Oxford, whose commitment to Bernard as an author and to high standards of editing, design, production, and marketing is so valuable at a time when scholarly publishing faces complex financial challenges.

Finally, I should like to acknowledge the publishers who have kindly given their permission to publish material in this volume.

1. "Tertullian's Paradox." Reprinted with permission of Scribner, an imprint of Simon & Schuster Adult Publishing Group, from *New Essays in Philosophical Theology*, ed. Anthony Flew and Alasdair MacIntyre. Copyright © 1955 by Anthony Flew and Alasdair MacIntyre.

2. "Metaphysical Arguments" in *The Nature of Metaphysics*, ed. D. F. Pears (London: Macmillan, 1957). Reproduced with permission of Palgrave Macmillan.

3. "Pleasure and Belief" in *Proceedings of the Aristotelian Society*, suppl. vol. 33 (Oxford: Blackwell, 1959).

4. "Knowledge and Reasons" in *Problems in the Theory of Knowledge*, ed. G. H. von Wright (The Hague: Nijhoff, 1972). © 1972 by Martinus Nijhoff, The Hague, Netherlands. With kind permission of Springer Science and Business Media.

5. "Identity and Identities" in *Identity*, ed. Henry Harris (Oxford: Oxford University Press, 1995). By permission of Oxford University Press.

6. "The Primacy of Dispositions" in *Education and Values: The Richard Peters Lectures*, ed. Graham Haydon (London: University of London Institute of Education, 1987).

7. "The Structure of Hare's Theory" in *Hare and Critics: Essays in Moral Thinking*, ed. Douglas Seanor and N. Fotion (Oxford: Oxford University Press, 1988). By permission of Oxford University Press.

8. "Subjectivism and Toleration" in *A. J. Ayer: Memorial Essays*, ed. A. Phillips Griffiths (Cambridge: Cambridge University Press, 1992).

9. "The Actus Reus of Dr. Caligari" in *University of Pennsylvania Law Review* 142 (1994).

10. "Values, Reasons, and the Theory of Persuasion" in *Ethics, Rationality, and Economic Behaviour*, ed. Francesco Farina, Frank Hahn, and Stefano Vannucci (Oxford: Oxford University Press, 1996). By permission of Oxford University Press.

11. "Moral Responsibility and Political Freedom" in *Cambridge Law Journal* 56 (Cambridge: Cambridge University Press, 1997).

12. "Tolerating the Intolerable" in *The Politics of Toleration in Modern Life*, ed. Susan Mendus (Durham: Duke University Press, 2000).

14. "Political Philosophy and the Analytical Tradition" in *Political Theory and Political Education*, ed. Melvin Richter (Princeton: Princeton University Press, 1980).

15. "Philosophy and the Understanding of Ignorance" in *Diogène* 169 (1995). Also published in English by Berghahn Books, Oxford.
16. "Philosophy as a Humanistic Discipline" in *Philosophy* 75 (Cambridge: Cambridge University Press: 2000).

Introduction

A. W. Moore

Bernard Williams (1929–2003) was one of the greatest twentieth-century British philosophers. His work, which was unusual in its range, was always marked by an equally unusual combination of rigour, imagination, and depth, as well as by a thorough humanity. The essays published here bear copious witness to these and other facets of his extraordinary intellect.

Between them they span Williams's entire career. Essay 1, "Tertullian's Paradox," was his first publication. It appeared half a century ago. Essay 13, "The Human Prejudice," was given as a lecture shortly before he died.

Williams himself brought out three collections of essays during his lifetime: *Problems of the Self*,[1] *Moral Luck*,[2] and *Making Sense of Humanity*.[3] He did preparatory work on a fourth, in the history of philosophy, and this, supplemented by a few other pieces, including some pieces on Nietzsche, which he had intended to be part of another work, is published posthumously under the title *The Sense of the Past*.[4] A fifth collection, consisting of hitherto largely unpublished essays on politics, which together roughly chart a projected book on politics for which he left behind a sketch, is also published posthumously, under the title *In the Beginning Was the Deed*.[5] The present collection, which does not overlap with any of these, in effect completes the set.

It does not, however, contain everything that it might have contained. There remain both published and unpublished essays by Williams that have never been anthologized and that I have not included here, either because they overlap with other published work of his or because they were too occasional. (I say a little more about this in a note on the selection at the end of this introduction.)

---

[1] *Problems of the Self: Philosophical Papers 1956–1972* (Cambridge: Cambridge University Press, 1973).

[2] *Moral Luck: Philosophical Papers 1973–1980* (Cambridge: Cambridge University Press, 1981).

[3] *Making Sense of Humanity and Other Philosophical Papers 1982–1993* (Cambridge: Cambridge University Press, 1995).

[4] *The Sense of the Past: Essays in the History of Philosophy*, ed. Myles Burnyeat (Princeton: Princeton University Press, 2006).

[5] *In the Beginning Was the Deed: Realism and Moralism in Political Argument*, ed. Geoffrey Hawthorn (Princeton: Princeton University Press, 2005).

In the prefaces to his own collections Williams cites similar grounds for excluding material. But he also cites thematic grounds. In the preface to *Problems of the Self* he writes, "I have left some papers out on grounds of subject matter (what is here all relates to two or three themes)." This means that one of the virtues of the present collection is that it provides a welcome opportunity to reprint early essays by Williams on topics about which he otherwise wrote very little; essays in which we find some of the finest examples of his analytical dexterity and his clarity of vision.

Not that the present collection is a farrago. There is a unity of concern that runs throughout Williams's career which prevents it from being that. One of the reasons why I have appropriated the title of Essay 16 for the collection is that it precisely expresses this unity of concern. Williams's way of conducting philosophy is always profoundly self-conscious, in the sense that, even when he is not explicitly reflecting on the character of the discipline, his work is informed by an acute sense both of its possibilities and of its limitations; both of how to exploit its potential as a humanistic discipline and of how to curb its pretensions to be anything else.

To give a better sense of what I mean by this, I will begin by saying something about the three groups into which the essays are divided. I eventually resisted the temptation to give these groups the labels "Hard Philosophy," "Soft Philosophy," and "Meta-Philosophy"—though I think that the very absurdity of these labels, combined with the fact that they do, in their own crude way, convey what is intended, would have appealed to Williams. One function that these labels would certainly have served is that of highlighting how the first two groups map the terrain of ground-level philosophical enquiry while the third provides a bird's-eye view of that terrain. But there are many dangers that the labels would have incurred, of which the danger of depreciating the second group is merely the most obvious. Another—or rather, a danger that the grouping already incurs and that the labels would have exacerbated—is that of suggesting that the divisions between the groups are much sharper than they are. Several of the essays would not have been out of place in different groups. For that reason, among others, I toyed with dispensing with the grouping altogether and presenting the essays purely chronologically. What is striking is how little difference this would have made. The list as it stands is within a few minor adjustments of being purely chronological. This seems to me significant.

As Williams advanced from the "harder" enterprise of trying to make sense of our thought and experience in general, to the "softer" enterprise of trying to make sense of our ethical thought and experience, he became increasingly self-conscious about what claim philosophy had to be worth serious attention when the magnitude of its questions was not just the magnitude of sheer generality, characteristic of metaphysics, but the magnitude which is (or should be) characteristic of ethics: the magnitude of *importance*.[6] Williams was never prepared simply to take for granted the relevance of abstract rational argument to important questions. In *Ethics and the Limits of Philosophy*, whose very title of course speaks volumes, he began with what may be the most important question of all, the question of how one should live, and made clear from the outset how little we should expect from philosophy with respect to this question: help in understanding it, perhaps; an answer to it, certainly not. (It is one of the ironies of Williams's moral philosophy that, while it serves as a glorious illustration of how much moral philosophy can achieve, it is devoted in large part to determining how little moral philosophy can achieve.) Small wonder, then, that the self-consciousness that had always been at least implicit in Williams's work should have become more and more explicit as his philosophical interests became more and more concrete, until eventually one of his chief concerns was neither with any of the great "hard" questions of philosophy nor with any of the great "soft" questions of philosophy, but with the nature and prospects of philosophy itself.

I should say straight away that, although this way of characterizing the evolution of Williams's work has something almost Hegelian about it—with its suggestion of a growth in self-consciousness actualized through an ever more concrete concern with the realities of ethical experience—any resemblance to the Hegelian world spirit is purely coincidental. One thing, certainly, is clear. However affronted, discomforted, or amused Williams might have been by being associated with Hegel in this way, he would have strenuously resisted any implication that his work was an endeavour to attain something that merits the title "absolute knowledge."

Not that he denied the possibility of such a thing. On the contrary, it is one of the best known and most fiercely contested of his philosophical views that something meriting the title "absolute knowledge" is possible, namely knowledge "which is to the largest possible extent independent of the local perspectives or idiosyncrasies of enquirers."[7] (This definition, though less demanding than others that have been ventured, is still pretty demanding. It excludes, for instance, any knowledge that depends in some essential way on sensory apparatus that is peculiar to certain enquirers, say our knowledge that grass is green. Our concept of greenness, linked as it is to our visual apparatus, "would not be available to every competent observer of the world.")[8] But although Williams believed that such absolute knowledge is possible, he also believed that, if it is to be attained

---

[6] For a discussion of this idea of importance, see *Ethics and the Limits of Philosophy* (London: Fontana, 1985), pp. 182 ff.

[7] Essay 16, p. 184.

[8] *Ethics and the Limits of Philosophy*, p. 139.

anywhere, then it is to be attained in science. It is not to be attained in philosophy. That is one of the principal contentions of the eponymous essay in this collection, Essay 16.

This extraordinary piece serves as a kind of manifesto for Williams's conception of his own life's work. It is here that he most explicitly addresses the question of what philosophy can and cannot contribute to the project of making sense of things. He denies that philosophy can issue in absolute knowledge because he denies that it is even an objective of philosophy—as it is, in his view, an objective of science—to issue in absolute knowledge. But, he insists, the objectives of philosophy are simply different, not inferior. He cleverly identifies the latent scientism in those who, in a show of anti-scientism, deny that even science can issue in absolute knowledge; but who do so with a wistfulness, or with a sense of relief concerning any potential comparison with their own non-scientific endeavours, or indeed in defiant reaction to the arrogance of science, thereby betraying their conviction that, if only science *could* issue in absolute knowledge, then it could achieve the holy grail of any intellectual activity. From each, Williams urges, its own. What philosophy can most quintessentially contribute to the project of making sense of things is whatever it can contribute to the project of making sense of *being human*; and that is not a contribution that is best served by abstracting from "the local perspectives or idiosyncrasies" of human beings.

These ideas about absolute knowledge constitute one of Williams's most significant legacies. But they have been seriously misunderstood, and misrepresented, by countless critics. In this piece (Essay 16) Williams unpicks some of the misunderstandings. In particular he scotches the surprisingly common misunderstanding that, in championing the idea of absolute knowledge, or the idea of an absolute conception of the world as he sometimes puts it, he is championing the idea of a conception without concepts. (He never explicitly advocates any such absurdity; but that is what his idea is often reckoned to come to.) One source of this misunderstanding is the thought that any set of concepts must involve its own distinctive principles of assimilation and discrimination, which must reflect certain concerns and interests, which must in turn depend, to some non-minimal extent, on certain local perspectives and idiosyncrasies. But it is precisely this last step that Williams repudiates. An absolute conception is not a conception without concepts. It is a conception with concepts of a special kind.

A somewhat subtler misunderstanding is that Williams is championing the idea of a conception with concepts by whose means, and only by whose means, "the facts can directly imprint themselves on our minds, without need of mediation by anything as historically conditioned and open to dispute as canons of good and bad scientific argument."[9] Any such mediation is again thought to implicate local perspectives and idiosyncrasies. But why? Unless "directly" is interpreted in a way that begs all manner of questions, there is nothing in Williams to suggest that the facts need imprint themselves on our minds any more directly when we conceive of them in absolute terms than when we conceive of them in any other way. The concepts involved in an absolute conception are still concepts, and they mediate in whatever way concepts do mediate between the facts and our minds; while knowledge which is not absolute is still knowledge, and any knowledge, or at least any propositional knowledge, can be said, however pleonastically, to be knowledge of the facts.

This last point deserves elucidation. Propositional knowledge, to borrow Williams's own definition in Essay 4, "Knowledge and Reasons," is "knowledge whose paradigmatic expression in language-users is the confident assertion of truths, and where the claim that it is knowledge that is being expressed involves as a necessary condition that what is asserted is true."[10] This excludes such "practical" knowledge as my knowledge of how to tie my shoelaces, whose paradigmatic expression is my actually tying them. On the other hand, it includes plenty of knowledge which is not absolute, such as (to revert to the earlier example) my knowledge that grass is green. And unless "fact" is understood in some specially ambitious way, "truths" in Williams's definition can be replaced by "facts" and "is true" by "is a fact," which is as much as to say that any item of propositional knowledge is knowledge of some fact.

Williams says nothing, then, to suggest that absolute knowledge involves peculiarly unmediated access to the facts. In particular, he says nothing to suggest that such knowledge can be attained without mediation by canons of good and bad scientific argument. True, canons of good and bad scientific argument are "historically conditioned," just as other parts of our intellectual life are. This is something that Williams himself would be the first to insist, as indeed he does in Essay 16. He reminds us that scientific concepts have a history. The point, however, is that their history is "part of the history of discovery."[11] The advance from one set of scientific concepts to another, or from one canon of good and bad scientific argument to another, can be seen from both the earlier perspective and the later perspective as just that: an advance. It is an improvement.

---

[9] This is a quotation from John McDowell, "Critical Notice of *Ethics and the Limits of Philosophy*," in *Mind* 95 (1986): 380.

[10] P. 47.

[11] P. 189.

This is one of the many respects in which scientific concepts differ from concepts of another kind that we frequently use to report the goings-on around us: what Williams has famously dubbed "thick" ethical concepts.[12] The idea of a thick ethical concept is another of Williams's most significant legacies. It is of great importance to him: witness the fact that it features in no fewer than seven of the essays in this collection (though not always with that label). By a thick ethical concept, Williams means a concept which (unlike a scientific concept) has an evaluative aspect—but which also (unlike a "thin" ethical concept such as that of wrongdoing, which in Williams's view cannot serve, in any straightforward way, to "report" anything) has a factual aspect. Thus to apply a thick ethical concept in a given situation is, in part, to appraise the situation, but it is also to say something straightforwardly false if the situation turns out not to be a certain way. An example is the concept of infidelity. If I accuse you of being unfaithful, I thereby censure you; but I also say something that I am obliged to retract if it turns out that you have not in fact gone back on any relevant agreement. Other examples are the concepts of blasphemy, chastity, courage, and sloth.

The differences that Williams recognizes between scientific concepts and thick ethical concepts are reflected in differences that he recognizes between scientific beliefs and ethical beliefs. He holds that scientific beliefs enjoy a kind of objectivity which ethical beliefs lack. This is connected to the prospect of our reaching principled agreement about scientific issues, or, as Williams sometimes puts it, of our *converging* in our scientific beliefs,[13] as opposed to the prospect of our reaching principled agreement about ethical issues or converging in our ethical beliefs. But the view is not that, whereas we can reasonably expect to do the former, we cannot reasonably expect to do the latter. Still less is it that we do sometimes do the former but never do the latter. Nor does it have to do with whether or not, where there *is* convergence, the beliefs in question constitute knowledge. It has to do with the different ways of explaining whatever convergence there is.

Williams's view is as follows. People sometimes converge in their ethical beliefs, and those beliefs sometimes constitute knowledge. This can happen precisely when the beliefs in question involve a thick ethical concept. Thus people who embrace the concept of blasphemy might have no difficulty in agreeing, and indeed in knowing, that a certain work of art, say, is blasphemous. The crux, however, lies in what is involved in their embracing the concept of blasphemy in the first place. Granted the concept's distinctive combination of evaluation and factuality, embracing it

---

[12] See, e.g., *Ethics and the Limits of Philosophy*, p. 140.
[13] See, e.g., ibid., p. 135.

is part of living in a particular social world, a world in which certain things are prized and others abhorred. People need to live in some such social world. But, as history amply demonstrates, there is no one such social world in which people need to live. They certainly do not need to live in a world that sustains the concept of blasphemy. Thus any good reflective explanation for why people converge in their beliefs about what is blasphemous must include a social-scientific explanation for why they embrace the concept of blasphemy at all; why they live in *that* social world. This explanation cannot itself invoke the concept of blasphemy, because it must be from a vantage point of reflection outside the social world in question. So it cannot conform to the schema "These people converge in their beliefs about *x* because they are suitably sensitive to truths about *x*." That is, it cannot represent them as agreeing about what is blasphemous because of insights that they have into what is blasphemous. By contrast, a good reflective explanation for why people converge in their beliefs about what (say) nitrogen is like, to take a standard scientific example, *can* itself invoke the concept of nitrogen and hence, provided that the beliefs have been arrived at properly, *can* conform to the schema specified above. It can represent these people as agreeing about what nitrogen is like because of insights that they have achieved into what nitrogen is like; because of what they have discovered about nitrogen.

This is of course a variation on the theme that ethical knowledge is dependent on "the local perspectives or idiosyncrasies of enquirers," whereas scientific knowledge may not be. Which ethical concepts people embrace is certainly part of what determines their local perspectives and idiosyncrasies. A good reflective explanation for how people have the ethical knowledge they have must therefore include an explanation for how they have some of the local perspectives and idiosyncrasies they have; and it cannot do this unless it detaches itself from those perspectives and idiosyncrasies. By contrast, a good reflective explanation for how people have the scientific knowledge they have, where such knowledge may be absolute, need not involve the same kind of indirection.

These reflections on reflection bring us back to the question of philosophy. Philosophy, clearly, involves reflection. And reflection, in turn, involves detachment. What degree of detachment is appropriate in any given exercise of reflection is commensurate with the aim of the exercise. (In the case that we have just been considering, where the aim is an explanatory one, and where various local perspectives and idiosyncrasies are themselves the explicanda, the requisite degree of detachment, at least from those local perspectives and idiosyncrasies, is total.) Very well; what degree of detachment is commensurate with any of the multifarious objectives of philosophy? Not, given what was said above, the absoluteness to which scientists might aspire. But enough, in many cases, for our thick ethical concepts to cease to be among the items that we think with and to come to be among the items that we think about, as indeed they just have done. The project of making sense of being human requires recognition that our thick ethical concepts are contingent phenomena, whose histories typically do nothing to vindicate them, whose contributions to our lives are continually being modified by all sorts of shifting social forces, and whose very futures may be open to question[14]—and which therefore, though they may be able to support certain kinds of objectivity in our ethical thinking, are unable, for reasons that we have just been considering, to support others.

The problem, as Williams emphasizes in Essay 16, is that this can be very unsettling. Becoming aware of the frailty of our thick ethical concepts, and of the existence of alternatives, can loosen our grip on them. Moreover, since some philosophical objectives demand less detachment than this, indeed little enough for us to retain our grip on our thick ethical concepts and to think critically and imaginatively *with* them, it follows that there is a certain tension within philosophy itself. This is a tension to which Williams's work has constantly returned. It is related to one of the tensions to which he says, in the postscript to *Ethics and the Limits of Philosophy*, the argument of that book constantly returns: the tension between reflection and practice.[15] There is, contending with the disengagement that makes it possible for our ethical thought and practice to become objects of enquiry in this way, the engagement that makes it possible for us to have any ethical thought and practice at all, an engagement grounded in what Williams has variously identified as commitment,[16] conviction,[17] and confidence.[18]

It is a commonplace that self-consciousness and self-confidence do not go easily together. Williams's insights take us beyond that commonplace in various ways. One of these is by locating the same uneasy relationship in the domain of the social. Another is by locating it in the domain of thought, specifically ethical thought. And a third is by setting it in the context of a pluralism of values. For there are, in Williams's view, competing goods here. Reflection is a good, as is famously stated, if perhaps overstated, in Socrates' dictum that the unexamined life is not worth living.[19] And confidence is a good, without which there would not be any

---

[14] I take it that the relevance to this of the title of the Gauguin painting used as a cover illustration for *Moral Luck*, namely *D'où Venons Nous . . . Que Sommes Nous . . . Où Allons Nous?*, is no accident.

[15] *Ethics and the Limits of Philosophy*, p. 197.

[16] Essay 16, pp. 192–93.

[17] *Ethics and the Limits of Philosophy*, pp. 168–70.

[18] Ibid., pp. 170–71.

[19] Plato, *Apology* 38a.

such thing as living a life, or not in any interesting non-biological sense. But neither of these goods is a supreme good. Each consumes the other. Each "has a price, and the price should not be set too high."[20]

How to balance these goods is itself a practical question, and properly addressing the question itself requires a suitable balance of reflection and confidence. It is largely because of Williams's awareness of this that his work in philosophy has always been informed by such an acute sense of its possibilities and limitations, its potential benefits and its potential dangers. This is especially clear in Essay 16, and in the other essays in the third group, where precisely what Williams is doing is reflecting on philosophy. But there is evidence of it throughout the collection, where Williams is also of course a practitioner, and where his practice is marked, not by an indiscriminate confidence in philosophy, but by a confidence in what he himself succeeds in producing: philosophy at its best.[21]

Note on the Selection

There are essays by Williams, both published and unpublished, that I have not included in this collection even though they do not appear in any of his other collections. I have excluded them on various grounds:

- overlap with the essays that I have included (for example, I have excluded several essays on toleration, large chunks of which appear verbatim in Essay 12, "Tolerating the Intolerable");
- overlap with, or supersedence by, other published work by Williams (for example, I have excluded several essays which are in effect early drafts of chapters in *Truth and Truthfulness*,[22] or whose principal ideas have been incorporated into that book);
- being too occasional (for example, I have excluded several essays which are direct responses to other people's work and which would make too little sense in isolation).

A full list of Williams's published essays, including all those that I have excluded, appears in the bibliography at the end of this collection. (This bibliography also includes a list of Williams's reviews, only a few of which have so far been anthologized. A separate volume of these may appear at a later date.)

---

[20] *Ethics and the Limits of Philosophy*, p. 170.

[21] I am very grateful to Miranda Fricker, Geoffrey Hawthorn, Ian Malcolm, and especially Patricia Williams for their advice and encouragement.

[22] *Truth and Truthfulness: An Essay in Genealogy* (Princeton: Princeton University Press, 2002).

All but two of the essays published here have been published before (though many of them were relatively inaccessible).[23] The two exceptions are Essay 13, "The Human Prejudice," and Essay 17, "What Might Philosophy Become?", which was delivered as the inaugural lecture for the Centre for Post-Analytic Philosophy at the University of Southampton.[24] The origins of the remaining essays are given in the acknowledgements section at the end of the preface.

[23] They are published here exactly as they originally appeared, except for some minimal standardization and the correction of minor errors (which I have signalled whenever the correction seemed to me anything other than routine). I am very grateful to Lauren Lepow, senior editor at Princeton University Press, for her help in identifying these errors.

[24] There is a published German translation of this essay under the title "Die Zukunft der Philosophie," in *Deutsche Zeitschrift für Philosophie* 48 (2000).

PART ONE

Metaphysics and Epistemology

ONE

Tertullian's Paradox[1]

> Non pudet, quia pudendum est . . . prorsus credibile est, quia
> ineptum est . . . certum est, quia impossibile.
> —Tertullian, de carne Christi, v.

(1) This paper does not deal directly either with Tertullian or with his paradox. In considering the most famous and most widely misquoted of Tertullian's paradoxes, I do not try to explain it, still less to explain it away; but take it as the starting-point and end of a discussion of religious language and of its relations to theology and to the kind of philosophical inquiry with which this book* is principally concerned. In particular, I try to bring out a certain tension, a pull between the possible and the impossible, a sort of inherent and necessary incomprehensibility, which seems to be a feature of Christian belief, and to locate this point of tension more exactly within the structure of the belief. This tension Tertullian seems to have felt very strongly, and characteristically proclaimed it with vigour; but it is only by this rather thin string that my remarks are tied to what Tertullian said, the strict interpretation of which would require something quite different.

As the path of this paper is rather circuitous, a rough map may help. After stating the paradox (2), I go on to a short discussion of paradoxes in general, their uses and demands (3). I then leave Tertullian for a while, and attempt to show some features which distinguish religious, or at least Christian, language from other kinds of language (4); this is done by pre-supposing the existence of God, which may seem a rather peculiar procedure for a sceptic, but which will, I hope, serve for a discussion which tries to show something about religious language as used by believers. The thesis is then proposed that Christian belief must involve at least one statement which is about both God and the world, and that this statement must be partly incomprehensible—which I hold to be suggested by Tertul-

---

[1] This paper, substantially in its present form, was read in May 1954 to the Oxford University Socratic Club; I should like to express my gratitude to the Chairman of that club and the editor of its publication, the *Socratic Digest*, for allowing the paper to be printed here.

* This is a reference to Anthony Flew and Alasdair MacIntyre, eds., *New Essays in Philosophical Theology* (London: SCM Press, 1955), in which Williams's essay first appeared.—Ed.

lian's paradox, if given its head (5). Some remarks are then made on theology, and its relations to religious language and to the philosophy of religious language; these raise considerations that stop an incipient discussion of the incarnation, and suggest some rather disheartening conclusions about both the philosophy of religious language and theology (6). I end (7) with some observations about faith and about what one may or may not be said to believe on faith.

Tertullian's paradox I represent as a paradox both about Christian belief and about theology, but it is the former that is the more important point. In both cases I consider it as a paradox about meaning rather than about truth; that is, it is with questions of what is being said in religious language that I am concerned, rather than with questions of whether what is said is true, although the two sorts of question are not (and cannot be) kept clinically apart.

(2) Tertullian, the first Latin father of the Church, started his career as a lawyer and ended it as a heretic. After his conversion from heathenism in 196 he remained for only five or ten years a member of the Orthodox Church; both then and after his lapse into the Montanist heresy, he produced a series of theological works remarkable for vigorous reasoning, an unabashed use of legalistic rhetoric against his opponents, and an intransigent acceptance of paradoxical conclusions. The paradox I want to discuss comes from a work entitled *de carne Christi* which he wrote in the year 208, '*libris*', as the *Patrologia* (*Vit. Tert.*) elegantly puts it, '*iam Montanismam redolentibus*'—'at a time when his writings were already stinking of Montanism'—but the work is not itself, I believe, heretical. He is attacking Marcion, who believed that Christ was not actually born of the flesh, but was a 'phantasma' of human form. Marcion's refusal to believe in a genuine incarnation, Tertullian argues, could come only from a belief either that it would be impossible, or that it would be unworthy, a shameful degradation of the divine nature. Against the view that it would be impossible he produces the sweeping and general principle '*nihil impossibile Deo nisi quod non vult*'—'nothing is impossible for God except what he does not wish to do'. In particular Marcion had argued that the idea of the incarnation of God involved a contradiction, because being born as a human being would involve a change in the divine nature;[2] but a change involves ceasing to have some attributes and acquiring others; but the attributes of God are eternal; therefore he cannot change; therefore he could not have been born as a human being. Against this Tertullian says that this is to argue falsely from the nature of temporal objects to the nature of the eternal and infinite. It is certainly

----

[2] For a similar argument see Ch. XI below—Editors. [This is a reference to C. B. Martin, "The Perfect Good."—Ed.]

true of temporal objects that if they change they lose some attributes and acquire others; but to suppose that the same is true of God is just to neglect the necessary differences between God and temporal objects (*de c. C.* iii). (I shall in section (6) of this paper say something about this, perhaps not immediately convincing, argument.) Finally, against the view that, even if it were possible, God could not wish to be incarnated, because it would be unworthy of him, Tertullian, summing up his objections to Marcion in a passage of great intensity, accuses him of overthrowing the entire basis of the Christian faith: his argument would destroy the crucifixion and the resurrection as well. 'Take these away, too, Marcion,' he says (*ibid.*, v), 'or rather these: for which is more unworthy of God, more shameful, to be born or to die? . . . Answer me this, you butcher of the truth. Was not God really crucified? And as he was really crucified, did he not really die? And as he really died, did he not really rise from the dead? . . . Is our whole faith false? . . . Spare what is the one hope of the whole world. Why do you destroy an indignity that is necessary to our faith? What is unworthy of God will do for me . . . the Son of God was born; because it is shameful, I am not ashamed: and the Son of God died; just because it is absurd, it is to be believed; and he was buried and rose again; it is certain, because it is impossible.' '*Non pudet, quia pudendum est . . . prorsus credibile est, quia ineptum est . . . certum est, quia impossibile*': that is Tertullian's paradox.

(3) People who express themselves in paradoxes are in a strong position; and the more outrageous the paradox, in general the stronger the position. For an objector who insists on pointing out the absurdity of what has been said is uneasily conscious that he is making a fool of himself, for all he is doing is pointing out that the paradox is paradoxical, and this was perfectly obvious already: he is like a man who has missed the point of a joke or an ironical remark or an imaginative comparison, and insists on taking it literally. But ironical remarks and imaginative comparisons can have their point, and so can paradoxes; so it will not do, either, for the objector to dismiss the paradox in the hope that its evident absurdity makes it unworthy of discussion; for this is again to suggest that the person who uttered the paradox had overlooked its absurdity, but on the contrary he knew that it was absurd, and that was one reason why he uttered it. Because people do not in general utter absurdities unless they make a point by doing so, it is felt that the paradoxographer must have been saying something important. He not only prevents the critics answering, but makes them feel that in some mysterious way he is in a better position than they are; he is rather like a normally well-dressed man who appears at a function in a black tie and tails: the others present can't mention it to him, they can't overlook him, and they feel uneasy about their own turn-out. Or, again, he is something like a man

who firmly closes a door in one's face: not only preventing one from going on, but making one feel one has no right to.

So far the paradoxographer has everything on his side, but it is not entirely so. For, as the man in the black tie, to make his effect, has usually to be well-dressed, and the man who closes the door has to be someone one respects, so the paradoxographer has to have some other claim on the attention of his audience: for in general a paradox, however suggestive in itself, does not represent solid earnings—it draws a little on yesterday's credit or mortgages a little of tomorrow's. This claim on one's attention can be possessed in various ways: positively, by the utterer being a good and impressive and genuine person whose life commands love and respect, or by other utterances of his being original and profound; and negatively, by other conflicting, or apparently conflicting, claims on our attention being confused and unhelpful, or made by persons whose way of life seems trivial, evil or disastrous. If this is so, we might expect to find the beliefs of a religion, for instance, being put forward with a particularly defiant paradoxicality in two sorts of situation: first, when its believers are intensely bound together by a new and compelling faith, and fighting for survival in a hostile but decaying society whose beliefs they utterly reject; and second when, whatever the divisions and discredit that have fallen on the belief itself, those who reject it, their own hopes perishing, seem to have little to offer in its place except *angst*, tyranny or imminent thermonuclear annihilation.

This, however, so far as it goes, suggests only why people, and in particular religious believers, should tend at one time rather than at another to express themselves in paradoxes; it says little about why anyone should ever at all choose to speak in paradoxes, or suggests at most that they do this as a striking way of getting people to listen to or consider something else. Often it is not much more: to say, for instance, that the Holy Roman Empire was not Holy, nor Roman, nor an Empire, is, or should be, a brisk way of preparing for a new historical analysis. But there are other paradoxes which seem more important and significant; where to grasp the paradox seems an essential part of understanding what is being said. Here we have the feeling that a paradox, granted that it has to be understood against a background of other beliefs or a way of life, itself tells us something: that it is in a certain way the essence of what is to be believed. This is particularly so in the case of religious beliefs, where the feeling has itself been expressed in many ways: perhaps by saying, that there is an infinity of things that are beyond our comprehension; or that our reason cannot embrace the deepest truths; or that what we say can only be an unsatisfactory (or, perhaps, analogical) account of what we believe on faith. I shall try to show how such a point of tension, of failure of language, must occur in religious belief, and I think, therefore, that we should take Tertullian's paradox seriously; not as just a rhetorical expression of his objections to a particular doctrine, but as a striking formulation of something which I shall suggest is essential to Christian belief.

(4) There has been much discussion in recent years of religious language and its relations to other types of language; a good deal of this discussion has been concentrated on religious *statements*, and a good deal of this on the one statement 'God exists'. I think it is now time to consider whether such concentration has not been too narrow: for in each respect it has had undesirable results. First, there is an unclarity in the idea of a language—meaning by this, of course, not a national or dictionary language, such as French or Esperanto, but a logically distinguishable language or type of discourse. Second, the concentration on religious statements, as distinct from other types of religious utterance, has produced a string of disruptive effects: it has overemphasized the difference between the apparently unfalsifiable religious statement and the falsifiable statement of the sciences, which is indeed important and will appear later in what I have to say, but which taken by itself leads to an *impasse* which looks a little like a reduplication in linguistic terms of the barren nineteenth-century dispute between science and religion; and efforts to get out of this *impasse* have involved, in some cases, attempts to reduce statements of religion to statements of something else, for instance, of mystical experience, and in others attempts to reduce statements of religion to other things that are not statements at all, such as commands or exhortations to a religious way of life—all of which either involve an evident circularity or omit the peculiarly religious character of the statements altogether. Third, there has been the concentration on the logic of the particular statement 'God exists'; this shows a kind of hopeless courage. It shows courage because this statement seems to be the lynch-pin of the whole system: to uncover what is involved in believing this should be to uncover the whole nature of religious language and the essence of religious belief. But it is just the peculiar importance of this statement that makes hopeless an inquiry that starts with it. Its peculiarity is such that it is extremely untypical of religious statements; a peculiarity emphasized by Collingwood, for instance, when he said that it was not a religious statement at all, but rather the presupposition of any religious statement. We might say that the statement of God's existence has indeed great logical power, but that it is the power not so much of a lynch-pin as of a lever: if we knew, from outside the religious system, how to work with it, we might move heaven and earth; but from outside we do not, because we know neither where we may fix a fulcrum nor where we can insert the other end of the lever. So rather than attempt such a direct approach, we must obey the Boyg, and go round.

I cannot hope to go far round, but perhaps something can be said. First, then, I think we must always bear in mind the fact that religious language is not used just for making statements, but that there are many other kinds of religious utterance: commands, for instance ('Thou shalt not take the name of the Lord thy God in vain'), and, very importantly, prayers, and expressions of trust ('Though he destroy me, yet will I wait for him'), and promises, and reprimands, and many others. Furthermore, none of these utterances, including the statements, is made *in vacuo*: sometimes they are used as part of a religious ceremony or observance, sometimes as part of a religious person's deciding what to do in a practical situation; and generally as part of the activities of life. This as a general point is one constantly emphasized by Wittgenstein; and in considering religious language it is, I think, particularly disastrous to ignore it.

But what is religious language? Is there one thing which is religious language? With what is it being contrasted? One thing, certainly, with which we must be wary of contrasting or comparing it is that nebulous and pervasive substance, 'ordinary language'. For one thing ordinary language should be the language used by most of us in going about our ordinary occasions, and the question of how religious that is, is the question of how religious or professedly religious most of us are; and if some of us all of the time, and most of us most of the time, do not bring talk about God into our affairs, that seems to be at least as much something about us as something about talk about God. This raises the question of dispensing with talk about God, of what is involved in doing without it; and about that I shall later say a little.

So one might ask, 'What are in general the distinguishing marks of a language, of a type of discourse?'; and in attempting an outline of an answer, one can think at once of at least five possible distinguishing marks. For one language might be distinguished from another by the types of logical relation holding within it; by its subject-matter; by its use of technical terms; by its purposes; or, more generally, by the activities with which its use is associated. But it would, of course, be an illusion to suppose that these five, even if they were satisfactorily distinguished one from another, would be competitors for the position of the one and only distinguishing mark of one language from another; it is rather that from the inter-relation of features like these we can, in particular cases, justifiably claim to distinguish one type of discourse from another. Which of these features one would particularly consider is a question partly of at what level the distinctions are being drawn. If we concentrate on distinctions between the sciences, at a low level of generality, we tend to fasten on distinctions of subject-matter, for we all learn at school that mycology is the study of fungi, and geology the study of rocks, and so on. But it is clear that in doing this we presuppose already a distinction between scientific and other discourse, and between one type of science and another: for not all talk about plants, for instance, and not even all scientific talk about them is botanical talk. Nor will the distinction of subject-matter apply at all to any but the most naïve distinctions between subsidiary sciences, the distinction elsewhere—for instance, between physics and physical chemistry—lying rather in the scope and terminology of the laws formulated and employed.

But it is not to the present purpose, even if it were possible, to attempt the high Aristotelian task of characterizing the differences between organized bodies of knowledge. For while it may be possible to characterize the language used by some type of scientist in his professional work, or to characterize a professional scientific activity to distinguish it from some other professional activity, such as that of the historian, this is beside our purpose, which is to characterize some *unprofessional* uses of language as distinct from others. It does seem clear, however, that when we, as laymen, speculate on the distance of a star, for instance, we are using language differently from when we remark on how beautifully it now shines; and that if we say that the first is a scientific use, part of what we mean is that we are asking a question to which the professional scientist is in the best position to give an answer—it is the sort of question he is asking. So we can at this point reintroduce the idea of a professional use of language, and say at least this much: that some of our utterances ask or involve questions that are properly to be answered by techniques and methods of inquiry professionally employed by some types of specialist, and others do not do this.

This distinction does not apply in any simple way to our investigation of religious language. In the case of religious belief, there is indeed the notion of a person who is a religious authority, but this is something quite different from a scientific authority. For first, the religious authority, if there is one, is at least not just someone who has a good training in the methods of answering certain sorts of question, but someone who *has* the authority to *lay down* what is to be believed or done. Second, the question of whether there is a religious authority even in this sense and, if so, who it is, has been the occasion of violent dispute, and many people have been killed in the attempts to settle it. But the dispute was about the settling of admittedly religious questions, so a reference to the authority cannot come into the characterization of a religious question. Third, even if we were to say that a specialist or professional use of religious language was to be found in its theological use (and about theology I shall have something to say later), it is clear that the relation of religious language to the theologian is different from the relation of scientific language to the scientist; one who speaks scientifically is at least an amateur scientist, but one who speaks religiously is not necessarily a theologian, even an amateur one.

How, then, can we attempt a characterization of religious, or at least of Christian, utterances, made in their ordinary occasions by persons other than professional theologians? Could we say, for instance, to take up one of the suggested criteria, that certain language was to be characterized as religious, or more specifically as Christian, by reference to certain practices or observances in the course of which it was used? It is clear that such a reference could not give us enough. For, first, the ceremonies would themselves have to be characterized as religious ceremonies, and if we could do this, we should already have a clearer idea of what religious language was. Second, many religious utterances are made outside such ceremonies; unless everyone speaks religiously only on Sundays. The ceremonies might in the end have to be mentioned in a full characterization of a religious life; but what we are looking for must first be found elsewhere. We have seen that in attempting the characterization of other kinds of language, the distinction of subject-matter, of what the language is used about, did not take us very far; but in the case of religious language perhaps we should after all return to it. For religious language, we might say, is, peculiarly, language about God; and by 'peculiarly' I mean not only that all religious language is language about God, but—and this seems to me an important point—that all language about God is religious language.

But to say that religious language is language about God immediately raises three related difficulties. For first, the word 'about' is misleading. In the most normal linguistic sense of 'about', it is statements that are about things or persons; but, as we have already seen, not all religious utterances are statements—a prayer, for instance, is not about God, but is addressed to him. If we are to say, then, that religious language is language about God, we have to take 'about' in an extremely wide sense. I take it that it would not be disputed by Christians that every religious utterance in some sense comes back to God, perhaps in the sense that if the purpose of the utterance is to be explained, God has in the end to be mentioned. In something like this sense, the word 'about' must be understood. I think we have to say, further, that the mere occurrence of the *word* 'God' in an utterance does not mean that it is actually about God, and so religious; for the most devout may use the word 'God' in idle phrases and not mean really to speak about God. An utterance which includes the word 'God' must be seriously meant to be about him for it to be actually about him.

Conversely—and this is the second difficulty—it is not the case that the word 'God' *has* to occur in an utterance for it to be religious. We could put this by saying that the distinction of subject-matter cannot be reduced to another distinction I mentioned, that of technical terminology. For there are many utterances that are religious even in the sense of 'Christian' but do not involve the *word* 'God'; and, more widely, there is religious language that is not the language of Christianity. To say that this other religious language is language about God, where 'God' is understood in a Christian sense, is at least to prejudge a particular theological issue, concerning the reference and truth of religious beliefs other than Christianity; but the fact that there is an issue here shows that there must be some characterization of a religion, and so of religious language, which is independent of the beliefs of Christianity. Thus we have to say that our characterization is one not of religious language in general, but of that of Christianity; and this will do for the purposes of this discussion.

But is it even this? For—and this is our third difficulty—saying that Christian language is language about God evidently presupposes the truth of Christianity in a far more radical sense, for it presupposes the existence of God. Therefore it looks as if we have to say that, if God exists, the language of Christianity is language about God, and this seems useless as a characterization of such language. For if we start from the statement of God's existence, the characterization is vacuous unless we already know that statement to be true; but if we know that statement to be true, the characterization appears superfluous. If, however, we start from the evident existence of Christian language, in the sense of language used by Christians, we might be tempted to arrive at the statement of God's existence, and so involve ourselves in a kind of ontological proof which might well be considered suspect. This all illustrates the peculiar relation to religious language of the statement of God's existence, which I have already mentioned. If we were seeking an independent characterization of Christian language these difficulties would be damning; but my present aim is not to do this, but to leave on one side the question of God's existence, and to try to show something about Christian language as used by Christians. So perhaps this rather paradoxical approach will not prove entirely useless. I shall therefore continue to speak of Christian language in a way that involves a suspension of disbelief, the suspension being achieved, evidently, by our own bootstraps. I have suggested, then, that all Christian language is language about God. I suggested before that all language about God is religious language, and this must stand, if it stands at all, in its original form: for to say that all language about God is *Christian* language is to prejudge to the opposite effect the theological issue, which I mentioned before, about the status of other religions.

But here perhaps we have an important point about religious language: for we saw before that, while the language of botany is language about plants, not all language about plants is botanical: for poets, painters, ramblers and so on may also speak of plants, but not botanically. But I want to suggest that all language about God is religious language—one cannot speak non-religiously about God. It does not follow from this that atheists are necessarily speaking religiously: for they are denying the statement

'God exists', and to do this goes behind the presuppositions of the present discussion. It does, however, follow from the present thesis that blasphemy is a kind of religious language, and such it must be—for how else could it give so much offence? Blasphemy is the misuse of religious language: it is to say things about God, or to ask things of him, but the wrong things. Yet there seems to be a sort of paradox here: for the blasphemer says, for instance, that God is wicked, and gives offence by so speaking of the Christian God. But the Christian God is good; so must not the blasphemer be speaking of some other God? But if he does this, he either gives no offence, because it was not of the Christian God that he was speaking offensively, or gives offence only by suggesting that there is another God—a line of argument that might lead to the intriguing conclusion that the only form of heresy is polytheism. Perhaps here we must say something like what we say about disagreements concerning characters in the historical past, that there must be some beliefs, and in the case of religion some practices, in common, between the blasphemer and the orthodox to support the idea that they are both talking about the same God: when Housman referred to 'Whatever fool or blackguard made the world', the description 'He who made the world' provided the place from which the offence was to be taken.

If we say, then, that all language about God is religious language, we have said something about religious language and its subject-matter which distinguishes these from, say, botanical language and its subject-matter. We must next consider one type of utterance which, very importantly, occurs within the body of religious language. I have stressed the fact that religious utterances can be of very various types: statements, commands, prayers, etc.; but it is important also that when we consider only those religious utterances that are statements we find that they as well can be of very various types. Some may be statements directly about the nature of God: 'God is three Persons'; some about historical events: 'God sent the Jews into exile'; some about human nature: 'God has given men free-will'; and so on. That is to say, there are many religious statements that are not just religious—although they are about God, they are about something else as well, something involving the affairs of men.

(5) We must now look more closely at the way in which some religious statements, to confine ourselves to statements, are not purely about God, but about human affairs as well; for by doing this we may become clearer about the range of religious language, its relation to other language and to theology: and we shall return, at long last, to Tertullian's paradox. Because religious statements are so various, many different ones should be discussed, but here I shall mention only one. It raises in itself some well-flogged issues, but these I do not want to discuss: I take this example only to illustrate a more general point.

If a people suffer from occasional failure of their crops and subsequent starvation, a person of rather Old Testament faith might say: 'God makes the crops fail to punish the people for their wickedness.' Such a statement is certainly a religious statement of a sort, but it is also a statement about certain events in human life, and seems in fact to provide an explanation of them; and it seems most clearly to do this, and looks logically like a non-religious explanation of the same events, because it connects with each other two sets of human events—the wickedness of the people and the failure of their crops—with God, as it were, as a middle term. As such, the statement seems also to be in a crude sense falsifiable. For when the agriculturists arrive, the irrigation is improved, the crops never fail, and the people riot in wickedness in the midst of plenty, the man who said that the crops failed because of the people's wickedness notoriously falls into discredit. People will cease to talk of God in explaining the success or failure of the crops: one sort of religious statement will cease to be made. This is the familiar phenomenon of the elimination of religious language from a context; and it has been eliminated here not just because people have come no longer to speak in a certain way—as a people might cease to write some sort of poetry—but because the religious statement, in this particular crude example, was a kind of explanation, and was run over by a rival and better explanation. We mentioned before a distinction of languages in terms of specialists and their techniques, and where a language in the specialist sense can clash with religious language, religious language tends to be driven out; because the specialist techniques give explanations which are recommendations for effective action, and where religious language claimed to do that, it failed: for either it gave an 'explanation' which wasn't an explanation in this sense at all, and provided no recommendation, or it gave an explanation, as in the case of the crops, but a very bad one—for if anyone believes that the best way to prevent natural disasters is to live a better life, he appears to be in error.

It would, of course, be a crude mistake to suppose that these antique considerations could, in some sense, 'disprove religion'. What they do show is that if religious language is used to give certain sorts of explanation, it clashes with a more effective explanation and tends to be eliminated. Such elimination has its effect, too, on the theology of the user of the language. For the religious explanation, as we have seen, was a statement both about certain events and about God; and if these statements are seen to be inapplicable to events, they are seen to be inapplicable also to God. Hence it will come to be seen, perhaps, that certain things cannot be said of God: for instance, that he produces particular disasters as a punishment to men. This in turn leads to new speculation about the nature of God and his relation to the world; so that a change in the possible uses of religious language is connected with a change in the views about the nature of God. This works also the other way; for it would be false to represent the situation as one of the constant retreat of religious language, with consequent trimming of theological doctrine. Undoubtedly this has happened; but there may also be new thoughts about God and new moral views and following from these, changes in what can be said in religious language; as with the coming of Christianity less was said about the anger of God and more about his mercy, and as there comes with a change in religious belief a change in what it is considered proper to ask of him in prayer. An attempt may be made at each stage to co-ordinate the implications of what men think they can and ought to say in religious language, and such co-ordination takes the form of a series of statements about the nature of God: and this is systematic theology.

But although the changes in the range of religious language are not to be described entirely as a retreat, the retreat, as we all know, has its dangers for the religion. The supposed religious explanation that we mentioned was in its rough way one statement about both God and the world; and if all statements that are about both God and the world were to be abandoned, what would be left? Such statements would not need to be, as that one was, explanatory of what goes on in the world, and indeed could not be; but there are connections other than explanations, and some such there must surely be. Wittgenstein said (*Tractatus*, 6.432): '*How* the world is, is completely indifferent for what is higher. God does not reveal himself *in* the world.' But if all talk about God were talk only about God, and all talk about the world talk only about the world, how could it be that God was the God *of* the Christian believer, who is a toiler in the world of men? Would not the views about the nature of God retire more and more away from the world of men: his existence would become like that of the gods of Epicurus, 'far remote and cut off from our affairs' (Lucretius, *de Rerum Natura*, II, 648). And if that happened, it could not be of much concern whether he were there or not.

(6) This is where we return to Tertullian. Tertullian's paradox is relevant to this question both because it is a paradox and because it is about the incarnation. For the incarnation seems to be the point for the Christian faith, where there must essentially be an intersection of religious and non-religious language; it has to be said not only that a certain person was crucified, but that that person was the Son of God. This has to be said, as Tertullian clearly saw, if there is to be a Christian faith; and as he equally clearly saw, it is a paradox. The paradox comes about because, although we must have some statement which says something about both God and the world, when we have it we find that we have something that we cannot properly say. For when God is spoken of in purely religious language, he is said to be a Person eternal and perfect, that is, we do not

speak of him in terms appropriate to the temporal and imperfect objects and persons of this life; or if we do, it is notoriously by the analogy of which theologians speak, and therefore imperfectly. For there is no language for God's eternity and perfection beyond the statement of it: it can be said *that* God is eternal and perfect, not *how* he is, for God's eternity and perfection must be beyond the reach of our understanding. So when we come to a statement that is about both God and temporal events, it must be unsatisfactory; for if it were not, we should have adequately described the relation of the temporal events to God in terms appropriate only to the temporal events: and this would mean either that we had described only the temporal events, and left God out, or had described God as a temporal being, which he is not.

The difficulty seems to follow not from the eternity of God by itself, but from the conjunction of this with his perfection as a personal being. For some have held, for instance, that the numbers are eternal objects, although mathematical statements about things in the world can satisfactorily be made. One difference of this case from that of God could be marked by saying that, leaving aside the question of application, the nature of the numbers in themselves can be adequately expressed in the language appropriate to this, the language of pure mathematics, but the nature of God cannot be adequately expressed in any human language. But if we say this, it looks as though we were defending now a different thesis about religious language. For this seems to say that any statement about God, whether we say that there is a relation between God and the world or not, will be unsatisfactory, just because it is made in the words of human language; but the thesis was that it is the fact that there must be a relation between God and the world that made religious language unsatisfactory. But it is not really a different thesis; for it is just the fact that there is at some point such a relation, and a statement or set of statements that try to express it, that makes religious language elsewhere also unsatisfactory. The question of the applicability of mathematics to the world does not affect the question of the expression of the nature of the numbers by pure mathematics; but the question of the relation of God to the world does affect the question of the expression of the nature of God in religious language. The actual effect is that God is said to be a perfect personal being; because, for instance, prayers are addressed to him, and because he has a Son who was born into the world. The statement of these relations will be itself unsatisfactory, and will involve others that are so: because the concepts required—of fatherhood, for instance, and of love, and of power—are acquired in a human context; the language of these things is a language that grows and is used for the relations of humans to humans. To say that, while this is so, religious language requires merely an extrapolation from the human context,[3] is not to solve the problem but to pose it again. For the extrapolation required is an extrapolation to infinity, and in even trying to give a sense to this we encounter the incomprehensibility. This incomprehensibility Tertullian has brought out in his paradox.

In fact, it is a double paradox: 'because it is shameful', Tertullian says, 'I am not ashamed . . . it is certain, because it is impossible'; that is, there is something that is morally outrageous about it, and there is something intellectually outrageous. The two paradoxes can perhaps be seen by considering the incarnation from two different directions. That God, a perfect being, should be willing to be born and to be crucified, is morally astonishing; that this man on a cross should actually be God is intellectually astonishing. Of these, the moral paradox is perhaps the more readily comprehensible to the unbeliever; for this at least he has a model, in the ideas of humility and sacrifice and the finding of the greatest value not where the worldly are looking for it. So the unbeliever, perhaps impertinently, may feel that he sees a point to the moral paradox—that it has turned upside down the standards of what is to be admired and loved. The feeling is easier, perhaps dangerously so, because we have a Christian tradition: to the educated Roman, for instance, it must have been deeply shocking. In this case, too, we can understand to some extent what is in fact the centre of the paradox, Tertullian's saying not just that it was absurd and he believed it, but that he believed it *because* it was absurd. It was just the outrageousness of the crucifixion that pointed the new way one had to try to follow in one's life,[4] and how can any of this be applied to the second part of the paradox, to the fact of the incarnation? How can it be certain, because it is impossible? How can we come to understand, how can we give any sense to, the statement that this man who was crucified was God?

Here I encounter fully a difficulty that has been gradually making itself felt throughout. For the examination of the meaning of statements about the incarnation is, or certainly has been, a task for the theologian; and not being a theologian I cannot feel competent to undertake it. And yet, by starting out to look at religious language I seem to have reached a point at which it is necessary to turn into a theologian. I think we can see the reason for this if we consider what has already been said about religious language and theology. I suggested before that there was a relation between what can and cannot be said in religious language and systematic

---

[3] The connection of this with the idea of an immortal soul will be obvious, and is basically important; but it cannot be pursued here.

[4] But clearly we cannot properly understand the first part of the paradox unless we understand the second.

theology; that a contraction or extension in the use of religious language leads to changes in the theology; and that the systematization and explanation of the implications of what can be said about God is a task of theology. But this seems to have two consequences. For the theology examines and changes by reference to the logical consequences of speaking in this or that way about God: if we cannot say 'God sent the drought to punish the people', we must say that God does not intervene in the operations of natural law; if we say this, are we to say that God's power is limited or that he himself is willing not to intervene?—and so on: all traditional problems of theology. And if we say that God was incarnated, are we to say that he changed?—Marcion's problem. But if the raising of these questions is a task of theology, then theology seems to include the logical analysis of religious language; for surely the logical analysis of religious language is just this, asking how, and with what implications, utterances are made in religious contexts. So the philosopher who regards his task as the logical analysis of language and who sets out to examine religious language will find himself, I suspect, as I have done, doing theology. This, which is the first consequence, seems to me not too happy a one for the supposedly independent analyst of religious language. For I have a suspicion that as a theologian he will turn out rather poorly; as some indeed have, supposing themselves to be raising for the first time logical difficulties in Christian language which have in fact in one guise or another been the concern of theologians for centuries. If he is not a believer at all, his case will be worse still, for the utterances are not just *there*, to be pulled to pieces without understanding of the context in which they are used; but can he understand what is the context and importance of a prayer, for instance, unless he understands what it is to pray? Any more than a man can write on the language of aesthetics who cannot see beyond a coloured photograph of 'The Laughing Cavalier'.

The first consequence I suggest, then, of the status of theology is that there is not much hope for an independent logical analysis of religious language; and the second is its converse: that if one task of theology is such an analysis, theology is committed to making itself coherent, and coherent not only with itself, but outside as well. We have already seen how religious language might retreat from human affairs into an Epicurean remoteness, and that this must not be, if it is to be of any use. So it is that theology must show how religious language can gear into other language, and must lay bare the points of intersection. Yet in the end, it seems, it cannot be successful in this; for the points of intersection, as I have tried to say, must contain something incomprehensible. In saying this, I am only saying what theologians and other religious people have nearly always said; and this shows, what in any case follows from the nature of the thing, that while one should be a believer to be a theologian, being a believer does not eliminate the incomprehensibility. For if the belief is true, it is a belief in an eternal but personal God with a concern for the world, and it is from this that the incomprehensibility follows.

Having just disqualified myself from becoming a theologian, I shall not pursue the question of the logic of statements of the incarnation. I shall say, however, that I think it is clear that one cannot deal with the difficulties in the summary way which, in the work under discussion, Tertullian takes. It will be recalled that Marcion had said that if God had been incarnated, he would have changed; but change involves losing some attributes and gaining others; and God cannot do this. Tertullian briskly replied that what Marcion had said was true of temporal objects, but God is not a temporal object, and that therefore what Marcion said did not apply. But this is to counter one's opponent's move by smashing up the chessboard. For Marcion's objection, we might say, is a point about the logic of the word 'change'; we only understand the word 'change' in terms of the losing or gaining of temporal properties: so how can we use it of God? So something else must be said; but then, again, if the beliefs are true, nothing can be said that will really do. Tertullian's paradox is also a paradox of theology: it seems committed to what on its own premises must be an impossible task.

(7) If it is impossible, what is to be done? Here it may be said that we must have faith; and further that the incomprehensibility I have been discussing is not only a necessary feature *of* Christian belief but necessary *to* it, for it is this that provides a place for faith. Tertullian himself I take, on my freewheeling interpretation, to suggest this in the core of his paradox: it is certain, he says, *because* it is impossible.

We must distinguish here several things that may be meant by having faith. For we may have faith in a person, in the sense that we continue to trust their honesty, good intentions, wisdom, etc., despite perhaps an apparent perversity in their actions. Or we may believe on faith a statement that such-and-such is the case, despite all the evidence being to the contrary. Or we may have faith that such-and-such is what ought to be done, despite the fact that actions and the results of actions involved in carrying out this policy are such as otherwise we should consider wrong. These kinds of faith are, of course, found together: when, for instance, Lenin asked the Bolsheviks before the Revolution to have faith in him, although many of his actions would appear to them inexplicable, he was asking them to believe, among other things, that the aims of the Party would be effected by his policies, although often they seemed to be moving in the opposite direction; and a humanitarian member of the Party had to continue to believe that the Bolshevik state was the right thing to aim at, although murder and misery were involved in doing so. These kinds of faith can be paralleled in the case of religious beliefs; but in the former cases, one thing at least seems to be clear, *what* it is that is being believed; for if a man had faith in Lenin as leader of the Party, or in the belief that his policies would forward the Revolution, he knew what it was he was believing, although he might be able to give very little in the way of rational grounds for believing it. But it is a stranger request to ask someone by faith to believe something that he does not properly understand; for what is it that he is being asked to believe? Faith might be a way of believing something, as opposed to believing it on evidence; but how could it be a way of stepping from what is understood to what is not understood?

Well, it might be said, faith can be a way of coming to understand something; and here it might be suggested that there is an analogy in the arts. 'You think this stuff is all nonsense,' someone might say about a poem; 'but just believe that the poet is not trying to fool you, take it seriously, and you will come to see what it is about.' The eighteenth-century hymnologist, in slightly more utilitarian terms, made something like this point when he wrote: 'O make but trial of his love; Experience will decide How blest are they, and only they, Who in his strength confide.' But the analogy is not good enough. For here again the initial faith is in a belief that is itself comprehensible: the belief that the poem has a meaning, if one can only find it. But in the case of religious belief it is just the belief itself, and not a prior belief about its comprehensibility, that one has, on the position being discussed, to take on faith, in the hope that afterwards it will become clear what it means. Here again I encounter the same difficulty: for if you do not know what it is you are believing on faith, how can you be sure that you are believing anything? And *a fortiori* how can such belief be the means to something else, viz. coming to understand?

In any case, this is beside the point; for the original argument was that certain religious beliefs must be inherently mysterious and remain so, and that it is the part of faith to accept them. My difficulty is that, if the belief is incomprehensible and necessarily so, one cannot see what is being accepted, on faith or otherwise.

St. Paul (I Cor. 1.20 f.) writes: 'Where is the wise? Where is the scribe? Where is the disputer of this world? hath not God made foolish the wisdom of this world? For after that in the wisdom of God the world by wisdom knew not God, it pleased God by the foolishness of preaching to save them that believe . . . the foolishness of God is wiser than men'; and in explanation a French commentator, F. Godet, has said: '*l'évangile n'est pas une sagesse, c'est un salut*'—'the Gospel is not an intellectual system, but a salvation'. It might be objected that my argument has been treating Christian beliefs too much as a '*sagesse*', and that a system of coherent and comprehensible beliefs is not to the point. This might be put differently by saying that in the later part of this paper I have neglected what I emphasized in the earlier, that religious language is not used only to make statements but for many other purposes as well; that the statements of religious belief are to be understood only as part of a way of life, which includes prayer and religious observance and so on; and it might be said in connection with the previous discussion that what one chooses, when one chooses to believe, is to live in a certain way, in which the statements play a part. This is true; but the statements do play a part, and the beliefs must be there, and that is the point. We may consider again the possible contraction of religious language, the lessening of its scope, which I discussed before, God may cease to be mentioned in explanations of particular physical events, for instance, or in moral discourse, and they will continue as forms of discourse on their own. What would not make sense would be for God to cease to be mentioned in the forms of religious observance or in prayer, for then they would no longer exist at all. But religious observance and prayer stand for nothing, so far as I can see, unless there are also behind them some beliefs about God, some statements about him: for this would indeed be the end needle point of faith, to pray just to the unknown God, in complete ignorance of whether such an activity had any sense in relation to him or not—or rather, in such ignorance, one would have to say 'it' rather than 'him'; and could one even say that? Something must be believed, if religious activities are not just to be whistling in the dark without even the knowledge that what one is whistling is a tune; and something that connects God with the world of men. But such a connection must involve saying something about God that is interpreted not just in terms of other statements about God, but in terms of the life of men. If this is said, it seems that it must either be so like some non-religious statement, as in our crude pseudo-scientific example of the failure of the crops, that it can conflict with such a statement, which would make the central religious belief falsifiable and in no way what was required; or it must be sufficiently a statement about God, as it were, for it to be mysterious, as involving an attempt to express the appearance in, or other connection with, a human situation of the infinite perfection of God. If it is inherently mysterious, then it cannot be explained by reason; but to say that it is to be believed on faith, and not by reason, does not face the difficulty: for the question was not how it should be believed, but what was to be believed. If, then, the Christian faith is true, it must be partly incomprehensible; but if it is partly incomprehensible, it is difficult to see what it is for it to be true.

(8) This is only Tertullian's paradox with a converse: *credibile est quia ineptum; et quia ineptum, non credibile*. It follows further, if this is the case, that it is difficult to characterize the difference between belief and unbelief. We can indeed point out that the believer *says* certain things

which the unbeliever does not say; but we want not just this, but to know *what* it is that the believer believes and the unbeliever does not believe; but this we cannot properly do. But if we cannot adequately characterize the difference between belief and unbelief, we may not be able to characterize the difference between orthodoxy and heresy: for the difference between persons believing different ineptitudes is as obscure as that between those believing one ineptitude and those not believing it. Tertullian, as I mentioned at the beginning, became a heretic.

TWO

Metaphysical Arguments

Metaphysicians do not just assert their positions. They attempt to support them by argument, and to give proofs of their conclusions. Some consideration of these proofs must form part of any enquiry into the nature of metaphysics; for it is the attempt to give a proof for his conclusion, to show by logical argument that such-and-such must be so, that chiefly distinguishes the philosophical metaphysician from the mystic, the moralist and others who express or try to express a comprehensive view of how things are or ought to be.

It may well be that the thorough-going metaphysician does not often, psychologically speaking, start with his proofs; he may start rather with a view of the world, and find subsequently demonstrations that articulate his thoughts in the required shape. In this sense, the arguments that he gives may be described as rationalizations—so long as this description does not mean that the arguments are therefore summarily to be dismissed as baseless, invalid or contemptible. Part of the word 'rationalization' is after all the word 'rational', and it is in virtue of their logical structure, their claims to logical validity, that metaphysical theories are marked off from mere intuitive and unformulated insights into reality.

However, the resemblance of metaphysical theories to rationalizations in the psychoanalytical sense does go rather deeper than this, and it may make one wonder whether the arguments that the metaphysician produces really *matter*. To some recent writers, metaphysical theories and arguments have seemed to be just symptoms of a kind of intellectual neurosis or 'mental cramp'[1]—the metaphysician is a man with an *idée fixe* which he projects on the world in the form of an ambitious and distorted theory. So, just as it is no good reasoning with a neurotic, it is no good arguing with a metaphysician—what one must do, in both cases, is to cure them. Hence there goes with this view of metaphysics a corresponding view of the proper duty of philosophy. The philosopher should play psychoanalyst to the tortured and theory-ridden metaphysician and, by-passing the arguments in which he rationalizes his worries, use analytic technique to get to the roots of the worries themselves.

[1] This phrase, and the underlying idea, come from Wittgenstein. The most thorough-going exponent of the theory is John Wisdom—see his collection of articles, *Philosophy and Psychoanalysis*, published by Blackwell.

In its extremer forms, this view seems to be a wild exaggeration. What it rightly emphasizes is that many important metaphysical arguments are not the sort of arguments that can just be accepted as valid or rejected as invalid by certain and generally agreed rules, and that their value or their faults are likely to lie deeper, in some central concept or idea which the metaphysician is trying to articulate through them. The weakness of this therapeutic view, if taken a long way, is that there seems to be no reason why it should not be taken all the way, so that metaphysics comes to be regarded, not just as *like* a neurosis, but as being indeed a particular sort of neurosis. If it were so regarded, of course, the use of philosophy or philosophical analysis to cure it would be a frivolous pursuit—what would be needed would be real psychoanalysis. One cannot seriously believe that metaphysics is as non-rational as this, or that philosophers should really hand over to the clinicians. The analysis that is required is philosophical, not psychological, and what requires it is not the metaphysician himself but his arguments; which should be taken seriously as rational attempts to prove a point of view.

Of course, metaphysicians vary in the extent to which they try to give proofs of what they say; and in the extent to which the proofs that are given are precisely and rigorously expressed; and in the extent to which the proofs, however expressed, form an essential part of the thought, and are not just there for decoration. To take two comparable British metaphysicians, for instance, there is a marked difference between McTaggart and Bradley: while McTaggart seeks knock-down forms of proof and hard coal-like knobs of argument, Bradley tentatively adumbrates. Yet allowing for all these differences, there is in practically any Western metaphysician of importance a core of argument, an attempt to support his position or raise his questions by a movement from premises to conclusion.

All theorists employ arguments and make inferences, for all are concerned to get from one place to another, to move from a set of premises or collection of facts to a conclusion. But, equally notoriously, not all theorists make the same kind of inferences, and a movement from premisses to conclusion can be made according to very different sorts of rules. Logicians, who have been concerned to examine, classify and formalize the different types of inference, have divided them by a basic distinction into two broadly different classes—inductive and deductive inferences. Deductive inferences are such that if you accept the premises, you must accept the conclusion, or else contradict yourself—the conclusion follows with rigorous logical necessity from what implies it. Such are the arguments, for instance, of mathematicians. Inductive arguments, on the other hand, have no such absolute rigour; one who accepted the premises would not *contradict* himself if he refused to accept the conclusion, although he might look pretty silly. Most practical inferences of everyday life are of this type: thus if a man arrives from personal experience at the conclusion that it is always unwise to play cards with strangers on race trains, he is making an inductive step.

This example points to one further important feature of inductive arguments. The man who arrives at this conclusion is *generalizing*—he is saying something to the effect: 'Seven times I've been asked to play, and seven times they've tried to swindle me—so probably next time, or any other time, I'm asked, it will be the same'. His argument so far is very sound, but of course he may be wrong in his conclusion; it is always *possible* that the next card-playing stranger may be honest. This is a general feature of inductive arguments. Just because it is their function to lead from some matter of fact already accepted to some wider, or at least different, assertion, their conclusions are always in a sense only probable. An inductive inference is empirical, and it is always conceivable that its conclusion should turn out to be untrue, however carefully it has been considered.

In the case of deductive arguments the situation is more complicated. Deductive arguments can have conclusions that are necessary and certain—such are the conclusions of mathematical arguments. But they will be so only if the premisses are certain as well, just because a deductive argument gives you no more in the conclusion than what is already tied up or implied in the premisses. If the premisses are only probable, then so will the conclusion be. The immediate point for the present discussion, however, is that inductive arguments can lead only to empirical and probable results.

What is the relation of metaphysical arguments to these two sorts of argument? An enquiry into this relation should at least help us to see what a metaphysical argument is not, and may help us to see something of what it is. It is clear, first, that metaphysicians do not characteristically make straightforward inductive inferences: they do not say things of the form 'such-and-such is true in these instances, so it is probably always true'. It would be absurd, for instance, to suppose that a metaphysician would reach the conclusion 'men have freewill' by an argument like 'all men we have observed have freewill, so men in general do' as one might argue 'all the men we have observed have eyebrows, so men in general do'. The *a priori* quality of a metaphysical conclusion, its necessity, by itself makes such a procedure inappropriate: there could be no need of *that* kind of support from experience.

Yet it must be said that some arguments that metaphysicians have employed do look remarkably like inductive inferences. Such, for example, is the simplest form of the theological argument from design, once well known under the name of 'Paley's watch'. Paley's form of it was just this: 'If we found by chance a watch or other piece of intricate mechanism we should infer that it had been made by someone. But all around us we do find intricate pieces of natural mechanism, and the processes of the universe are seen to move together in complex relations; we should therefore infer that these too have a Maker.' There are some general difficulties about an argument from analogy of this type; but the immediate point is that it does seem just to be a kind of inductive argument. Paley's reasoning is simply this: 'wherever in the past we have found intricate mechanisms we have found a maker, so in this case, too, we can infer one'. But by being an inductive argument it seems too weak for its purpose. For, taken by itself, it can lead only to an inductive type of conclusion; and so the statement of the existence of a God, to which it is supposed to lead, will have the status only of a quasi-scientific hypothesis; and for any such inductive hypothesis, as we have seen, the opposite involves no contradiction, and is logically possible. So one who from *this* type of argument accepted the existence of God would have to admit that it was at least possible that God did not exist after all. But in general one who believed in God would not admit that it was in any way possible that God did not exist; he would insist that the statement of God's existence must have some sort of absolute necessity. Thus Paley's watch, if it is to be called a metaphysical argument at all, does not seem to be a characteristic one, nor yet a characteristic argument for the existence of God. It is only, as it were, a super-scientific inference.

Another way of saying that the metaphysician does not use inductive arguments is to point out that in metaphysical conclusions the notion of probability plays no part. As we have seen, it is a characteristic of inductive inferences that the word 'probably' can always slip into them. But the metaphysician does not offer his conclusions as being *probably* so; he argues that they *must* be so. Here again, we do meet what look like exceptions to this rule. In the earlier writings of Bertrand Russell, for instance, we find him saying things like this: 'there are arguments that try to show that the external world does not exist, but since these arguments are not conclusive, and we have a natural tendency to believe that the external world does exist, we are probably safer in going on thinking that it does'. Professor Broad and others have written in a similar vein, as if weighing the probability of one metaphysical thesis against another.

I should like to make two points about this type of example. First, I think there certainly is, or has been, a way of doing philosophy that tried to assimilate it to the natural sciences, and hence regarded its conclusions in the light of probabilities. Some philosophers in this century, impressed by the achievements of the sciences and depressed by traditional metaphysics, sought to apply scientific methods inside philosophy itself, and the results did include what look like metaphysical conclusions presented with an air of inductive probability. I think, however, that if these arguments are closely examined, they can be found not to be straightforward inductive arguments, as Paley's perhaps was; the language of theory and probability is little more than a dressing for a philosophical conceptual argument. Moreover, these philosophers are not typical metaphysicians; they themselves, I suspect, might have denied that what they were doing was metaphysics.

Second, there may be another reason, quite different from the last, why Russell, for instance, should qualify metaphysical conclusions with terms like 'probably'. We have already seen one reason why the conclusion of an argument should be thought to be only probable: that is, just that the argument is an inductive one, and a philosopher may want to mark the empirical nature of any inductive argument by inserting 'probably' into it. If this is what Russell meant, then certainly his argument is an inductive one. But this is only one reason why the word 'probably' should occur in an argument, and there are others. Another, and very familiar, reason is that the premises of the argument are themselves only probable, in the quite ordinary sense in which, for instance, it is (at best) only probable that the favourite will win the 2.30 at tomorrow's races. Of course, if my premises are only probable, then any conclusion I draw from them, even in deductive argument, will be only probable. As we noticed before, you get no more out of deduction than you put in at the beginning. Thus, if someone thinks that the favourite will probably win the 2.30, he can infer, validly if uninterestingly, that probably no other horse will; but he will get no conclusion that is itself certain, since his premises already are no more than probable. Here we have a reason why the word 'probably' should occur even in deductive arguments. But again, if we look back at Russell's argument, it is not of *this* pattern; his premises—*e.g.* that we believe in an external world—are not in themselves dubious, as forecasts about tomorrow's races are.

Still, there is yet another way in which 'probably' can come into an argument, and this may shed more light on Russell's. In considering an argument, we may be concerned not so much with the question of whether the premises and the conclusion are true or false, certain or probable, as with the question of whether the conclusion follows from the premises—that is, we may just want to know whether the argument is *valid*. Strictly speaking, there are no degrees of validity: the conclusion either follows from the premises or it does not, and there is no middle way. It makes no sense to say that a conclusion 'more or less' or 'just about' follows. Yet one often meets the situation in which one is not *sure* whether a given argument is valid. The premises may be complicated or unclearly expressed, the chain of reasoning subtle, and so on, and one may be in genuine doubt whether the conclusion does follow or not. In such cases, one may express one's doubts by saying that the conclusion 'perhaps' or 'probably' follows from the premises.

This sort of doubt, and hence this sort of 'probably', can come in, of course, with any sort of argument, inductive or deductive: a piece of mathematics, for instance, may be so complicated and so little self-evident that the best one can say, pending a lot of further investigation, is that the conclusion is probably reached by valid argument. Russell's argument, and some other metaphysical arguments that involve the notion of probability, may be of this last type. The notion of probability comes into them not because the philosopher thinks that either his conclusion or his premisses are inherently dubious, but because he is doubtful about the connection between them—he is not sure whether his conclusion in fact follows. Such doubts, as we have seen, can arise with any sort of argument; and the fact that a philosopher does not commit himself to saying more than that his conclusion *perhaps* follows, does not by itself show what sort of conclusion he is reaching, or by what sort of argument.

Anyway, metaphysical arguments do not seem to be characteristically inductive. Are they then deductive?

Deduction seems a better candidate for the metaphysician's professional tool, for deductive arguments can at least lead to conclusions of necessity, which are what he wants. It is commonly said that metaphysicians seek to deduce the nature of reality or some such thing; and so the impression may be given that the metaphysician's is a wholly deductive enterprise. This impression seems to get support from the great systems that some metaphysicians have constructed, which claim to show deductive relations between features of reality.

But the idea that the metaphysical activity consists just of making deductions in a system neglects a more fundamental question. Every deductive movement must be made from one place to another: one needs both premisses and conclusion. So in a chain or system of deductions there must be something at the beginning from which the whole series of reasoning starts. In a formal logical system what one has at the beginning are axioms; these are, relative to that system, unquestionable. They are not themselves derived in the system—there is nothing to derive them from. It is possible to have a number of purely formal systems, each with its own axioms, and for particular purposes one can take one's choice. But the metaphysician is not concerned to give us a choice. He wants to make a series of statements that will both have content and be necessarily true. But if his conclusions are, as he wishes, to be inescapable, and he is deducing the conclusions ultimately from axioms, then the axioms must be inescapable as well—inferences, unlike divers, do not gain in weight as they get nearer the bottom. But the axioms cannot themselves be proved in the system; so the metaphysician must have some other method of supporting his axioms, outside the system. He will try to show that one has to accept his axioms, for only so can he show that one has to accept his conclusions. The weapon he uses to try to make one accept the axioms is in the strongest sense the metaphysical argument.

The rationalist system-builders of the seventeenth century tried in their different ways to find axioms for their systems which would be inescapable; but their method was on the whole to look for axioms which needed no support of any kind, which were self-evidently true. So their metaphysical argument at this point is rather an appeal to propositions which need no argument at all. Thus Descartes, for instance, by his procedure of systematic doubt, whittled away the truths he believed in until he arrived at the apparently indubitable truth 'I am doubting', from which he took an immediate step to 'I exist'. Whether he regarded this step as purely deductive is to me unclear; at any rate, the indubitability of 'I am doubting' seemed to him to be established by the pure light of reason.

But not all system-builders use methods as simple as this to provide their axioms. And not all metaphysicians are, in this most ambitious sense, system-builders. Our argument has shown why there is no need for them to be. For if a metaphysical argument can be used to compel one to accept a statement which is then going to be used as the axiom of a system, it can also be used to make one accept the statement even if it is not going to be used as an axiom. Even metaphysicians not engaged in comprehensive system-building will try to show by constructive argument that such and such (which on the whole you didn't expect) must be so; or, very frequently, by destructive argument, that so and so (which on the whole you did expect) can't be so. I shall in a moment try to say something about the interrelation of these in a typical case.

In contrasting, up to this point, arguments used by metaphysicians with inductive and with deductive arguments, I have spoken as if there were one definite sort of argument that is metaphysical. I think in fact there is no one thing that is a metaphysical argument, just as there is no one thing that is a metaphysical statement. This does not mean, however, that absolutely no general remarks can be made about them; only that such general remarks will serve to characterize these arguments in outline rather than to state some one essential property of them. One essential property of them, however, can be and has been stated: that they are not the same as deductive or inductive arguments. For some philosophers, indeed, such as the so-called logical positivists, this is quite enough; all metaphysical arguments and statements are by them lumped together and dismissed as meaningless. But this skeletal unity tells us nothing about metaphysics; it is only the uniformity of all before the final leveller. The approach of these collectively anti-metaphysical philosophers is a kind of philosophical parallel to the attitude of a fanatically militarist person who divides all men into two classes only, combatants and non-combatants. Even from the military point of view, such a division would have its disadvantages:

among non-combatants, for instance, it fails to distinguish between the medically unfit and the conscientious objectors. A metaphysician, in relation to the positivist criterion of meaning, is more like a conscientious objector than like an invalid; it is his whole purpose to do something other than what the positivist wants him to do. And just as there are different kinds of conscientious objector, so there are different types of metaphysician and of metaphysical argument. Understanding can only be gained by taking individual cases.

Within the limits of this chapter it is possible to look at only one example of metaphysical argument in more detail. It has the overwhelming disadvantage of being only one example; but it is such a central and recurrent one that I hope it may yield some general lessons as well.

The stage is set for the argument I am going to consider by the facts of perceptual illusion. All around us we see objects which we recognize as being of certain sorts—trees, tables, people and so on. Occasionally, in the business of recognizing things, we are deceived, and take something that we see for something which in fact it isn't. Thus an old boot in the dusk might be taken for a small cat. Into this setting the philosopher steps. He may be concerned with any of a number of questions, such as 'What do we really know?'; 'How much reliance can be placed on perception as a source of knowledge?'; 'What really exists?'; and so on. But whatever his particular question, his reasoning from the situation of perceptual illusion may well go something like this. 'You were deceived when you took that boot for a cat. Since you were deceived, there can have been no *intrinsic* difference between the experience you had at the moment of seeing what was in fact a boot in the dusk and the experience you could have had in really seeing a cat at that moment. The difference, after all, came out later—when you had a closer look, made a noise, or whatever it was. Clearly there can be no intrinsic difference between the two experiences, for if there were, you could have told the difference, and would not have taken the one thing for the other. So what was this experience you had? Clearly not that of seeing a cat, for there was no cat to be seen, but equally clearly the experience you had wasn't just that of seeing an old boot, either. For we have already agreed that it must have been the same experience as you could have had in really seeing a cat, for otherwise you couldn't have mistaken the boot for a cat; and if you could have had this experience in really seeing a cat, the experience can't just be that of really seeing a boot; for when you really see a cat you don't really see a boot. So the experience you have in both cases must be something neutral between really seeing a cat and really seeing a boot—it is something common to both and less than either. Moreover' (this philosopher might continue) 'the having of visual experience must be more basic than the seeing of real objects; for one can have visual experiences without in fact seeing the appropriate, or indeed any, sort of object, but we cannot see an object without having visual experiences.'

So runs the argument from illusion in one of its many forms. It contains both a destructive and a constructive movement; both are typical of metaphysical argument. The destructive movement consists of showing that something we should naturally say if asked to reflect on perception—that is, that we just see objects—is false. It may be said that there is nothing very surprising about this, and that anyone who said that we always, whenever we see anything, see a material object, would obviously be wrong; but that nevertheless we sometimes see material objects. But the destructive movement is stronger than this. The metaphysician does not in fact claim that there is *no* difference between being deceived and not being deceived; his argument is just that the difference is not where you expected it to be. For the argument purports to show that by reflection on the cases of illusion we can come to see that the cases of genuine perception as well are different from what we thought; that in these, too, the visual experience of the observer—which, the metaphysician will go on to argue, is private to the observer—must play a part.

To say this, however, is already to have started the constructive movement of the argument. It is characteristic of metaphysical arguments that the method of destruction already points to what is to take the place of the things destroyed. Hence it is that what is in one sense the same argument—an argument, at any rate, generated by the same facts of experience—can appear in different forms in different philosophers to suit their several purposes. The form in which I have presented the argument from illusion (and some particular form had to be chosen) is in fact one that can lay the foundations for an empiricist metaphysic using the notion of an 'idea' or a 'sensation'.

But the same argument can be used for ends quite different from those of the empiricist metaphysician. Plato, for instance, accepted something like the first stage of the argument, and reasoned from this that our beliefs about the material world must be personal, fleeting and unstable. He added the premisses that true knowledge must be of the unchanging and stable, and that we can up to a point have knowledge, and reached the conclusion that there must be a world of unchanging things, the world of Forms. What he and the empiricists have in common is the use of the argument to destroy a world taken for granted and to substitute something else for it—in his case, a world of Forms, in theirs a succession of experiences from which objects have in some way to be inferred or constructed. Here we see a prime characteristic of metaphysical argument—its use to establish propositions of existence or non-existence. 'The world of Forms is the world of genuine existence'; 'the ultimate constituents of the world are sense-data': these are (very different) metaphysical statements a main prop of which is the argument we have been examining.

How is this argument related to the distinction between inductive and deductive arguments? Clearly it is not just inductive: the empiricist metaphysician, for instance, is not just saying 'there are illusions, so probably objects don't exist and individual experiences do'. Yet he is making a movement beyond what he started with. By examining the concept of perceptual illusion, he arrives at a general conclusion about perception as such; a conclusion which is to be attacked, not by the production of any straightforward empirical counter-examples, but by an enquiry into his concepts, in particular the rather dubious concept of 'an experience'.

'Well', someone might say, 'all we have in this argument is a contingent fact and a set of deductions. The deductions are made from the concept of a perceptual illusion; the contingent fact is that the concept has application—that is, we are sometimes deceived.' But this would be a complete misunderstanding. For neither is the supposed contingent fact just a contingent fact, nor are the supposed deductions just deductions. When the metaphysician says, with a disingenuous air of factual simplicity, 'We are sometimes deceived, and take one thing for another', he is not just stating a contingent fact, something that might well be otherwise. All he actually needs for his argument is the logical possibility of misrecognition, the existence of such a concept; and, very roughly, contained in the concept of recognition is the possibility of misrecognition. So long as we have the concept of recognizing things, we must also have that of failing to recognize them. Of course, we might *perhaps* have neither concept; but what our perception would then seem to be is totally obscure. In the relation of recognition and similar concepts to our experience lies a huge philosophical problem. Again, the deductions are not just deductions. If they were, there could scarcely be the disagreement there is with the conclusion; and, again, the metaphysician has acquired from somewhere *en route* a concept with which he did not start out, that of 'an experience'.

Yet the introduction of this concept is not just gratuitous. It seems to be somehow implied in what is already said, to be demanded by the facts as they stand, and one principal aim of the metaphysician's argument is to display the facts so as to show where the demand comes. The purpose of the argument is not just to deduce a conclusion from the facts. It is rather to show that the account of those facts, when we reflect on them, has a hole in it, a hole which is exactly fitted by the metaphysician's special concept. This concept may be one, like that of 'an experience', which exists already in a rough form in our ordinary language, and which the metaphysician takes up, dignifies and refines into a principle of explanation. Alternatively, if he is a very thorough-going metaphysician, the concepts he uses in this way may be much more technical and remote from ordinary thinking, like Leibniz's 'monads' or Kant's 'noumenal objects'.

The greatness of a metaphysician, it seems to me, is to be determined by three considerations: how arbitrary his special concepts are, how much they explain, and how much they distort our ordinary thinking. These considerations are not, of course, independent—they are bound up together like the design requirements of an aeroplane, where conflicting demands such as minimum weight, maximum capacity and the requirements of safety have to be reconciled by expert designers. The designer of genius gets as near as possible to having the best of all worlds, and so does the metaphysical genius. His concepts will explain a lot, by revealing important analogies between kinds of experience and thought which superficially seem widely different. These analogies must be real ones, and not the product of forced or over-distorting assimilations; and they must not be arbitrary, in the further sense that one must be led to recognize them, and with them the demand for the metaphysician's explanatory concepts, by clear and cogent argument.

But it is the argument that concerns us here, rather than the features of the metaphysician's enterprise when it is completed. Any account of such arguments in a few words is bound to be a caricature, but their standard features can be summarized like this. The metaphysician feels an inconsistency or difficulty or incompleteness in what we naturally tend to think about some feature of our experience, or rather in what seems to be presupposed by what we so think. In resolving this, he will try to show that some concept on which we rely is secondary to, or presupposed by, some other concept which he has introduced or extended from elsewhere. This concept of his may have a special place in the answer to the problem in question (like the empiricists' use of 'experience'), or he may use it widely elsewhere (like Plato's Forms) to solve other problems; the more widely he uses it elsewhere, the more systematic will his philosophy be.

The compulsiveness of his argument will come from his starting with concepts and features of experience which, it seems, must be there if we are to think about our experience at all. His attempt to show that some concept involves a difficulty, or is presupposed by some other concept, will often issue in statements of existence or non-existence. Yet his assertions of existence or non-existence, unlike assertions of either empirical or mathematical existence, are in a sense only comparative. For all metaphysicians agree that appearance, those features of the world which are metaphysically shown to be unreal, must eventually find *some* place in the account of things as they really are. We saw this before in the empiricist's preservation, in a different place, of the ordinary distinction between illusion and genuine perception. Even McTaggart's famous demonstration of the unreality of time (which is both philosophically spectacular and very hard to refute) is preparatory to an account of what it is that really does exist and presents itself to us confusedly as the passage of time. Hence it is that some have seen the metaphysician's activity as primarily one of reallocation: the extension of some favoured concept to a primary place in the account of things at the expense of more familiar concepts.

There is truth in this; yet the choice of such a concept, and the point of its application, is not just arbitrary—and we are left with the problem of why some work so much better than others. Metaphysical arguments are like trees. Their exact position, and their shape, are to a certain extent matters of preference: the metaphysician can choose where exactly to plant them, and how to trim them. But he cannot choose whether they will grow or not; some spots on the conceptual landscape are more fertile than others. If with the positivist axe we chop the trees down, they grow again. If with the Wittgensteinian spade we start digging up the roots, we shall, fascinatedly, go on and on. For even if we dig up one set of roots, there will be, if it was a stout tree, many others. Perhaps digging is the proper philosophical activity at this time—certainly mere pride in having grown a tree larger than anyone else's is no longer enough. But there was something that justified such pride—the knowledge that the metaphysician's green fingers had found the spot where acorns could grow. What spurs on the philosophical digger is the desire to know more. What makes metaphysical trees grow? Why from some features of our experience rather than others do metaphysical arguments spring up? The answer to that question would be the ultimate metaphysical answer.

THREE

Pleasure and Belief

We can be as pleased by what we only believe to be the case and is not, as by what we know to be the case. Thus I may be pleased because (as I suppose) I have inherited a fortune, when I have not. This fact deserves consideration, in particular because it raises the question of the relation of pleasure to its objects; it is with this question that this paper will be principally concerned.

If anyone is tempted to think that the object of my pleasure—what I am pleased by, or at—is the *cause* of my pleasure, this type of case should discourage him. For the object of the pleasure in this case seems to be an inheritance, but this, since it does not exist, cannot be a cause (as it used to be said, *non entium non sunt effectus*). Yet the cause of the pleasure cannot be something else quite different from the supposed inheritance. For one thing, if I am persuaded that I have not in fact inherited a fortune, my pleasure will disappear and so must have been connected with at least my previous belief in the inheritance. Moreover, in speaking retrospectively of the pleasure, I shall say that I was pleased because I believed that I had inherited a fortune; or something of this kind.

Hence, the only resort of a casual account of pleasure and its objects will be to say that the cause of my pleasure was my belief in the inheritance. Yet this account in its turn raises difficulties. First, if my belief in the inheritance was the cause of my pleasure, it must have been so in virtue of some law connecting such beliefs with pleasure. But what law? Evidently the belief in an inheritance is not the cause of *any* pleasure, but, at best, of *pleasure at an inheritance*; yet it is this last notion that the causal account was supposed to explain. However, it may be replied to this that there is no need to introduce this notion into the causal law: it will be enough to say that belief in an inheritance is among the possible causes of pleasure, pleasure itself being a state of feeling (for instance), which is much the same whatever the cause. So that when we say of someone "he is pleased because he believes he has inherited a fortune", what we mean is "he is experiencing pleasure, and the cause of this is his belief that he has inherited a fortune".

It would follow from this view that it was *always* the belief that caused the pleasure, even in those cases in which the thing I said I was pleased at really existed. For if not, the statement "I am pleased because I have inherited a fortune" would express a causal hypothesis different from, and incompatible with, the hypothesis expressed by the statement "I am pleased because I believe that I have inherited a fortune". But it is evident that at the time of believing in the inheritance, I could have no grounds whatever for preferring the second of these hypotheses to the first, since it is logically impossible for me to distinguish between what (as I believe) is the case, and what I believe to be the case. Hence there will be two incompatible hypotheses about my pleasure which in principle I shall not be able to distinguish. But it is clear that my retrospective description of the situation as my "being pleased because I believed . . .", and anyone else's description of it in these terms, are just based on my sincerely thinking or saying at the time "I am pleased because I have . . ."; thus it appears that a necessary condition of the assertion of the true hypothesis would be my previous belief in or assertion of a false one, and this is absurd.

Hence the causal account must hold that it is *always* my belief that is the cause, or at least the proximate cause, of my pleasure: and that the statement "I am pleased because I have inherited a fortune" must be taken to mean "I am pleased because I believe I have inherited a fortune". This is equally implausible, however. For first, it still looks, from the previous argument, extremely doubtful whether I am in a position to arrive at the correct hypothesis, and distinguish it from rivals—at the very least, it seems that it would be a necessary condition of so doing that I had engaged in philosophical reflection; second, it is impossible to see what evidence I could have for the hypothesis, or how I would set about collecting evidence; third, since the statement in question expresses, on this view, a causal hypothesis, it would be corrigible, and it would make sense to say that I had just been mistaken in thinking that it was a certain belief that caused my pleasure; but in general no sense can be attached to this. In fact, something like this incorrigibility extends even to the formulation which does not include an explicit reference to my beliefs. There are, indeed, ways in which I may be mistaken about, or ignorant of, the objects of my pleasure, and it will be one aim of this paper to investigate them; but I cannot be mistaken in saying "I am pleased because I have inherited a fortune" in the same way as I can in saying, for instance, "I have a stomach-ache because I ate some bad fruit".

Thus the object of my pleasure—what I am pleased at, by, or (in this sense) because of—is not to be taken as a cause: nor can my belief in so-and-so be made to function as the cause of my pleasure at so-and-so.

In fact, the whole idea of a man's beliefs' being a cause in such cases is a fiction, aided, though not inspired, by a misunderstanding of the form of words "he was pleased because he believed . . .". Now this form of words, and perhaps a similar misunderstanding, occur also in another connexion—that of a man's having mistaken grounds for an action. There are other obvious similarities between the two cases. Statements of the form "he did it because he believed that p" are, like the comparable statements about pleasure, ultimately based on the man's own statement, taken to be sincere, of the form "I did it because p"; and statements of the latter form are, again, not open to the charge of being straightforwardly mistaken. It is perhaps worth noticing that there are languages which, in both connexions, do not employ anything like the misleading formula "because he believed" at all, but perform the same function merely by the mood of a verb.

Thus in these respects, at least, there is some analogy between pleasure and its objects on the one hand, and actions and their grounds, on the other. But this analogy will not take us very far. For pleasure, like many other states with which similar difficulties arise, such as fear, is not an action, but more like, at least, a "passion" or something that happens to us. But even if this is denied, the analogy will not work out. Even if we agreed with Aristotle[1] and possibly Prof. Ryle[2] that pleasure in the standard case consists in or accompanies zestful activity, it would have to be the activity, if anything, that constituted the object of the pleasure, for it is this that I take pleasure *in*; but if it is the activity that constitutes the object of the pleasure, this will not be constituted by the grounds of the activity, if any; so that even in this case, the relation of pleasure to its object will not have been explained as the relation of actions to their grounds.

In fact, in many cases it is impossible to discover any activity, the zestful engagement in which constitutes the pleasure. The man who is pleased because he believes he has inherited a fortune may indeed enjoy such "activities" as imagining his improved style of life, planning expensive holidays, envisaging the gratitude of persons to whom he will be generous, etc. But even if we supposed, what seems to be false, that such "activities" were the logically necessary concomitant of being pleased at a supposed inheritance, their zestful performance cannot in fact constitute the pleasure in question. For a man can enjoy such activities (as day-dreaming) without believing that these things will come about. He will enjoy the activities quite differently, and much more, and will give a quite different answer to the question "why are you pleased?" if he really believes that these things will come about, and just *because* he so believes. Hence enjoying such activities is not a sufficient condition of being pleased because

---

[1] *Eth. Nic.* 1174a 13 seq.

[2] "Pleasure" *P.A.S. Supp. Vol.* XXVIII (1954), pp. 135. *seq.* I am unclear whether Ryle does subscribe to this view; some remarks in this article suggest that he does not, but concentration on the case of activity plays a large part in his arguments against the view that pleasure can be a feeling.

I believe I have inherited a fortune, and it does nothing to explain the peculiarities of the latter. So the only "activity" we are left with as the object of this sort of pleasure is the "activity" of believing in these future events, itself; and this will not do, for we give sense to "he takes pleasure in believing it" only where the man does not (really) believe it, or at least has made himself do so, or has refused to be unpersuaded, and these are quite different matters. An activity in which I can take pleasure is surely something in which I can engage or indulge, which I can take up or abandon, and none of these things can in general be done with belief.[3]

In such cases, pleasure certainly cannot consist in any zestful activity. Thus, for more than one reason, the slight epistemological analogy between the grounds of action and the objects of pleasure cannot be directly pursued. How then is the connexion between pleasure and its objects to be characterized?

Let us consider the notion of "pointing to". This will lead us, I am afraid, a long way round, but eventually back to pleasure. It is a familiar point that the mere fact that my finger may be pointing to something, in the sense that a line drawn from it meets that thing, does not mean that I am pointing to that thing.[4]

It is a characteristic of the sense of "pointing to" in which I point to things, that if asked what I am pointing to, I should be able to give an answer.

Further, that subject to certain qualifications I cannot be mistaken or ignorant, i.e., it makes no sense to say that I am mistaken or ignorant, about what I am pointing to.

Further, that I can point to things of various categories. Consider what can come after "look at . . ."—that thing, the size of it, the shape of it, the number of ants down there, what he is doing, the colour of the sky, the speed he is going, etc.

Last, that by pointing, I can draw someone's attention to these various things; and that the purpose of pointing is usually, if not always, to do just this.

Now it is not true to say without qualification that I cannot be mistaken or ignorant about what I am pointing to. For I can be mistaken, or at least something goes wrong with my account of what I am pointing to, in at least the following cases:—

(a) About the past, I may remember that I pointed, but misremember (or, less usually, completely forget) what it was that I pointed to. This is obvious and uninteresting.

---

[3] Though we should not underestimate our capacities in this direction; cf. Price "Belief and Will", P.A.S. Supp. Vol. XXVIII (1954), Inaugural Address.

[4] The point is made several times by Wittgenstein in the Philosophical Investigations.

(b) I may point to x, but mistakenly say that I am pointing to y, because I mistakenly believe that x is y. The first case of this is that in which the mistake does not matter, because it was not *as y* that I was pointing to x. The commonest case of this is where I want to point to the attitude, qualities, etc., of x, and identify x as y. ("Look at the wonderful colour of those hibiscus flowers."—"What? There are no hibiscus flowers."—"Oh, I meant the colour of that bush over there, whatever it is.")

(c) This case is like case (b), except that here the mistake matters, because it is *as y* that I am pointing to x. ("Look! The Queen!"—"It is not the Queen."—"Oh . . .") Here it is true that I pointed to something, and something of which I could have given another description (*e.g.*, "that lady who just walked in"), but here the pointing is, as it were, withdrawn; and attention drawn to the thing *pro tanto* lapses.

(d) I may point to x which does not exist at all, as Macbeth might have pointed to the dagger. Here the description given ("a dagger") has to be withdrawn, but in its place a different kind of description can be given ("I was pointing to the dagger I thought was there"). It is noteworthy that "the dagger which I thought was there" is not a description referring to an image, or any similar private thing. It is a description whose place of application is in the external world— for the dagger I thought was there is (if I may be allowed the expression) just the one that is not really there.

So much for mistakes that may arise with my descriptions of what I am pointing to, or drawing someone's attention to. If we consider now the correlative situation, of my having my attention drawn to something by somebody, we see that matters are different since of course I may be just mistaken about what he is trying to draw my attention to. Or the boot may be on the other foot, and I may know better than he about the application of the descriptions he gives, *i.e.*, may be able to correct his descriptions already. But now consider the situation of my having my attention drawn to something, not by a person pointing, but by the thing itself; I may have my attention drawn by and to any of the sorts of things to which I or someone else might point. Now here I cannot make the sort of mistake that arises when someone else does the pointing and I misunderstand him, for that is related to the description he would give, and that does not arise in the present case. Nor can I correct myself, as I can correct him, on the spot; though I may go on to correct myself, or if I share the object of attention with others by pointing, the situation is as described above. The situation is *rather* as with my own pointing; and here it is important that having my attention drawn to something is often a preliminary to my pointing to it, and that the description I would give in pointing to it is often the description under which, as it were, the thing draws my attention to itself. Having my attention drawn to something of course differs from pointing to it inasmuch as the latter is an action and the former is more like something that happens to me. This difference is important; but it is more important that the difference does not affect the status of the descriptions that occur in the two cases. The descriptions or identifications, misdescriptions or misidentifications, I could give of what drew my attention are just those that I might give if I were to draw your attention to whatever the thing is: and just as with pointing the description I give may in one of these ways go wrong, and yet it makes no sense to say that I was mistaken in supposing myself to be pointing to this rather than that, so when I characterise what drew my attention, I may misdescribe it, and yet it makes no sense to say that I was mistaken in thinking that it was this that drew my attention rather than that.

There is one peculiar sort of case that arises in connexion with "having my attention drawn" and cannot arise with "pointing", which may be added to the present list of examples, although it is not strictly speaking a case of mistake or ignorance at all:

(e) My attention may be drawn to some feature which I already know to be illusory, but which is striking and worth attention nevertheless. Thus, after I have taken mescalin, my attention may be drawn by the unusual appearance of my carpet. Here I know that I am under an illusion, so of course will not try to point to this extraordinary appearance.

One further case concerns ignorance:

(f) It may be that x has drawn my attention, but that I do not know exactly what it is about x that has drawn my attention.

There is no analogy for this last case, either, in pointing. There must, of course, be some determinacy about what draws my attention, if only because to have my attention drawn is to have it drawn to one thing rather than another; and under the description so proffered I shall be able to point (unless of course the case is otherwise peculiar, by being e.g., of type (e)). It makes no sense to say that I do not know what about it I am pointing to, but it does make sense to say that I do not know what about it drew my attention. There is nothing surprising about this difference: since my purpose in pointing is to draw someone's attention to x, the description I furnish of x will be one which I suppose will effect this purpose, and one that is indeterminate through ignorance would be unsuitable. It is of course true that I can point to, and draw someone's attention to, x (under some description) just because I do not know what (under some other, usually more specific, description) it is: "look at that bird—what is it?" or "that shape in the corner!" This is a partial analogue to having my attention drawn to something and not knowing precisely to what feature of it—but only a partial analogue. For in the pointing case, if I point to x, and ask what it is, any further description I go on to give of it in an attempt to answer the question is in no logically different position from anyone else's suggestion. But the situation is different with the thing that drew my attention. If I go on to try to decide what it was about the thing that drew my attention, it seems that, although others may make suggestions and have theories on the subject, it is for me to decide whether their suggestions are correct. If I do sincerely and wholeheartedly decide that it was a particular feature of this thing that drew my attention to it—e.g., a certain resemblance, even if only a fancied resemblance, of this lady's hat to a familiar landmark—it is doubtful what sense it makes to say that I was mistaken in this diagnosis. The fancied resemblance may turn out to be only fanciful; but I cannot be mistaken in saying that it was this fancied resemblance that drew my attention to the shape of her hat; or that it was the shape that drew my attention to the hat; or that it was the hat that drew my attention to her. At most, I might, in certain very complicated contexts, be said to be deceiving myself; for instance, an inhibited person *might* succeed in deceiving himself into thinking that what drew his attention to a certain girl was the unusual material of her dress rather than its provocative cut. But such cases are perhaps rare.

How it is that one can come to know on reflection that it was *this* feature that drew one's attention to something, I find an obscure question. That such conclusions are not reached by empirical inference, and that one is not establishing an ordinary type of causal proposition, is evident.[5]

Before we return to the direct discussion of pleasure, one further point must be made about "having my attention drawn to". Two importantly different sorts of case have not been distinguished. The first is that in which my attention is drawn to something because I am expecting or looking for something, and the thing which draws my attention does so as a supposed candidate for being the object of my expectation or search. In such cases, obviously, my attention to the object will lapse if it turns out not to be the object in question, and if it is the object in question it will become the object of attention of a different kind, *viz.*, of whatever sort of interest motivated the expectation or search. Second, something can attract my attention as being surprising or (rather differently) in-

---

[5] This *may* be related to a point made by Miss G. E. M. Anscombe about certain bodily movements: *cf. Intention* (Blackwell, 1957) para. 8. Her phrase "cause known without observation" does not fit the present case; but then I am not sure that it is a very happy description of the case she is discussing, either.

triguing. In this case, attention will lapse if the object turns out not to be a surprising thing at all; or if it is, but surprise is dissipated by explanation; or if, without explaining it, I just get bored with it or distracted by something else. The most important difference between these two sorts of case is that in the first the object draws my attention as supposedly matching a description (in the broadest sense) with which I am already prepared— a description which would figure in an account of what I was already searching for, expecting, etc. In the second case, the description is not already prepared; the object merely introduces itself, arriving without invitation. It follows from this difference that the situations (a)–(f) described above do not all arise equally with both types of case; for instance, (f) does not arise with the first sort of case at all.

To return, now, to the case of pleasure. It is obvious that there is a close analogy between the cases (a)–(f) in connexion with attention, and similar cases in connexion with pleasure. There is in fact a parallel for each case, on the following lines:

(a) First, and again uninterestingly, I may remember some occasion in the past on which I was pleased, but misremember or completely forget what I was pleased at. This is perhaps rare; but less so with the converse case of misery: I may remember the miseries of childhood or adolescence, but forget, because I would now regard as trivial, their objects. This case is not to be taken to include the situation in which present pleasure is based on misremembering— this will be considered later.

(b) I may be pleased at x, but say that I am pleased at y because I falsely believe that x is y; but this does not matter, because x's being y is no element in my pleasure. Thus, I may be pleased by this picture, as a picture, and say that I am pleased by this Giorgione, when the picture is not a Giorgione.

(c) More drastically, I may take pleasure in, or be pleased by, x which I mistakenly think is y, where x's supposedly being y is the basis of my pleasure. Thus, I may be pleased by this supposed Giorgione as being a Giorgione.

(d) I may be pleased at something that does not exist at all, for instance my supposed inheritance of a fortune.

Common to cases (c) and (d) is the feature that the discovery of the truth means the end of pleasure—at least, of *that* pleasure. The distinction between case (c) and case (d) is often merely a matter of expression, and with many cases it would be ludicrously scholastic to try to force them into one class or the other. For instance, I might be very pleased by the arrival at my party of a gentleman whom I took to be a certain distinguished author. This could naturally take its place in class (c); but someone might argue, very strictly, that what I was pleased at was the (supposed) occurrence of a certain event, *viz.*, the arrival of this author, and that this event has not happened, *i.e.*, does not exist, so that the case belongs to class (*d*). It would surely be frivolous to insist on a decision between these two accounts of the situation.

However, a rather more serious point does perhaps emerge here; for it may be objected that the frivolity of an argument on this last question shows a weakness or unclarity in speaking in this way of the *objects* of pleasure at all. Often the most natural formulation will be to say that I am pleased because . . . .: *e.g.*, that I am pleased because (as I suppose) this author has arrived, rather than that I am pleased at the (supposed) arrival of this author. Alternatively, the language of activity may be appropriate: I might be taking pleasure in looking at the supposed Giorgione rather than in the supposed Giorgione. Some genuine differences are marked by these different formulations, and the sort of distinction I have been drawing needs refinement to deal with them. But the language of objects of pleasure which I am discussing here is sometimes not reducible to the language of "because", and is rarely not a possible alternative to it; and, as I tried to argue at the beginning of this paper, the language of "because" is a cause of philosophical puzzlement—which the other formulation, properly understood, may help to solve. The language of activity, again, seems more independent, and in some cases not to be reducible to the language of objects; unless it is that in those cases the activity is itself the object of pleasure in the same sense. But, as was argued in the previous discussion of the case of the inheritance, it is also true that the language of objects or of "because" cannot be reduced in every case to the language of activity. I shall not further discuss here the language of activity, which I suspect to be more closely related to the concept of enjoyment than to that of pleasure; in any case, our present concern is with the problems of belief and knowledge in relation to pleasure, and these less notably arise with activities. In so far as they do, it may be that some of the present account can be adapted to deal with them. (Thus it seems true to say that if I am engaged in an activity or performing an action, there is one sense in which I must know what I am doing; but this only means that there is some description of what I am doing under which I know that I am doing it, and there may be many others which I might offer of what I am doing which do not in fact apply. It might be under one of these latter descriptions that I was enjoying doing what I was doing (case (*c*)), or alternatively the misdescription might not matter because it was not *as this* that the action or activity was being enjoyed (case (*b*)); and so on.

The analogy between the cases discussed in connexion with pointing and attention, and similar cases with pleasure, does not stop here. Similar analogies can be found for the cases (*e*) and (*f*):

(e) I may be pleased by some feature which I know to be illusory, but which pleases me nevertheless. Thus, owing to my myopia, I may find a strident picture agreeably muted; having a high fever, I may find the sour drink pleasantly sweet; after mescalin, I may find my old curtains an exciting riot of colour.

(f) As x may draw my attention, and yet I may not know what it was about x that drew my attention, so I may be pleased by x, and yet not know what it is about x that I find pleasing. Again, with pleasure, as with attention, one finds in such cases the puzzling phenomenon of my apparently being able to discover by reflection what it was.

Thus there does seem to be an analogy between the cases of mistake, ignorance, and illusion that can arise with objects that draw my attention, and such cases that arise with the objects of pleasure. Before leaving the detailed consideration of the analogy however, there is one feature of it that needs further investigation. One notable way in which mistakes can affect pleasure is that my pleasure may be founded on false beliefs about the past or the future. Thus I may be pleased because I suppose the remark I recently overheard to have been a compliment about me, though it was not; or I may be pleased because I think that I am going to see a certain person tomorrow, and, as it turns out, I do not. The case of the supposed inheritance, previously mentioned, is a kind of amalgam of the two, since it involves both the belief that somebody has made a will in my favour, and the belief that money will be arriving; though it is presumably the latter belief that is the more closely connected with the pleasure. Now, with the inheritance as we have seen, the language of objects can indeed be used; and this case was assigned to a certain class in the analogy, class (d), of objects which I think exist but do not.

But the situation is more complicated than this suggests. First, there is a certain asymmetry between the past and the future in this respect. In the matter of the future, we must distinguish between the pleasures of anticipation and the pleasures of the event. I can of course have the former without the latter happening at all: either because the event does not happen, or because the event, though happening, turns out not to be pleasurable. These last two possibilities come to much the same thing, so far as the "baselessness" of the pleasures of anticipation is concerned; for the pleasures of anticipation consist in the anticipation of pleasure.[6]

In the matter of the past, it is in general true, correspondingly, that the pleasure of memory consists in the memory of pleasure. The "pleasure of memory" here is not to be confused, of course, with the pleasure of

---

[6] Cf. Plato, Philebus 39d seq.

reminiscence, or even of recall; with these, the pleasure is taken in a present "activity", *viz.*, recalling or reminiscing about some past events which in themselves need not have been particularly pleasant. We are interested in the "pleasure of memory" in a different sense, of the continuation or revival of the pleasure associated with some past event. But even in this connexion, we must distinguish two quite different ways in which mistakes may arise. The first is the case in which the pleasure is continued or revived by the correct memory of a pleasure originally based on a mistake—as in the case of the supposed compliment. This presents no special difficulty: it is merely, as it were, the inheritance of a mistake. But there is another case, in which, through mistake of memory, I either "remember" a pleasant event which did not happen and which I did not at the supposed time of happening believe to be happening, or misremember as pleasant an event which did happen but was found by me at the time unpleasant; in either case, I may feel present pleasure at the supposed past event. This is not the inheritance of a mistake, but a mistake of inheritance. Of these, the latter is more like the case of a mistake about the future.

Now it is not entirely clear how the language of objects is to be taken in such cases, nor what the analogy with attention will be. The cases can, as was suggested, be crammed into class (*d*), thus corresponding to those in which my attention is drawn to the actually non-existent. But this is not very illuminating. However, by extending the notion of attention a little, some better analogies can be found. Where I merely continue or revive a past pleasure originally based on a mistake, this is like having my attention drawn to something and continuing to concentrate on it when the object itself, or rather what I took to be this object, has been removed. More difficult is the case of present pleasure based on mere misremembering; yet here there is the analogy of someone's directing his attention to some event he supposes to have happened, or this event, or perhaps its memory, forcing itself on his attention. With the future, I can indeed have my attention directed to a supposed future event, as I do in expectation or waiting, which (as we noticed above) may be the preliminary to my having my attention drawn to the thing's actual appearance. This, though the analogy is not perfect, is something like the pleasure of anticipation followed by the pleasure of the event. The point needs further investigation, but I should like to suggest that the distinction between the "invited" and the "uninvited" objects of attention has other applications in connexion with the concept of pleasure. For instance, it is connected with the distinction, first drawn by Plato,[7] between those pleasures that consist in the satisfaction of a desire, and those that do not.

[7] *Philebus* 50b *seq.*

In the course of this discussion we have traced some analogies between, on the one hand, the relation of pleasure to its objects, and, on the other hand, the relation of attention to its objects. It can now be suggested that these analogies are not merely analogies: they exist because attention is involved in pleasure, and because the relation of pleasure to its objects *is* the relation of attention to its objects. If I am pleased by something, my attention is, to that extent, drawn to it; and the more I am pleased by it, the more my attention is absorbed in it. It may be remarked here that there are perhaps cases of pleasure that have no object; where one merely feels full of well-being. In fact, the word "pleasure" seems very rarely to be used in such cases, but rather "cheerfulness", "content-ment", etc.; or, if it is, the "pleasure" is given a pseudo-object ("pleased with life"). But if they are cases of pleasure, it is noteworthy that they are also cases in which characteristically my attention is not directed to anything in particular.

This is not to say, of course, that being pleased by something just is attending to it, that finding something pleasant just is having my attention drawn to it and held by it, that the pleasures of anticipation just are anticipation; attention can just as well be directed to or held by the unpleasant. It is rather that pleasure is one mode or species of attention.

This connexion between pleasure and attention has been noticed before, *e.g.*, by Prof. Ryle.[8] But Ryle does not discuss what the relation is of attention to its objects, in particular to objects which are mistakenly believed to exist. I have tried to show that the concept of attention is itself sufficiently complex in these respects to illuminate the corresponding complexities of the concept of pleasure. Now it may fairly be asked how much this explains; for, it may be said, since not all attention is attention to the pleasant, the actual relation of pleasure to attention remains still to be explained. This is true—it does. But at least the relation of pleasure to its objects may be somewhat clearer if it is shown that this relation is that of attention to its objects, and if this relation is given some explanation. The last I have tried, very sketchily, to do, in suggesting that the idea of attending to a thing can be based on, though not straightforwardly derived from, the simpler notion of pointing to a thing. In particular, I hope that the introduction of the notion of something's drawing my attention to itself may help to explain how it is that, although pleasure is something that happens to me rather than something I do, nevertheless the characterization of its objects shares epistemological features with the characterization of the objects of pointing, which is something I do rather than something that happens to me. These categories of "something I do" and "something that happens to me" are, of course, much too crude; but

---

[8] *Op. cit.* pp. 139 *seq.*; for pleasure as one mode of attention, see p. 142.

it is significant that they are much too crude for the concepts both of pleasure and of attention, and in very much the same ways. For instance, it sometimes happens that my attention is unexpectedly drawn to something because in fact I have been subconsciously looking for it, and very much the same thing can occur with pleasure.

The type of relation to an object that I have been trying to investigate in the cases of pleasure and attention is one of those that some philosophers have investigated under the title of "intentionality"; and though I have deliberately avoided the word, I hope the present remarks may suggest a line for clarifying this obscure notion. Some of these philosophers (perhaps Husserl) seem to have held that each type of "state of consciousness" was in the end unanalysable. If not only the relation of attention to its objects, but that of pleasure to attention, could be clarified, it might be found that this view was too pessimistic.

FOUR

Knowledge and Reasons

One aim of this paper is to make some suggestions about the role of reasons in knowledge. The other is to sketch an approach to the nature of knowledge which will put that question into a correct perspective. That sketch will indeed be sketchy, and most of what I shall say schematic. My aim is to put the main issues into what seems to me the right overall shape.

1. PROPOSITIONAL AND PRACTICAL KNOWLEDGE

I shall be concerned only with what I shall call *propositional* knowledge, knowledge whose paradigmatic expression in language-users is the confident assertion of truths, and where the claim that it is knowledge that is being expressed involves as a necessary condition that what is asserted is true. This contrasts with *practical* knowledge, of which the paradigmatic expression is the skilful and successful performance of some task. (Success is not, however, related to practical knowledge as truth is to propositional knowledge: without truth of the proposition there is no propositional knowledge, but practical knowledge can be present and in action, though robbed of success through extrinsic causes.)

The distinction is not easy to formulate, and admits borderline cases. It is, however, both genuine and ineliminable, neither sort of knowledge being reducible to the other; this I shall assume here without argument. I shall make two further remarks about the distinction, both relevant to what follows. First, I use the term *propositional*, and not the term hallowed by history for this contrast, *theoretical*, because the latter too readily imports the notion of the systematic. Some propositional knowledge is indeed theoretical, in the sense of being general, systematically arranged, having a structure of laws, etc.; but much propositional knowledge is not. The idea that what contrasts with practice is in *that* sense theory, can generate serious confusion (present, I think, in the reflections of Michael Oakeshott in his *Rationalism in Politics* and elsewhere). Second, I do not think that the distinction is very happily labelled, as by Ryle, as a distinction between *knowing that* and *knowing how*. These labels are of course all right if merely labels. But their use can encourage the neglect of several facts, some of them important. For example, not every ascription of propositional knowledge need, or even can, take as it stands the form "A knows that. . . ." "Know" importantly governs indirect questions (as in, notably, "A knows whether . . ."). The philosophical relevance of this fact will come up in (2) below. On the other hand "A knows how . . ." can represent propositional knowledge ("A knows how a nuclear power station works"); what represents practical knowledge is rather "A knows how to. . . ." But then there is no peculiarity with "how": practical knowledge can equally be represented by "A knows when to . . . , what to . . ." etc. Following from that, some cases of "A knows that . . ." can represent practical knowledge, if they further involve "to" (or equivalent construction) and (something like) a demonstrative: "A knows that this is the time to add the salt," "A knows that the one to use is the one that looks like this" etc.

I should perhaps add that I do not regard peculiar properties of the English language as very illuminating for the concept of knowledge; but they can serve to remind one of the misleading possibilities of labels themselves drawn from that language.

2. "Knowing That" and the Examiner's Situation

Philosophers who have addressed themselves to the third-personal issue (and have not, like Descartes, concentrated on "What do I know?"—a concentration which raises its own problems) have tended to stick to the question of the truth-conditions of "A knows that p." That is to say, they have looked for conditions sufficient for giving an affirmative answer to the question "does A know that p ?". In actual life, one very natural implication of asking that question is that the speaker himself knows that p, and is asking whether A does. One immediate effect of taking as central that question, which has that implication, is to push into the background an important class of cases: the cases, namely, where the speaker does not know how things stand with regard to p, and wants to find someone who does—a situation in which he could ask "who knows whether p?" or "does A know whether p?". We have already a concentration which helps us to forget a banal and important fact: knowers are, for others, sources of information.

Even in sticking to "A knows that p," however, the concentration tends to go in one only of several possible directions. The one favoured is that in which the point of the question is whether A's cognitive relation to the truth that p is adequate: in particular, the case where A is admittedly convinced of the truth that p, and the question is whether that conviction is adequately based. This situation, and more generally the situation in which informed questioners are concerned with A's credentials with regard to a piece of knowledge, we might call the *examiner's situation*. It is far from typical in practice. For instance, another and frequent situation with respect to the question "does A know that p?" is that in which the point of the question is to ask whether the information that p has *got out* to A, or *got round* to him: one of our interests in knowledge is where it has got to. Where such is our interest, the stress on credentials (the relevance of which to the examiner's situation is self-explanatory) is less to the fore. When my interest is whether A has come to know something which, for instance, it would be better for me if he did not know, the central question is whether the information has got to him, and he believes it, and less whether the reasons with which A would support his belief are strong or adequate reasons. Yet even in such a case, there is a contrast with A's merely having come to believe the proposition in question, a contrast embedded in the thought that the information has "got to" him. If he has come to know, then at least it is the case that he has not merely guessed—there must be a route by which the information has come to him, and the fact that what he believes is true must have contributed in some appropriate way to his having come to believe it. In this last consideration, obscure though it is, we shall see a central condition on the concept of knowledge.

Let us return to the cases in which our interest in another's possession of knowledge concerns a matter about which we lack knowledge: our concern (unlike the examiner's) is to find out, not so much about this person, as about the matter in hand. If "p" represents some sentence which may be used to make a statement of fact, let "wh-p" represent in general direct and (with any necessary grammatical modification) indirect questions that may be formed out of that sentence. The simplest example of an indirect question, available in every case, is "whether p." But there are of course many other and various possibilities; if "p" mentions some time ("the train leaves at 15.00 hrs") "wh-p" can be a "when"-question ("when does the train leave?" ". . . when the train leaves"); if "p" mentions a place, "wh-p" can be a "where"-question, etc. Now the following statements all seem to me to be true:

a. In many standard situations, all that is necessary for it to be the case that A knows wh-p—besides his actually being right in this case (see (b) below)—are such things as that A is almost always right about matters of this kind, because e.g., in the matter of the train, he has learned up the time-table; or that we know, what perhaps A himself does not know, that A has come by his beliefs on this subject by reliable means. Thus it may be that A has come by his beliefs from having been told by B, and we know that B is a reliable authority on these matters, though A himself may not, never (for instance) having reflected on that question.

b. If conditions of this kind are satisfied, then all that is further necessary for it to be the case that A knows wh-p is that the beliefs he
has with regard to the question be true, i.e. that he actually be right.
(I shall assume throughout this paper that *belief*, involving a fair
degree of conviction, is a necessary condition of knowledge. I doubt
whether that is true without qualification, but the assumption will
serve for the present discussion.)

c. If A knows wh-p, and P is the class of correct answers to the question
"wh-p?," then for some member of P, q, A knows that q. This rather
cumbrous formulation is intended to allow for such facts as that if
"wh-p?" is a "who"-question—say, of the form "who did X?"—A
may know of a certain person under some descriptions that he did
X, but not under other descriptions.

If the statements (a)–(c) are all true, then it is possible for A to know
that q without its being the case that A can rehearse reasons, or at least
adequate reasons, for q. For the sorts of conditions mentioned in (a) do
not necessarily imply anything, or anything very substantial, about A's
consciousness of reasons for q, or of his own relation to the truth of q.
They are conditions *about* A, rather than conditions *on* A; we may call
them (to use a phrase I owe to discussion with Mr G. O'Hare) *external*
conditions. If (a)–(c) are true, then the satisfaction of such external conditions can, together with true belief, be sufficient for knowledge.

3. Knowledge without Reasons

One might hope that it would be so. For if we consider the classical tripar-
tite analysis of propositional knowledge, namely that A knows that p if
and only if (i) p is true, (ii) A believes that p, (iii) A has good reasons for
p, there is a notorious difficulty, that a regress is likely to be generated,
and in more than one way.[1] For if A's reason for p is constituted by some
other proposition which supports p, then it seems that this in turn must
be something that A knows, unless we are to embrace the not very inviting
conclusion that the difference between true belief and knowledge is basically the difference between believing one true thing and believing two
true things which are connected. Moreover, the fact that this other proposition supports p must itself (it seems) be something that A knows, which
generates a further regress.

[1] The difficulty has been well discussed by Gettier: see his article reprinted in Phillips
Griffiths, ed., *Knowledge and Belief*, Oxford 1967; and also Griffiths' introduction to that
book. The present discussion is also indebted to Martin and Deutscher, "Remembering",
Philosophical Review 1966.

Some formulations of the third condition (such as Ayer's "A has the right to be sure" in *The Problem of Knowledge*) are designed to be general enough to allow of at least some cases in which the appropriate grounding of A's true belief does not take the form of another proposition which A knows or believes. But the purpose of such attempts has generally been to accommodate some class or classes of propositions which supposedly possess some specially evident or ground-level character: the regress is to be stopped by *foundations*. Whatever may be said about the foundations of knowledge, I do not believe that they are thus to be brought in, as an answer to this difficulty in relation to the account of what knowledge in general is. Rather, we should acknowledge that if we are speaking *in general* about knowledge, not only is it not necessary that the knower be able to support or ground his true belief by reference to other propositions, but it is not necessary that he be in any special state with regard to this belief at all, at least at the level of what he can consciously rehearse. What is necessary—and what represents the undoubted fact that knowledge differs from mere true belief—is that one or more of a class of conditions should obtain, which relate the fact that A has this belief to the fact that the belief is true: conditions which can best be summarised by the formula that, given the truth of p, it is no accident that A believes p rather than not-p. This formula is vague and over-generous, but it gets us, I think, on the right line; in particular, in the consideration that the notion of its being "no accident" is basically the same notion as is employed in a causal investigation.

Suppose a spiritualist medium or some such is thought to have clairvoyant powers. She makes claims, of which she is convinced, about the whereabouts of certain objects, or states of affairs elsewhere. Let us suppose that her claims are clear and determinate and, moreover, true. Two questions might now be raised: is it just an accident, extraordinary good luck on her part, that she is right in this series of cases? and—does she know? My thesis is that these are the *same* question. If we are convinced that it cannot just be luck, that the probability of chance success at this level is vanishingly small, then the question arises of how the success comes about: which is the same question as, how does she know? (The difference in English, that we ask why he believes, but how does he know, a difference remarked by Austin and other philosophers, is indeed indicative of a truth.) Perhaps we shall not be able to find out how it happens: in that case, we shall not be able to tell how she knows. If we are left in that position, we shall not (*pro tanto*) be led to deny that she knows, any more than we shall deny that the correlation indeed exists, is too good for chance, and demands an explanation. We shall just be left with the admittedly puzzling fact that she does know, but there is an utter obscurity about how she knows.

We may take also a familiar real-life example. Someone in close relations with another may often know how the other feels, what thought has occurred to them, how they are about to react, why they reacted in a certain way. Their grounds for these convictions are often, at the conscious level, virtually non-existent or at least hopelessly unspecific. But if it is true that such a person is usually right—and not, as sometimes, merely passing over the negative instances—then we have little hesitation in ascribing knowledge. In this case, we also have a general idea of how they know: there is an explanatory schema available, which could in principle be further filled in, no doubt, by careful investigation of what they are subconsciously "going on."

It is worth saying in passing that the existence of such unreasoned knowledge; the existence, further (though this is not the present point), of personal and social knowledge which the subject cannot even adequately express, let alone justify: these things do not stand opposed, in some mystical way, to a rational and scientific picture of what the world is like. That humans can understand the human in ways in which the non-human is not to be understood, does not show that man stands apart from nature, but rather shows something about what kind of system in nature he is. To think, moreover, that unless unreasoned human understanding is magic, it must be possible to *replace* it with articulate and reasoned procedures in a scientific style, is again a *non-sequitur*, and in good part a scientistic illusion. To insist on thinking about personal situations in such terms makes, after all, a concrete psychological difference to the thinker, a difference which may perfectly well destroy, without replacing, the knowledge he would otherwise have. The role and importance of the reflective and self-conscious in human affairs is indeed a serious issue, but it is not to be thought of in terms of replacing weather-magic with meteorology.

4. The Difficulty of Producing a Criterion

I claim, then, that it is not a requirement *in general* on knowledge that the knower be in some special conscious state in relation to his true belief; the requirement rather is that it be no accident, granted the truth of p, that he believe p rather than not-p. But if this is considered as an *analysis* of knowledge, there is no doubt that it will not serve, since it is too vague and (on natural interpretations) over-generous. For suppose that A, being from Guinea, tells B falsely that he is from Ghana; but (let us fancifully suppose) owing to features of A's spoken English which are peculiar to Guineans, B takes him to have said "Guinea" when he said "Ghana." Then B has come truly to believe that A is from Guinea, and (in an obvious sense) it is no accident, relative to A's being from Guinea, that this has come about; but B can scarcely be said to have acquired knowledge in this way, as opposed (for instance) to a situation in which, familiar with the Guinean accent, he sees through the pretence. Or again, the firm's accountant, being depressed over personal matters, is influenced by that to give a gloomy picture of the firm's affairs. The manager is depressed by this account; being disposed, when depressed, to think that everyone else is, he forms the (true) belief that the accountant is. This can hardly count as the acquisition of knowledge, either.

These, and other, cases do seem to be counter-examples to the "no accident" account taken without further restriction as an analysis, since they do seem (unless we covertly assume some unexplained restriction) to satisfy the general condition that the acquisition of the belief was no accident relative to its truth, and yet these are not cases of knowledge. Further investigation may be hoped to provide some appropriate types of restriction, such as those needed to distinguish the passage of a piece of information (in a propositional sense—not in the generalized sense used e.g. in the biological sciences, though that is not irrelevant), from the more general notion of a causal chain with the same proposition at each end of it. In the absence of the required restrictions, I offer the "no accident" clause not as part of an analysis but (as I said before) as a label for a class of conditions, the general requirements on which need to be spelled out with greater precision.

One general requirement indeed is that the route from fact to belief should *in general* be a truth-producing or truth-preserving route—that beliefs engendered by this *kind* of process should have a good probability of being true. But that, while correct, does not actually get us very far. For the difficult question remains: at what level of generality of description is a process or kind of process to be determined to have or lack the truth-producing feature? Or—another way of putting it—what is to count as the same, or a different, process? Thus it may be said with regard to the two cases just described, that what is wrong is that the processes of belief-production involved—mishearing in the one case, being influenced by a mood in the other—are not in general truth-producing processes. Well, regarded at this level of generality, they are not. But regarded at a more specific level, with the distinctive features of the cases put in, they are, and the question is why the first and not the second level of description should properly represent our view of the situation.

Very similar problems arise with the characterization of *reasons*. A fact which, described at one level, constitutes a good reason for believing something (e.g. "being told by Jones, a reliable authority") will have many other descriptions under which it will appear as a bad reason, or no reason at all ("being told by somebody," "being told by a man who has never been to Paris"). This unsurprising parallelism between the problems of finding the right application of "no accident," and the problems of assessing reasons, is one of several grounds for supposing that the sort of difficulty presented by these cases is not one of principle with the "no accident" account, but only demands refinement of it.

5. The Place of Reasons

None of this is to deny that the possession of reasons plays an important role in the economy of the concept of knowledge. It would be highly paradoxical if there were no such role. But the present account enables us to see the nature and point of that role more clearly than does an account which merely insists on the possession of reasons.

In many cases, it will be highly probable, and in some cases, it will be necessary, that the only way in which a subject could reliably and (relative to the truth) non-accidentally acquire true beliefs is via the *thought* of considerations which support the truth-claim, that is to say, via reasons. It is likely to be so with knowledge of matters remote to the subject in space and time; though here it is worth remembering the platitude that we all possess information about the past (and leaving aside the special case of our own pasts) which is rightly accepted as knowledge yet whose credentials lie in no adequate reasons that we can muster for these propositions, but in the "external" fact that we have acquired the information from presumptively reliable sources, which we cannot now, usually, remember. A special sort of requirement for reasons comes into view with propositions of certain logical types. Concerning mathematical propositions, for instance, save of the simplest kind, there is strong pressure behind the Platonic view that the distinction between knowledge and true belief lies in the possession of an *aitias logismos*, a chain of proof. Plato himself claimed (at least in the *Meno*) that the point of this demand, and thereby the superiority of knowledge, lay in the greater permanence of beliefs so tied down. It may or may not be psychologically true that such beliefs are more permanent, but it hardly goes to the heart of the matter, which is surely more the point that the access to mathematical truth must necessarily lie through proof, and that therefore the notion of non-accidental true belief in mathematics essentially involves the notion of mathematical proof (the points which the Platonic model of *recollection* precisely serves to obscure).

Now I can truly believe a mathematical proposition, which I cannot demonstrate, because I have been authoritatively told that it is true. This would be widely agreed not to constitute knowledge—knowledge, that is, that p, where p is the mathematical proposition. But there is another piece of knowledge that I might well be said to have in these same circumstances—the knowledge that p is a mathematical truth. It will seem paradoxical to take apart in any way knowing that p, and knowing that p is true. But if these two are kept logically tied together, then the line must come between knowing that p is true, and knowing that p is a truth of a given science. To be a truth of a given science is to be, in a special sense, a part of *knowledge*; and to know that a proposition has that status is to know that it is, by the standards of that science, to be counted as *known*, as opposed to its being, for instance, a matter merely of plausible conjecture.

This consideration brings us to a last and different sort of connection between knowledge and reasons. So far, I have been discussing knowledge as, in a certain sense and in part, a psychological concept, one to be applied to individuals with respect to their hold on true propositions. But there is such a thing as impersonal knowledge, as when we speak of the state of knowledge in a given field, or of something's now being known which was not known 20 years ago, or of the structure of a certain molecule not being known though there exist various theories or hypotheses about it.

That there should be radically impersonal knowledge seems, on the face of it, impossible: if p is known, then somebody surely must know it. But this apparent platitude is in conflict with other things we are also disposed to accept, and at least one of them has got to give. Let "Kip" stand for "it is known that p," in the sense under discussion, and "Kap" stand for "a knows that p." The apparent platitude is

(1) If Kip, then, for some a, Kap.

The following, further, seems to be plausible:

(2) If Kip and Kiq, then Ki(p & q).

But certainly this is not true:

(3) If Kip and Kiq, then, for some a, Ka(p & q);

If (3) were true, the age of the universal polymath would not be behind us. But (3) is entailed by (1) and (2), since "p & q" will of course be a substitution instance of "p" in (1). I will not explore this problem here, beyond pointing out that we must resist the temptation to defend (1) on the basis of the two assumptions (a) that the logic of "Kip" will be revealed by concentrating just on true assertions of the form "Kip," (b) that anyone who truly asserts or, at least, who knows, that Kip must himself know that p. Neither is true. A proper understanding of "Kip" will take into account, for instance, questions whether Kip; and as to (b), we have already seen in the mathematical case that it is false.

I have mentioned this problem only to show that the relations between impersonal and personal knowledge are not as simple as may at first appear. Now, impersonal knowledge certainly has a special commitment to reasons. Bodies of knowledge are essentially, if to varying degrees with different subjects, systematic. There is both a pure and an applied reason for this. Pure, because the aim is not just to know but to understand, and in scientific cases at least understanding necessarily implies organization and economy. Applied, because a body of knowledge will only be freely extensible and open to criticism if rationally organized. And there are of course other considerations which support the same point. So knowledge, in this sense, must have reasons. It may, even, have foundations, though that is an open question. What it is an open question *of*, however, is the philosophy of science; these are different issues from those of epistemology in general, that is to say, the study of knowledge as such, and in particular personal knowledge.

Whatever is to be said about the relations between personal and impersonal knowledge, it is of course true that what is known is fragmentarily known by various persons; the *savant* has internalised some part of a body of knowledge. Insofar as this is true, his personal knowledge will satisfy the standards of rational organization which are appropriate to a body of knowledge. But we must not take that special case as *the* clue to the account we should give of the ordinary business of personal knowledge.

FIVE

Identity and Identities

In 1955, there appeared an ingenious and enjoyable novel by Nigel Dennis called *Cards of Identity*. It introduced an organization called the 'Identity Club', which engaged in making people over, giving them a new past and a new character—a new identity. There was much discussion of the *name* that any given character should have. This gives the flavour:

> 'Has he been with us for long?'
> 'A good many years. He came straight here from the Navy. I found him, dead-drunk, in a Portsmouth gutter.'
> 'And he likes his name?'
> 'He took to it immediately. Would you care to construe?'
> 'I should love to. We begin with the premise that every butler believes he was born to command a fleet.'
> 'That is correct. Go on.'
> 'Nelson, you felt, was too common a name . . . But in Jellicoe you found *everything*—a bellicose, echoing, challenging suggestion discreetly balanced by an opening syllable indicative of a nature congealed and wobbly. In short, though he is for ever partly something pink, shaking guiltily on a plate, he has, in whole, the stuff of leadership.'
> 'That is first-class, Beaufort. Thus it was, exactly. Incidentally, it may interest you to know that at first I toyed with the idea of an identity from the race-course. But when I put out a few racy feelers, he shrank in horror. That is an important thing to know, by the way. Never, except in rare cases, build on the existing disguise. Imagine the horror of this wretched man if I had taken up his crop and cord breeches and named him Donoghue.'
> 'And *too* Irish,' murmured Mrs Mallet sleepily. 'Not the streak we want here at the moment, with so much to do.' (Dennis 1955:* 40–1)

In this connection 'giving him a new identity' means making him a certain *sort* of person. Although he is not merely an imperious butler, but an imperious butler called Jellicoe, born in a certain town on a certain day, and so forth, this is still a type, though a very individuated type. Underly-

---

* This is a reference to Nigel Dennis, *Cards of Identity* (London: Weidenfeld and Nicolson).—Ed.

ing the type, in the sense of the identity that is applied to a particular human being, we have the idea of that human being, and his particular identity. The person who gets the new identity in the type-sense still has his old identity in the particular-sense: he is, unchangeably, the same human being as the one who was found in the gutter and was made into a dignified butler by the Identity Club.

Many philosophical problems about identity concern the criteria for the identity of particular things. In the first part of this essay I shall consider a number of different philosophical problems that are associated with the concept of the identity of a particular thing. This leads to a particularly important case of the relation of particulars to types, which I shall take up in the later part of the essay: this is the notion of a person's social identity.

I start with more strictly metaphysical questions. Identity intimately involves counting, either synchronic or over time, and problems of identity are connected with what, in ancient terms, may be called questions of the One and the Many, of how many things of a certain sort there are at a certain place or over a certain period. As Frege helpfully insisted, the question 'how many?' always demands an answer to 'how many what?' What we have in front of us may be one wood and 500 trees, or one library and 2,000 books. In these cases, the more numerous things, the trees or books, constitute, make up, or are parts of the one thing, and the one thing indeed looks like an aggregate of particular things. But sometimes, the one may be a great deal more obvious than the many. This is a significant point in biology. There are many species of animals, for instance jellyfish of the order *Siphonophora*, such as the notorious Portuguese man-of-war, with which the manifest individual is, in fact, a colony of smaller and rather different individuals joined together: there is one Portuguese man-of-war, which is a colony or association of many constituent animals. Since the colonial participants may be functionally differentiated to some extent, this raises questions about the boundaries of an individual, and also what counts as a biological type. With the Portuguese man-of-war, it is not quite the case that one jellyfish consists of many jellyfish, and quite certainly it does not consist of many Portuguese men-of-war. In other cases, however, the one and the many may collect the same name.

This is characteristic of cloning. There is a species of desert bush that grows in an increasing circle, and parts in the middle, and parts between clumps on the circumference, then die off. This process can yield a circle, in some cases a very large circle, of separate bushes which are in a sense one bush. Is the result one bush with spatially separated parts, or several bushes? In this case it may not matter much. It is easy to answer that it is both one and many, or that it does not matter which one says. But one should not get too attached to the description in terms of 'one thing'. It can run into real difficulties, particularly when we are concerned with motile species. Identity questions typically and unsurprisingly sharpen up when things can move about.

This is obvious in the case of the amoeba. The amoeba divides, and it is extremely important that its division constitutes a form of (asexual) reproduction; the function of this process is to produce two amoebae. If there are two amoebae, then they are not each identical with the one that was there in the first place. If they were identical with that, they would be identical with each other, which means that there would be only one amoeba. This would yield the discouraging result that however hard the amoeba reproduced, it would never increase the population of amoebae. There would simply be parts of the amoeba which turned up in different places. We have good reason to resist this description.

Splitting may look like a particularly good way of preserving one's identity through time. If I could split, it might seem that I would not only go on existing, but do so twice over. But in fact, division is typically destructive of identity through time. The amoeba does not appear in two places at once, but rather gives up its existence so that there will be two amoebae.

An equally ancient metaphysical puzzle concerns form and matter. This in fact leads back quite soon to the One and the Many, and a case in which we end up with more things than we wanted. The fact that a thing of one kind can be made up of or consist of parts or pieces of stuff means, familiarly enough, that the parts can change while the whole remains the same. In the case of creatures, such as ourselves, which consist of living cells which are almost all replaced over a periodic cycle, some find it tempting to say that 'we are not really the same' at the end of this period. This is simply not correct, for a reason which shows that the phenomenon in itself does not yield a puzzle. A living body may be a thing made of cells, without its being the case that the same body is a thing made of the same cells. All that follows is that the same body is the same thing made of cells. The puzzles come not from this in itself, but from cases that involve peculiar items, or again ordinary items that have peculiar histories. A paradigm of identity through time is provided, as so often in philosophy, by standard physical objects, the sort of thing that J. L. Austin used to call 'middle sized dry goods'. There are many sorts of things which by comparison with those material objects are peculiar with respect to identity. They have a history and some sort of location but their criteria of identity seem to be vague or stipulative: there are things such as clubs, regiments, rivers, and so forth. In these cases, it is very obvious that the parts or constituents change, but vague what counts as continuity. Regiments merge, clubs cease and revive, and there are related questions of what counts as their existing at all. Items of these sorts may even be thought to have discontinuous existence, an idea which from a logical point of view is quite awkward. The river dries up for a bit or, like rivers in Australia, regularly dries up for long periods. Is there then no river? Or a dried-up river?

It is not a sign of good sense to make too much of such questions. I do not mean by that, as scientists and others may be disposed to think, that it is philosophy but not good sense; I mean that it is not philosophical good sense. But it is not always easy to rest on the point of conventional decision. As we saw before, with regard to the bush and the amoeba, identity questions can move very quickly from the seemingly trivial and verbal to the genuinely puzzling, and this fact itself is revealing. It is only what is on the surface of how we speak that can be easily rearranged.

An example of this is provided by the famous ship of Theseus, a vessel in which the hero is supposed to have come back to Athens, and which was preserved, but had its constituent planks replaced gradually over a long time until none of the original material remained. This gave rise in ancient times to a question of whether the end-product was the original ship. Thomas Hobbes brilliantly introduced into this not very interesting puzzle the further idea that the original planks were kept and then reassembled into a ship exactly like the original, with the result that there were then two candidates for being the ship of Theseus.[1] As Hobbes pointed out, and as we may recall from the case of the amoeba, they could not both be that particular ship. In the case of the amoeba, it had two descendants both of which arrived by exactly the same means; in the case of the ship, it might be said that there were two descendants which had arrived by different means, that of form and that of matter.

Rather than asking which, if either, is the original ship, it may be more interesting to ask the following question: if either of these things had existed without the other, would that have been the ship of Theseus? This suggests the idea that the answer to such identity questions is to be given in terms of the best available candidate. In these terms, the continuously repaired ship will indeed be the original if the planks have not been retained and reassembled, but equally the ship made of the original planks would, if the other had been destroyed, be that original ship. This seems, in its own way, quite sensible, but there is something counter-intuitive about Best Candidate Theory.[2] It leads to the result that something can stop being, or become, exactly the same thing as an original item. The

---

[1] de Corpore 2. 11. I am indebted on this question to David Wiggins: see Wiggins 1980: 92. [This is a reference to David Wiggins, *Sameness and Substance* (Oxford: Blackwell). —Ed.]

[2] It is defended (under the name 'Closest Continuer Theory') by Robert Nozick (1981, ch. 1). [This is a reference to Robert Nozick, *Philosophical Explanations* (Cambridge: Harvard University Press).—Ed.]

ship which Hobbes regarded as the winner—the one made of the original boards—was the worse candidate when it was not even a ship, but a pile of boards. When they were reassembled into a ship, did the other one cease to be the ship of Theseus? Moreover, if there is a contest between two items which results in a tie, this can lead to a merely arbitrary choice of one item to be the original thing. I think that a theory in these terms is a recognizable account of something, but not of numerical identity. What we should rather say about Hobbes's example is that the description 'the ship of Theseus' refers not to a particular ship but to a *role*, rather like the role of the Admiral's flagship; as in that case, the role can be discharged by various particular ships at different times.

The type of example for which Best Candidate Theory is particularly implausible is personal identity. Imaginary or science fiction cases are often discussed in this connection, in which one person's memory and character end up in another person's body, and the question is raised whether the person with Smith's memory and character (the psychological continuant) or the person with Smith's body (the bodily continuant) is Smith. In such a case, Best Candidate Theory seems absurd. From the outside, indeed, we might seem to be left just with a decision whether to say that the bodily continuant was indeed Smith who had lost his memories and so forth, or alternatively to say that the psychological continuant was Smith in a different body. But from the inside—that is to say from the perspective of the original Smith—it can scarcely seem like a matter of conventional decision. If unpleasant treatment, for instance, is to be applied after such a change to *this* body (the body that the original Smith originally has), should he or should he not expect to be hurt? It is hard to see how the answer to that question could depend upon what decision an observer might arrive at under Best Candidate Theory.

Conventionalism about identity is very tempting, as we saw with the bush, and the regiment, and the river, and the ship of Theseus discussed in antiquity. But faced with Hobbes's two ships of Theseus, and indeed with the amoeba, we are brought to see that conventionalism about identity does not come cheap, and that we have more commitments than we may suppose to dividing the world up on some lines rather than on others. When, further, it comes to myself and the proposed torture, conventionalism seems to lose its grip entirely. Here, conventionalism and Best Candidate Theory seem not to offer an invitation, but merely to demand that we understand our own thoughts better.

Questions at this level about persons are, in a metaphysical sense, questions what or who a person is. Such questions can themselves be related to ethics and politics, in a number of ways. They can bear, for instance, on the ethics and politics of euthanasia. But there is another kind of ethical and political question that can be expressed by asking the question 'what am I?' This kind of question concerns one's identity as a person who belongs to a certain family, group, or race; they are questions of social identity. In these connections 'identity' has a sense which, as in Nigel Dennis's story, relates to a type or a general thing. A gay or lesbian identity, a native American identity, or that of a Lombard as opposed to an Italian, are all type things, because such an identity is shared. Indeed, it is particularly important that it is shared, and an insistence on such an identity is an insistence on the ways in which it is shared. There is something else that it may have in common with Nigel Dennis's identities; it may be constructed. It will not of course be constructed by the intentions of a club, but by social processes; and again in common with Dennis's Identity Club, some of the construction may be demonstrably fictional.

At this point, it is easy to say that social identity is simply a benign self-applied stereotype, one that is favourable, supportive, and applied to oneself, rather than one that is unfavourable and applied to us by others. There is a grain of truth in this, and it reminds us how a negative stereotype may be by political action converted into a positive identity. But this simple account rides over an essential difference. A stereotype deployed against me by others impinges on my self, and if it gets into it, it is an obstacle to my living freely or effectively or in a convinced way. But an identity that I embrace is an aid to living in such ways. The difference between an identity which is mine and which I eagerly recognize as mine, and an identity as what someone else simply assumes me to be, is in one sense all the difference in the world.

But what is it for a general character or role or type to constitute my identity? Here the relations between type and particular individual are crucial. It is very important that an identity of this kind is not my identity in the particular-sense. If it were, then if I were separated from the life and allegiances which expressed that identity I would cease to exist. Moreover, if the form of life that embodied that identity were destroyed, the people who possessed it would cease to exist. But it is not so, and to insist that it is not so is not merely a piece of pedantry or an affirmation of abstract metaphysics. The point is included, rather, in the thoughts of the people who have such identities themselves. If those disasters happen, the particular people will still exist, because it is they who will have been damaged or wronged by this happening. If, for instance, native Americans on reservations are conscious of the loss of an identity, they are conscious precisely of *their own* loss. The destruction of a culture is often said to be a kind of genocide, but, while putting it like this has a point, it significantly misplaces the wrong or damage of which it is complaining. The loss of a culture can be seen, from a conservationist point of view, as the loss of variety or of a human possibility; but that is an external point of view on it, as it is with the extinction of a species.

An essential part of the idea of social identity is that a particular human being can find or lose identity in social groups. Henri Tajfel, the founder of modern social identity theory, defined social identity as 'the individual's knowledge that he or she belongs to certain social groups together with some emotional or value significance to him or her of the group membership'.[3] This account is enough for many of the questions that are pursued in social psychology under this general title, such as the relations of group membership to self-esteem, perceptions of salience, the relations between in-groups and out-groups, and so on. However, it goes rather wide as a definition of what might be called more strictly an *identity*. Thus someone may be very conscious of his or her membership of MENSA or of the Royal Society, and derive self-esteem from this, without its constituting or powerfully contributing to his or her identity. Indeed, a person who found his or her identity fundamentally in the membership of one of these organizations might be thought to be in a bad way.

One feature of the general or type classification that can help it to contribute to someone's identity is that it is thought to explain or underlie a lot of the individual's activities, emotions, reactions and, in general, life. It is from the point of view of those who endorse it a deep social classification. This in itself, of course, does not make it into a 'sortal' concept—that is to say, a fundamental concept for counting: the number of Quebecois people present is the same as the number of human beings present who are Quebecois. 'Human being' is, roughly, a term of nature, and 'Quebecois' a term of culture. But for those to whom 'Quebecois' is a powerful term of social identity it is as basic a classificatory term in culture as 'human being' is in nature.

However, it is also typical of such identities that they are not just analogous to the classifications of nature, but closely related to nature. You are, for instance, typically *born* in some relation to Quebec that makes you a Quebecois. When people of some minority cease trying to assimilate and opt for a culturally distinct identity, they seek to affirm an *origin*.

It is not always simply like this. Thus people may find their identity in a religious sect which they voluntary join. But it is typical in such cases that they have some sense that this is not just opting for one group among others but constitutes finding something that was there; or coming home—one kind of obedience to Nietzsche's splendid instruction 'become what you are'. In such a case, though I may feel that I have come there voluntarily, what I have come to lies outside my will: something is given, even though I must choose to take it up. This is true, of course, also of those other cases, of national or racial or tribal identification; the will

---

[3] Quoted in Abrams and Hogg 1990: 2. [This is a reference to Dominic Abrams and Michael A. Hogg, eds., *Social Identity Theory* (Hemel Hempstead: Harvester).—Ed.]

may be exercised in coming to coincide with something that I already unchangeably am.

This is one reason, also, why there is a special complexity to sexual identity. The self-conscious adoption of a gay or a straight life has its significance, surely, because it is not just joining one or another club but counts as a recognition of something. At the same time, that consciousness requires also that being gay or straight should not just be a matter of genetic or developmental determinism. There must be a space for both nature and the will.

All this helps us, perhaps, to see why the politics of identity should be so essential to our life now. Ever since the Enlightenment a recurrent aspiration of distinctively modern politics has been for a life that is indeed individual, particular, mine, within the reach of my will, yet at the same time expresses more than me, and shapes my life in terms that mean something because they lie beyond the will and are concretely given to me. It is the politics, if you like, of self-realization. That term contains in itself obvious difficulties: it is even grammatically ambiguous between activity and passivity, and illuminatingly so. Those obscurities are the product not of mere semantic inefficiency, but of unresolved political and personal tensions. This is one application of a more general lesson about philosophical problems of identity, that if we find it systematically hard to know what to say, the problem lies probably not in our words but in our world.

PART TWO

Ethics

SIX

The Primacy of Dispositions

I

There are several ways of understanding a philosophical search for what is primary or fundamental in ethics. The search might be for conceptual priority or dependence; and one way of understanding such a priority would be in terms of definitions. Moore,[1] for a while, thought that *right* was to be defined as *productive of the greatest good*, and he understood this not as a stipulative definition but as an account of what the term actually meant. This implied that an evidently contentious position, generalized utilitarianism or consequentialism, was to be found not only in language, but on the surface of it. As a linguistic hypothesis, the suggestion was very implausible, and was open to the style of 'open question' argument that Moore himself used against suggested definitions of *good*.

There is a different kind of thought, introducing a different kind of priority, and it may perhaps have been this that Moore unsatisfactorily tried to express in terms of a definition. Such thoughts are concerned with ways in which different kinds of value, in particular the value of different kinds of thing, may be best understood, and they may try to establish priorities between them. They may be called 'explicative' thoughts. In the present case, this thought will be to the effect that the value of actions is entirely derived from the value of states of affairs.

There has been a linguistic suggestion also in the opposite direction, to the effect that *good* is to be defined in terms of *right* or *ought*. Here again, as purely linguistic hypotheses the proposals scarcely look plausible. Here again, it is likely that some other thought is being expressed in this form, and it may be an explicative thought. But what will the explicative thought be in this case? In the case of Moore's proposal, I suggested that the underlying thought might be that actions entirely derived their value from the value of states of affairs. But we cannot simply take the converse path with the present proposal. No one can suggest, with any plausibility at all, that actions alone basically have value, and that the value of every-

---

[1] *Principia Ethica* (Cambridge, 1903), sections 89 and 117. Moore later retracted the view.

thing else is derivative from the value of actions. Action is for some end, and the deliberations that issue in action are usually directed to securing some good other than the action itself. When agents deliberate, they often (though not always) want their eventual action to bring about something else to which they attach value. It cannot be true that the only basic value is that of actions. If there is any interesting explicative view that is misrepresented by the suggestion that *good* is to be defined in terms of *right* or *ought*, it cannot be this.

There is a difficulty in seeing what it might be. *Right* and *ought* certainly express notions that apply to actions. If the view says, in any form, that these notions are basic, while notions such as *good* are derivative from them, it does seem committed to saying that at any rate, all *thought* about value must in some sense be *thought* about the value of actions. How can this be, if it is not true—and it obviously is not—that all value derives from the value of actions?

If *right* or *ought* expressed some specifically moral notion such as obligation, it does not seem that there could be an answer to this question. Not even all thought about *moral* value could be reduced to thought about obligation. This is clear if one considers the thought that it would be a morally better state of affairs in which people did what they were obliged to do. People who believe in the basic moral value of obligation are not likely to dispute this thought, but its content cannot be rendered entirely in terms of obligation. In particular, those people need not accept, and will probably reject, a claim to the effect that each of us has an obligation to try to bring about that state of affairs.

However, *ought* does not have to be explained in terms of obligation. It can lead us to another, and broader, notion: the notion of what one has most reason to do or to promote. Can we explain our thoughts about what is valuable entirely in terms of what we have reason to promote? The answer seems once more to be 'no', since we meet the same sort of problem as we met before, that we often think that we have reason to promote some state of affairs *because* it is valuable.

If there is a way round this difficulty, it will have to lie in going outside the theory of value. We shall have to accept that one can have a reason for promoting something without necessarily thinking that it would be valuable; thus one can have reason to promote something simply because one wants it, without thinking that one's getting it would be valuable. If we want to explain the idea of the valuable in terms of what one has reason to promote, this is the point from which we shall have to start. We might say, for instance, that a state of affairs is more valuable than another just in case more people have more reason to promote it. Another suggestion, not very different in principle, might be that a valuable state of affairs is one that an agent would have reason to promote who had the power to do so and who acted solely on the basis of what most people had most reason to promote. This might yield a version of utilitarianism, recognizably like Hare's theory. It is a question for further enquiry, what variations on this structure might be introduced by interpreting more or less generously the idea of what people *have reason* to promote. But it has to be remembered, of course, that if the structure is to serve the purpose we are presently discussing, of explaining all value in terms of reasons for action, notions of value must not be taken for granted in laying down what are to count as reasons for action.

II

So far I have moved too easily between two different things: *dimensions of value*, such as rightness, goodness, etc., and the *categories* of things being valued, such as actions and states of affairs. These two matters are not related to one another straightforwardly. Thus there can be, obviously enough, not only actions that one ought to produce, but good actions; and one can say of states of affairs not only that they are good, but that they ought to come about. So one cannot discuss priorities among the dimensions of value simply in terms of the categories of things being valued. I do not want to deny this. My assumption up to this point has merely been that those who have wanted to make *ought* or some such notion basic will naturally start from actions, while those who see *good* as basic will, given this choice, prefer to see the valuation of states of affairs as primary. This seems reasonable enough. Once one leaves behind a preoccupation with definitions, in fact, the more interesting questions are not so much concerned with dimensions of value, as with the categories of items valued, and I shall now concentrate on questions of that type.

A reductive strategy in terms of categories of items valued is going to try to explain the value of everything in terms of the value of as few kinds of items as possible—at the limit, in terms of one kind. If any such monistic view is plausible, it must surely be in favour of states of affairs, because they alone cover enough ground. On the monistic view, then, the most fundamental question of value—I shall call it *the value question*—is going to be 'What state of affairs would be best?'

The value question is not itself a practical question. *The practical question* (as I shall call it), the basic question for agency, must be 'What shall I do?' (It cannot be an impersonal question such as 'What is to be done?' The impersonal question has not been answered as a practical question until the first-personal question has been answered by or on behalf of some agent.[2]) So we must ask how the practical question and the value question—monism's one basic value question—are related to one another. Two extreme answers to this have been given, as well as some less extreme ones. One extreme answer is that, on those occasions when action is to be guided by values, the practical question should be immediately guided by the value question (this is the answer of direct utilitarianism). The other extreme answer is that good states of affairs are best promoted if people, in considering the practical question, rarely or never try to answer the value question.

The choice between these answers, or between either of these and other less extreme answers, cannot be principally a philosophical question. Granted the terms of the value question, and given some concrete understanding of what makes states of affairs valuable, it must very largely be an empirical question whether the best states of affairs will come about if agents are generally disposed to ask the value question when deciding what to do. This point is recognized by those who argue for indirect utilitarianism by claiming that it is empirically implausible that the best states of affairs will follow if people try to answer the practical question directly in terms of the value question.

So empirical assessments are needed. In making them, we must take an external view of agents, one that links certain facts about them with the states of affairs that their actions are likely to produce. We shall need to know about the information they are likely to acquire, and their ability to assess consequences accurately, but we shall also have to know about some of their habits or dispositions.

This will not simply be a matter of their inclination or their disinclination to answer the practical question in terms of the value question. We have to consider the alternatives to their answering the practical question in those terms. If they are going to answer the practical question on many occasions without asking the value question, and (as the theorist hopes) their answers are going to issue in actions that lead to the best states of affairs, then those agents must have some other reliable characteristics that explain how these results can come about. If we could rely on the invisible hand, or if, again, we were concerned merely with a system of external rewards and punishments, those characteristics might, in principle, consist in no more than elementary self-interest, some pattern of hopes and fears. But we cannot believe in the first, and our interest is not in the second. We are concerned with an ethical or moral system. If we are to consider any possibility other than that of agents answering the practical question directly in terms of the value question, we shall have

---

[2] I have argued for this in 'Formal and substantial individualism', *Proceedings of the Aristotelian Society*, LXXXIV (1984/85).

to consider other and more determinate characteristics that agents might possess. If agents are to produce desirable states of affairs through the outcome of their deliberations, but the deliberations are not themselves simply couched in those terms, then the agents will need to have ethical dispositions.

There is a well-known instability in structures of this kind. The ethical dispositions are required in order to generate desirable states of affairs, but they cannot remain merely as a black-box mechanism for doing that. They necessarily go beyond that, and provide the agent with a point of view from which the world can be valued. From that point of view, it is typically not merely states of affairs that seem to have value. This extends to the way in which the agent will understand, from that point of view, ethical dispositions themselves. From that point of view, ethical dispositions will seem to have a value that goes beyond their capacity to generate, through action, valuable states of affairs. This instability provides a serious objection to such models. The objection need not take the form of saying that the models are inconsistent. They may rather be socially impracticable. Again, and most interestingly, they may not be impracticable under all possible social conditions. There might be a society, perhaps of an elitist character, that realized the model or an approximation to it. The objection will rather be that the model cannot be realized in a society that satisfies certain requirements of transparency and self-conscious rationality: in particular, it could not be realized in the kind of society that is presupposed by the expectations under which ethical theories of this kind are put forward—expectations of free publication, rational enquiry, open social criticism and so on.[3]

III

We have come to this point by considering ideas of priority in ethics that were expressed first in terms of definitions. That formulation was unsatisfactory; it gave way to the aim of finding one kind of value that might be basic, and explaining others in terms of it. The 'kinds' of value involved here could be understood either as dimensions of value (goodness as against rightness, for instance), or in terms of the categories of item val-

---

[3] The point that such theories need not be inconsistent is well made by Derek Parfit, *Reasons and Persons* (Oxford: Oxford University Press, 1984), who distinguishes various ways in which theories may debar belief, or widespread and whole-hearted belief, in themselves. He is less interested, however, in the social implications of these results, a matter that seems to me fundamental. I have discussed the ideal of transparency and related issues in *Ethics and the Limits of Philosophy* (London: Collins. Cambridge, Mass.: Harvard University Press, 1985), especially at pp. 101 seq.

ued. Reductive theories may address themselves to either of these matters, or to both, and there is some correspondence between what they are likely to say about the two matters, although the correspondence is not perfect. If one considers reductive theories that address themselves to categories of items valued, the most plausible such theory is that which makes states of affairs the basic item to be valued, and explains other types of valuation in terms of that. But it is a well-known difficulty that it needs only some highly probable contingent hypotheses to make the system that is based on this view very unstable. I believe that those hypotheses are true, that the theory is unstable, and that this is an objection to accepting it.

In fact there are several kinds of thing that we can evaluate in ethical thought, and there is a wide range—wider than I have so far suggested—of concepts in terms of which we can evaluate them. I have suggested that a reduction to *states of affairs* is not satisfactory. But if there is to be a monistic reduction of the objects of ethical evaluation, this is the most plausible form for it to take. The possibilities are left that there might be some less thorough-going reduction of categories; or that the dimensions of evaluation might be reduced without a reduction of its objects. But the most reasonable conclusion seems to be that attempts at reduction, in either manner, are misguided. Whether one considers the history, the phenomenology, or the social functions of ethical thought, there is no presumption that it will reveal any very general priorities of these kinds, and no reason to suppose that it does.

There are some local priorities. It is true, very roughly speaking, that so far as distributive justice is concerned, the justice of outcomes is prior to the justice that is a disposition of character: you have to explain the latter in terms of the former. With regard to other virtues, there are other things to be said: the relation between courage as a disposition and the courage of courageous acts needs to be explained, and the explanation will not be the same as in the case of justice.[4] In such cases there *is* a presumption in favour of some relation of priority, on the traditional Aristotelian grounds that it is certainly not an accident, a question of a mere homonym, that the same word can apply to actions and to persons, and there should be something illuminating (if not necessarily very simple) to be said about the relations between the different applications of the word. But if we raise some quite general question of priorities among kinds of ethical value, there is no particular reason to expect an answer, and if there is no particular reason, there is no reason. Some actions have value because they lead to valuable states of affairs, some because they express valuable dispositions, some because they are the actions they are, and so on.

---

[4] See David Pears, 'Courage as a mean', in Amelie Rorty (ed.), *Essays on Aristotle's Ethics* (Berkeley: University of California Press, 1980).

This is not to deny that there can be explanations of our ethical conceptions. Some of those explanations are philosophical. Thus it can reasonably be asked why we should have a special kind of ethical reason that we call an 'obligation', and the answer to that question will have to start by considering, in a philosophical way and relative to some philosophical assumptions about action and ethical deliberation, what an obligation is. We shall have to consider also what is likely to come about if we have a practice of recognizing obligations as a type of ethical consideration. In some part, those answers will be empirical, if not very demandingly so, and they can contribute to an explanation of this ethical conception. An explanation is indeed needed if our understanding of ethical thought is to be unmysterious (in the best sense, naturalistic).

Since such explanations involve an account of what obligations are, there are other understandings of what obligations are with which they will inevitably conflict. Since they aim to make our ethical consciousness unmysterious, they will particularly conflict with accounts of obligation that make it essentially mysterious. It may be that the pre-theoretical understanding of obligation does represent it as rather mysterious (though assuredly not as mysterious as it appears in some theoretical accounts of it). A successful explanation might help us to understand the point and value of living a life in which obligations counted as ethical reasons, but, equally, obligations might not come out of the explanation with quite the resonance they seemed to possess before. Although it is likely that, after we have understood and accepted the explanation, we shall be able to go on living a life in which obligations play some role, some people might feel that this role was not enough, and that obligation had died under the explanatory knife. There are certainly some cases in which the item that is explained does not survive because it does not deserve to survive; the explanation focuses criticism on the item, rather than serving to vindicate it or help us to accept it. Someone who accepted Hume's celebrated account of 'the artificial virtue of modesty and chastity',[5] for instance, could scarcely suppose that it left everything where it was (or at least where it was respectably supposed to be).

IV

One's ideas of what is mysterious or unmysterious, for instance in relation to obligation, will of course be affected by one's general picture of what ethical convictions are. Explanations of our ethical conceptions must in-

[5] D. Hume, *A Treatise of Human Nature*, L. A. Selby-Bigge (ed.) (Oxford: Oxford University Press, 1975), Bk. III, pt. ii, section 12.

volve explanations of the convictions in which they figure; and that cannot be detached from epistemological issues, since knowledge is itself an explanatory notion. So far as the issues of pluralism are concerned, however, most of what has been said so far should be compatible with a variety of meta-ethical views about the nature and the epistemology of ethical convictions. The pluralism I have recommended does not imply any particular position at that level. Someone who had strongly realist views might, I suppose, have a special motive for asking reductionist questions: they could be a tool helping him or her to find out what kinds of ethical facts there were. But that motivation is not going to alter the phenomena, and the answer to his or her question, if I am right, will have to be that there are several sorts of ethical fact.

While ethical pluralism of this kind does not imply one epistemology rather than another, implications do run in the opposite direction. Our epistemological conclusions will affect our reflective understanding of the pluralism and the range of items involved in it. In particular, they may yield a ground for accepting a certain kind of priority or basicness, one quite different from those already discussed.

Some meta-ethical positions, including those that are, to my mind, the most plausible, have the following consequence: the characteristics that people acquire and exercise in ethical life and which are distinctive of it are not best understood on the model of cognitive or perceptual capacities, but rather on the model of dispositions of character. Let us call any view that has this consequence a *disposition view*. It is natural to say that disposition views are non-cognitivist, but this is too sweeping, if at any rate non-cognitivists are committed to holding that there can be no such thing as ethical knowledge. A disposition view can hold that there is some ethical knowledge, but it is knowledge that you come to acquire and exercise only in acquiring certain dispositions of character.[6] What is excluded by a disposition view is a realism about ethical facts or properties; I take this to be excluded *ex hypothesi*, since the only accounts of ethical realism that are at all intelligible try to make one understand the basic ethical capacities as close analogues of sense perception or intellectual intuition.[7]

Granted a disposition view, it follows that dispositions have a certain kind of priority. This is not a priority *within* ethical thought: it is no more correct than it was before to say that all ethical value is the value

---

[6] Cf. *Ethics and the Limits of Philosophy*, op. cit., on the subject of knowledge through 'thick' concepts. I have suggested there that the possibility of such knowledge tends to retreat in the face of reflective criticism; but that is, of course, a separate point.

[7] It is perhaps worth adding that it is only if objectivism is understood, narrowly, in terms of realism, that a disposition view has to be non-objective. Such a view may quite consistently seek an objective grounding of ethical life by trying to show that a life characterized by some structure of ethical dispositions was the life most worth living.

of dispositions. What is true, rather, is that all ethical value rests *in* dispositions. Dispositions are basic because the replication of ethical life lies in the replication of dispositions. They are themselves among the objects of ethical evaluation, and are characteristics in virtue of which people themselves are thought to be better or worse; but, uniquely among those objects, they make the evaluation of all of them possible. In a certain sense, they give the value of those other objects, even though the value of those objects cannot be reduced to theirs.

I have said that these are the dispositions of individuals, and it is as the dispositions of individuals that they are replicated and sustain ethical life. It is of course also true that a form of ethical life is a social thing, and that it involves social institutions, relations and roles. Moreover, there is no reason to suppose that these social items are reducible in any sense to individual terms. Nothing in the disposition view implies that they should be. It is not inconsistent to hold both that ethical life is a social item with much irreducible social content, and that it exists in the form of individuals' dispositions. The second point concerns the location and realization of the relevant thoughts, desires and attitudes, while the first concerns their content and their explanation.[8]

There are important practical consequences of the disposition view, and of the priority that it accords to dispositions. If ethical life is to be preserved, then these dispositions have to be preserved. But equally, if the ethical life that we have is to be effectively criticized and changed, then it can be so only in ways that can be understood as appropriately modifying the dispositions that we have. Indeed, only a disposition view, it seems to me, can give a socially and psychologically realistic account of ethical criticism and its effects, an account that gives enough weight to the fact that we can actually explain and understand the occurrence of ethical attitudes that we find variously prejudiced, limited, confused, barbarous and so on. Those views, on the other hand, that see the basic ethical characteristics as more like purely cognitive powers need a theory of error, and they do not have one. Without a convincing theory of error, they are bound to find that large-scale ethical criticism is either impossible for them, or doomed to be purely moralistic.

---

[8] For some further discussion of this point, see 'Formal and substantial individualism', op. cit.

SEVEN

The Structure of Hare's Theory

1 I hope that Dick Hare is disposed to accept seriously intended criticism as an expression of interest and respect, since I have expressed in this form my interest in and respect for his work at what he may reasonably regard as excessive length. Trying in a recent book (Williams, 1985)* to describe moral philosophy and some significant modern contributions to it, I found it appropriate to criticize his views at various points of the argument. Here I shall try to examine the structure of his theory as I understand it, and in the course of this I shall make some of these criticisms again, but in a different form, responding to what I take to be the overall shape of his theory. The design of this book** gives him the opportunity to reply and this is the best reason for my repeating some of my points.

2 I take Hare's theory[1] to have a structure that (allowing for some compressed formulations) can be set out in the following way.

(*a*) Moral language has certain necessary features.
(*b*) It is necessarily (i) prescriptive and (ii) universal; and (iii) these features are enough to determine the nature of moral thinking at a basic level.

Because of (*b*i) and (*b*ii),

(*c*) moral thinking involves identification with everyone's preferences;[2]

and because of (*b*iii), this is all there is to basic moral thinking. Hence,

---

* Here and hereafter "Williams, 1985" is a reference to Bernard Williams, *Ethics and the Limits of Philosophy* (London: Fontana).—Ed.

** This is a reference to Douglas Seanor and N. Fotion, eds., *Hare and Critics: Essays on Moral Thinking* (Oxford: Oxford University Press, 1988), in which Williams's essay first appeared and in which there is a reply by Hare.—Ed.

[1] I shall discuss the theory presented in *MT*. [Here and hereafter "*MT*" is a reference to R. M. Hare, *Moral Thinking: Its Levels, Method and Point* (Oxford: Oxford University Press, 1981).—Ed.] I shall not be concerned except in 7 with the development of Hare's views.

[2] Hare makes simplifying assumptions about the class of preferences to be considered: see *MT*, ch. 5. This is an important matter, raising questions about the motivation of utilitarian theories in general (cf. Williams, 1985:86–9; Sen and Williams, 1982, Introduction), but I shall not pursue it here. [The latter is a reference to Amartya Sen and Bernard Williams, eds., *Utilitarianism and Beyond* (Cambridge: Cambridge University Press).—Ed.]

(*d*) basic moral thinking is equivalent to a quasi-first-personal deliberation, governed by decision-theoretical criteria, over all preferences.

Basic moral thinking, that is to say, is properly represented by what I
have called the *World Agent model* (Williams, 1985:83f.). But,

(*e*) within the World Agent model, items of different levels can be eval-
uated: particular actions, type-actions, policies, principles, dispositions, etc. In particular, its criteria can be applied to the activity of
this basic moral thinking itself.

When they are so applied, the result is that

(*f*) everyday moral thinking should not all take the form of basic ('critical') moral thought; some of it should involve an 'intuitive' expression of dispositions. The result is a two-level theory.

3 I have presented (*f*) as a consequence of the rest of the theory: immediately, of (*e*) together with some supposed empirical facts. I think that this
is correct in terms of the theory's logical structure, but it does not adequately reveal the importance of the part played by the two-level view in
recommending the earlier parts of the theory. (*c*) and (*d*) are not obviously
true. Moreover, even if some conception such as that of an *impartial consideration* of all preferences followed from moral language or, independently of that, was thought to constitute basic moral thinking, it might
still be thought that (*d*), and (*c*) when taken in a corresponding sense,
involved an implausibly strong interpretation of that conception. In face
of such objections, the two-level view helps to make (*c*) and (*d*) acceptable, by saving the appearances that seemingly tell against them. Various
features of moral experience that suggest a different view are conceded
their place at the 'intuitive' level, while (*c*) and (*d*) hold true at the basic
or 'critical' level.

This is the same strategy as Sidgwick adopted, to try to show that utilitarianism, properly understood, did not have the unpalatable consequences that it seemed to have when advocated as a simple one-level theory. However, the doubts about (*c*) and (*d*) have wider effects. The fact
that (*c*) and (*d*) are not accepted by many careful thinkers makes it not
merely unobvious but implausible that they follow from the nature of
moral language:[3] it casts doubt, that is to say, on the role of (*b*). If the
two-level strategy helps to defend (*c*) and (*d*), does it thereby defend the

---

[3] For this objection, see Mackie, 1977:97; Nagel, 1982. [These are references respectively
to J. L. Mackie, *Ethics: Inventing Right and Wrong* (Harmondsworth: Penguin), and
Thomas Nagel, "Review of *Moral Thinking*, by R. M. Hare," *London Review of Books*,
15 January.—Ed.] On Hare's very demanding conception of impartial concern for others'
preferences, see Williams, 1985:89–92.

role of (b)? Here there is an interesting contrast between Hare's position and Sidgwick's. Sidgwick believed that (c) and (d), or something of the same sort, followed from a purely rational intuition to the effect that there could be no antecedent reason to prefer some one part of attainable good over any other part, and he thought that one came to see this truth by concentrating one's mind on it. His theory was intended to produce an acceptable balance between very general principles on the one hand and, on the other, spontaneous moral reactions to familiar types of situation. In particular, it was meant to help the theorist in justifying, and in that sense understanding, those reactions in terms of the general principles; it was also to help in defending the principles against the apparently contrary force of the reactions. While the epistemology of intuitions remains incurably obscure, Sidgwick could put this process into some relation to one's grasp of the basic principles as he conceived of it, by saying that the two-level theory, in giving a place to experiences that seemed to tell against the basic principles, helped to concentrate one's mind on those principles.

Hare's use of the two-level theory to make (c) and (d) more acceptable is much like Sidgwick's. But Hare's use of it has nothing to do with the way in which he derives (c) and (d) in the first place. The two-level theory does nothing to make more plausible the claim *that they follow from the nature of moral language*—that is to say, to justify the role of (b). Suppose that it is true that if one thinks hard about (c) and (d), with the help of the two-level theory, one will become convinced of them: that is not enough. It is enough for Sidgwick, but it is not enough for Hare, if he is to justify the role of (b). What needs to be true is that by thinking harder *about moral language* one will become convinced of them, and the two-level theory offers no help in that.

Besides asking whether considerations about language will yield this result rather than some other, we can ask why something called 'moral language' should be expected to reveal anything, or anything reliable, about these matters at all. Language consists in human practices; human beings (as the theory itself insists) have suffered and do suffer from many illusions about the relations of value to the world and so forth; if language can embody or imply any propositions at all about such things, why should it not embody illusions?

Merely as a moral theory, it might seem that Hare's system could do as well without involving (a) and (b). It could proceed by seeking what Rawls calls 'reflective equilibrium', by balancing the general theoretical material against features of moral experience, with the help of the two-level theory. In fact, Hare has strongly resisted this method, for reasons that I shall come back to in 7.

4 The two-level theory has its own difficulties. In what way are 'critical' and 'intuitive' thinking supposed to be embodied? In Sidgwick's version of indirect utilitarianism, the two styles of thought correspond to a social distinction between two classes of people, the utilitarian élite and the rest. In that version—'Government House utilitarianism', as it may be called— there are clear distinctions between the thoughts of the two classes of people. For one thing, the purely logical or semantic distinction between first-order and second-order thought is mirrored in the fact that the élite thinks about the practices of the others, but the others do not reflect on the special thoughts of the élite—in particular (as Sidgwick makes clear) because they do not know about them. Moreover, the élite are special not merely in the sense that they have second-order thoughts; they also think in a different way about particular practical issues, since more of their thoughts about those issues express direct utilitarianism, and fewer express common-sense principles.

This is not how Hare represents the distinction between the two levels of thought. Elsewhere (Williams, 1985:106–10) I have said that he regards the distinction rather as one between two times, that of practical activity as contrasted with the cool hour of reflection. However, this is not quite right. His distinction is indeed intended as a psychological rather than a social one: it picks out two styles of thought, both of which can be represented in the mind of one person. But it does not merely pick out two times of thought corresponding to those styles, since Hare supposes that a person can think in both styles at one time. Moreover, he believes that there are in this respect various kinds of people, who approximate in different degrees to one or the other of two archetypes, revealingly called the 'archangel' and the 'prole'. The first of these characters uses only critical thinking—which means, his powers are such that he needs no other. The second uses only intuitive thinking, because he is incapable of critical thinking (*MT* ch. 3, especially 3.1 to 3.3). Thus there are some people—more like the archangel, and more like Sidgwick's élite—who can think at the critical level more of the time; and this is seen as a valuable capacity, while thinking at the intuitive level is seen rather as a necessity and an imperfection. How much of the time it is advisable to think in one of these styles or in the other is a question that Hare seems to think depends on empirical factors and is of no philosophical interest.

I do not believe that this account is coherent, or that the styles of thought Hare seeks to describe could provide what his theory requires. It is important to make clear what the objection is. It is not an objection (how could it be?) to all styles of reflective or second-order thought, nor to the mere idea that such thoughts might be interwoven with other thoughts in the course of practice. Hare is of course right to say that a general in action can jump between tactical and strategic levels of thought

(*MT* 52). But strategic and tactical thoughts, unless the general is in a muddle, do not conflict, nor is there any conflict between the activities of thinking in the one style or the other. Nor do reflections of moral philosophy necessarily have to conflict with first-order practical thoughts: those of contractualism, for instance, characteristically do not. The objection is specifically to Hare's kind of theory, which represents the intuitive responses as deeply entrenched, surrounded by strong moral emotions, sufficiently robust to see the agent through situations in which sophisticated reflection might lead him astray, and so on; and yet at the same time explains those responses as a device to secure utilitarian outcomes. The theory ignores the fact that the responses are not merely a black-box mechanism to generate what is probably the best outcome under confusing conditions. Rather, they constitute a way of seeing the situation; and you cannot combine seeing the situation in that way, *from* the point of view of those dispositions, with seeing it in the archangel's way, in which all that is important is maximum preference satisfaction, and the dispositions themselves are merely a means towards that.

In saying that you 'cannot combine' these two things, I do not mean that as a matter of psychological fact it is impossibly difficult. People indeed have thoughts that they describe in these terms—Hare himself has said that he does. The point is that the thoughts are not stable under reflection; in particular, you cannot think in these terms if at the same time you apply to the process the kind of thorough reflection that this theory itself advocates. That is not a merely psychological claim. It is a philosophical claim, about what is involved in effective and adequate reflection on these particular states of mind.

It might be said that the difficulty arises only because the depth and strength of the 'intuitive' dispositions have been exaggerated. If the intuitive responses are seen only as presumptive rules of thumb, then the difficulty disappears, or at least is less severe.[4] That is right, but the position it provides is not Hare's. Moreover, it would not allow Hare to make all the use he does make of the two-level theory. Like Sidgwick, as I said earlier, he uses the theory to save the appearances, explaining people's ordinary reactions in relation to the basic utilitarian principles. But the more the theory represents the intuitive reactions as merely superficial, provisional, and instrumental, the fewer appearances it saves: it does not explain what people do feel and think, but suggests something else in the same area that they might usefully feel and think.

---

[4] If a utilitarian theory is not to raise the difficulty at all, it should not go much beyond the 'gas bill model' discussed in Williams, 1972. [This is a reference to Bernard Williams, *Morality: An Introduction to Ethics* (Cambridge: Cambridge University Press).—Ed.]

5 It is important that the two-level theory in its present form is not a unique solution, given the rest of the material, to the problem of what everyday moral thought should be. Its logical status, I suggested earlier, is that it is supported by the basic position together with some empirical material, and if there are difficulties with it, then some other solution may turn out to be better supported. If basic moral thought is defined in archangelic terms, then *some* stand-in for it is needed in everyday practice, since full archangelic thought requires an indefinite amount of knowledge and deliberative power (it is all the more exacting because Hare interprets so ambitiously the idea of being impartially concerned with everyone's preferences). Yet Hare himself cannot see critical, non-intuitive, thought exclusively in archangelic terms, since he thinks that it is something that most of us can conduct some of the time, and when it is seen in that light, it indeed becomes an empirical question, as he claims, to what extent a stand-in is needed. But then it must also be an empirical question what the stand-in should be.

It is obvious (as indeed it is from the history of utilitarianism) that there are many candidates for the stand-in, many styles of everyday moral thought that might in practice produce the best results. Deep dispositions, which Hare favours and which produce their own special problems, are only one. There are rules of thumb, direct utilitarianism applied to a limited constituency of beneficiaries, and others. Proceeding downwards from the account of basic moral thought, and taking the appropriate empirical facts into consideration about the effects in practice of different kinds of moral practice, one might arrive at any of these solutions. The fact that Hare arrives at this particular stand-in rather than some other may not simply be the product of empirical belief. It may be that he is drawn to this solution because it is at least prima facie better than others at saving the appearances of moral experience. But further argument is needed to show that the position one gets to by proceeding downwards from the top of the system, and the position that best saves the appearances of moral experience, are likely to be one and the same. If the method of reflective equilibrium is adopted, then of course there is a rationale for saving the appearances—that is part of the idea. But if the method is that of travelling down from moral language to basic principles, and from them, in the light of empirical facts, to the most desirable forms of everyday moral thought, there is simply no guarantee that the appearances deserve to be saved.

6 I raised (in 4) a difficulty with the two-level theory in its present form, in which it favours deep dispositions. The difficulty is, in summary, that one could not think at the 'intuitive' or everyday level in the way that the theory requires while one was fully conscious of what one was doing: in particular, while one fully understood in terms of the theory itself what

one was doing. This is, if real, a difficulty; but why exactly does it constitute an objection to Hare's theory? It might be seen as not yielding an objection, but merely as showing something about the theory, that it cannot work if people, in full reflection and all the time, believe it. Such properties of ethical theories, in particular of utilitarian theories, have been studied by Parfit (Parfit, 1984, Part I),*** who argues that they do not necessarily mean that such theories should be rejected. But this still leaves problems of who is to accept such theories, and in what spirit; and if it is not possible that any, or many, people should accept them, what the status of the theory then is, and the purpose of the theorist in announcing it.

In the case of Government House utilitarianism, the answer to these questions is straightforward. The theory is addressed to the élite, and there is no problem about the élite's fully believing it, all of the time. The hard problem is a political one, of how to run a modern society that is controlled by such an élite—in particular, running it decently, in accordance with values that the élite might (otherwise) be expected to endorse. Hare's theory, however, is addressed to people who are expected themselves to have dispositions which they cannot both exercise in the way that the theory requires and at the same time understand in the terms that the theory provides. If they are being asked to attend to this theory, they are also being asked, in some significant degree, to forget it. There could be a theory that asked to be treated in that way, but it is obvious that Hare's does not. On the contrary this is meant to appeal to and to sustain a spirit of critical reflection and self-enquiry, and Hare makes it clear that he intends his philosophy to contribute to moral improvement through self criticism. It is because the theory has these aspirations that the difficulty is also an objection.

7 Hare in his earliest theory separated his description of moral language from any determination of the content of moral principles. He was also disposed to see that separation as an application of the fact-value distinction—indeed, more than that, as a prime expression of it. Philosophy itself had to be on the 'fact' side of the distinction: both because that accorded with a general picture of philosophy as linguistic analysis, and, in particular, because philosophy's announcement of the fact-value distinction would lack the critical force it was supposed to possess if it were itself an expression of value.

In the later theory which I am considering, the description of moral language, together with empirical information, is thought to determine the content of moral principles; and the degree to which the description

*** This is a reference to Derek Parfit, *Reasons and Persons* (Oxford: Oxford University Press).—Ed.

of moral language determines the nature of moral thinking, even without empirical information, certainly serves already to eliminate substantive alternatives. (Hare says that what is determined at this level is the *form* of (basic) moral thought: but then many substantive questions about it must be questions about its form.) Because Hare associated his earlier formulations so closely with the expression of the fact-value distinction, these developments have led some critics to say that Hare has changed his mind about that distinction. However that may be—I think in fact that Hare can answer this claim—the relevant points here are that he has not changed his mind about what philosophy is, and that he has a stronger view now than earlier about its powers.

Hare has always wanted, and earnestly wanted, moral philosophy to have a practical effect, to make a difference. He does not think it an obstacle to this that on his view moral philosophy is, roughly, a branch of philosophical logic. On the contrary: moral philosophy can make a difference only because it has authority, and it can have authority only because of its neutral status as a logical or linguistic subject. He has always held this in some form, but his present theory gives a very special explanation of what this authority is. The crucial belief now is that this neutral subject can yield foundations.

It is this belief that explains his scorn for those who use the method of seeking reflective equilibrium and start their moral philosophy from people's 'moral intuitions'. Hare does not primarily object to this, as some utilitarians do, because these intuitions are too conservative; the 'intuitive' principles that he puts back at the end of his enquiry tend, in some areas, to be more conservative than those that would have been elicited in the first place. Similarly, the objection cannot simply be that their method is not critical or radical enough, if this is taken in some general sense: in a general sense, some of these philosophers are notably critical or radical. His objection is that, whether conservative or radical in the outcome, the intuitions and the theories elicited from them by these philosophers are mere prejudices: which means, they lack any foundation. This provides one sense in which he does think that these enquiries are not sufficiently critical or radical—the Cartesian sense, that they have not gone back to foundations.

Hare's present view of moral philosophy and its relation to practice has, then, several strands, with different histories. He now believes:

  (i) moral philosophy is (roughly) a logical or linguistic subject;
 (ii) it provides foundations;
(iii) it helps us to reflect clearly on our moral thoughts, and in particular—because of (i)—to think about what we mean;
(iv) when we do so, we discover (ii).

Hare has always believed (i). He has not always believed, as he now believes, (ii) and (iv). However, he now believes that in some part the authority of moral philosophy derives from (ii); as we have just seen, his rejection of other methods rests on this.

I earlier discussed the difficulty about the two-level theory and I suggested, in 6, that the reason why that difficulty was an objection to Hare lay in the view that he took of philosophy. In terms of the present schema, it is an objection in virtue of (iii). Hare has always accepted (iii); indeed, before he came to believe (ii), it had to do all the work of explaining why philosophy, as a neutral study of language, had authority and relevance to practical life. (iii) in itself presents no difficulty, at least of this kind. Others may be less inclined than Hare is to stress its purely linguistic aspect, but everyone can recognize it as a worthy declaration of the Socratic impulse, an expression of the values of social and personal transparency. When Hare moved to believing (ii) and (iv), however, it became possible for (iii) to be in conflict with the conclusions of (i). It was bound to be an open question whether the foundations that (i) now yielded were such that the practice recommended by (iii) could be thoroughly carried out. Hare has always assumed that (iii) was an obvious statement of the aims of philosophy, and also that the results of philosophy, as the objective subject described in (i), could be consistently, and no doubt usefully, known by anyone. He now has no assurance that these two things, the external view of what morality is, and the internal representation of it in moral practice, will necessarily fit together.

Some other objections I have mentioned turn on rejecting the idea that a linguistic enquiry will yield foundations. I shall not discuss here the question whether morality should be expected to have foundations, nor the paradox that Hare (and he is not alone in this) should move to a foundationalist view of morality while philosophy has been moving to taking a less foundationalist view of everything else. The present point is only about method. I have already mentioned Hare's basic reason for thinking that philosophy should not proceed by reflection (in the first place, at least) on our moral 'intuitions', opinions, or experiences. His reason is that they are merely ours: as an objection, it rests on his belief in foundations. His particular insistence on a linguistic enquiry, as opposed to such reflections, rests in some part the general point (i); but the special form taken by his linguistic enquiry reveals that it is itself conditioned by the search for foundations, and by the desire to get away from what is merely 'ours'.[5]

---

[5] The point is explicit at *MT* 17 f. For the very special character of the linguistic enquiry, cf. Williams, 1985, ch. 7.

To those who do not agree with Hare that a linguistic method can yield foundations, he does not provide any purely methodological reason why they should not start from 'intuitions'—a reason, that is to say, independent of the substantial point on which he and they disagree. They may themselves believe in foundations, but think that the way to find them is by starting from our moral opinions. Or they may not believe in foundations at all, and merely be concerned with the implications, presuppositions, and incoherencies of those opinions. In relation to either of these groups, Hare is in a situation familiar in philosophy (it was Descartes' own situation), that his objection to their method rests only on what he believes to be the actual results of his own.

Just because Hare's conclusions govern his method, and his conclusions are so foundationalist, he does clearly answer in his own terms a question that other philosophers often merely ignore. Why should the critical reflection to which moral philosophy is committed be expected to issue in an ethical theory? Hare has a conception of moral philosophy and its aims that naturally issues in such a theory. Those who reject that conception, but still seek a theory to systematize our moral opinions, owe both him and the rest of us an account of why they expect our best understanding of our ethical life to take such a form.

EIGHT

Subjectivism and Toleration

Bertrand Russell said more than once that he was uncomfortable about a conflict, as he saw it, between two things: the strength of the conviction with which he held his ethical beliefs, and the philosophical opinions that he had about the status of those ethical beliefs—opinions which were non-cognitivist, and in some sense subjectivist. Russell felt that, in some way, if he did not think that his ethical beliefs were objective, he had no right to hold them so passionately. This discomfort was not something that Ayer noted or discussed in his account of Russell's moral philosophy and ethical opinions, at least in the book that he wrote for the *Modern Masters* series (*RS*).* Perhaps this was because it was not a kind of discomfort that Ayer felt himself. His own philosophical views about the status of ethics were at all periods at any rate non-cognitivist, and I think that he did not mind them being called 'subjectivist'. He did indeed argue that the supposed difference between objectivism and subjectivism in ethics did no work, and that philosophers who took themselves to be objectivists could not achieve anything more than those who admitted they were subjectivists. Ayer based this mainly on the idea that the claims made by objectivists for the factuality, objective truth, and so forth of moral judgments added nothing to those judgments—so far as moral conclusions were concerned, the objectivist was saying the same as the subjectivist but in a louder voice.

While, in this way, he thought that the extra claims of objectivism did no real work, Ayer did not conclude from this that the distinction between subjectivism and objectivism had no content at all. He did not reject the distinction altogether, because he thought that there was a meta-ethical view which he held and any objectivist would reject, namely that moral utterances were not fact-stating, were not (really) true or false. Indeed, in saying that no real work was done by claims to the effect that moral utterances could state facts, Ayer took himself to be disagreeing with an objectivist—so there had to be some difference between his own position and the objectivist's. The assertion of vacuity was not itself vacuous.

Ayer admitted that many moral utterances—the claim that someone was a coward, for instance—did have what on anyone's view would be a factual

---

* This is a reference to A. J. Ayer, *Russell* (London: Fontana, 1972).—Ed.

component: this, by a well-known style of analysis, was supposed to be separated out from the distinctively moral dimension of the utterance. He further admitted that in ordinary speech moral utterances were often called 'true' or 'false': this he traced to comprehensible prejudice. However, there is a problem about what more he supposed was necessary for them to be *really* true or false: that is to say, what it precisely was that, according to him, the objectivist believed and he did not. A diluted version of the verification principle was typically invoked here: if moral claims were really true or false, there would have to be some agreed procedures, inherent in the meaning of those claims, for checking up on them. This is what he had in mind when he attacked objectivism in the form of the intuitionism that was associated with the Oxford of his earlier days, in particular with Prichard and Ross. Because the intuitionsts' theory provided no way of verifying the supposed truths of morality, Ayer held that a claim that we could have knowledge of them or reasoned belief in them was false, and from this he perhaps concluded that it was equally false to hold that they were truths at all. Since Ayer agreed that one could indeed hold moral views, it was implicit in his position, as in any other that denies truth-value to moral claims but does not reject them altogether, that one can hold a moral position (assent to it, etc.) without holding that it is true. If the attitude to moral propositions that one holds can be called 'belief', then there are propositions that one can believe without believing them to be true.

Ayer resisted this conclusion by denying that the favourable attitude to moral propositions is, properly speaking, belief. He preferred to express his position on this in terms of speech-acts; the claim was that the moral utterer (as such) was not stating facts, but rather doing something else. In *Language, Truth and Logic* the candidate for the other speech-act was 'expressing one's feelings'; by 1949 it was such things as prescribing, giving leave, showing oneself favourably disposed, expressing a resolution, and so on. Indeed from at least 1949 onwards Ayer seems to have adopted a simple version of prescriptivism, the kind of theory that R. M. Hare was to express in a more complex form in *The Language of Morals*.

This appeal to an alternative speech-act may provide a formula for avoiding the difficulties about belief and truth, but it does not provide (as Ayer and others perhaps believed) any independent way of understanding the claim that moral utterances do not state facts or have a truth value. People when they make moral remarks do not typically think of themselves as just prescribing, expressing a resolution, and so on—this may be illustrated by their ordinary use of 'true' and 'false', which was mentioned before—and they usually think it about others only when they think the others' claims are baseless. The philosophical theory that what people are (really) (only) doing is prescribing, expressing resolutions, and so forth, gets any force it has from the view, independently supported, that they cannot be stating facts. Indeed the phenomenology of moral thought is in some ways notably resistant to a prescriptivist interpretation, a point I shall come back to.

Ayer did introduce in 1949 the idea of having reasons for a moral pre-scription; this was supposed to make a wider range of moral comments comprehensible than emotivism did. As he put it:[1]

> In saying that Brutus or Raskolnikov acted rightly, I am giving myself and others leave to imitate them should similar circumstances arise . . . Similarly, in saying that they acted wrongly, I express a resolution not to imitate them, and endeavour also to discourage others. It may be thought that the mere use of the dyslogistic word 'wrongly' is not much of a discouragement, although it does have some emotive force. But that is where reasons come in. I discourage others, or at any rate hope to discourage them, by telling them why I think the action wrong . . .

There are several implausible things in this passage, for instance the idea that it is up to me to give someone leave to imitate these characters. More generally, there is something very puzzling in the idea that the considera-tions it offers could be enough to give a sense to 'why I think the action wrong'. What Ayer goes on to say does not give that content, but simply explains when I may be able to modify someone else's attitude. The con-nections between having a reason, giving a reason, and trying to persuade someone else, are a great deal more complex than this implies. In part, this is a problem left over from emotivism, and in part, a problem shared by prescriptivism.

It was characteristic of Ayer's outlook that the shift to prescriptivism did not do much more than suggest new modes of persuasion. It could have done more, by alerting Ayer to a different idea of objectivity, associated with the possibility that moral statements might express objectively univer-sal prescriptions (as in Hare's later work and, in a different form, in Kant). Such a view of course separates the question of objectivity from the ques-tion whether moral discourse is as such fact-stating: on the Kantian view, the correct moral principles and their foundation, the Categorical Impera-tive, are *objective*, because supposedly grounded in the requirements of practical reason, but they are not fact-stating, because they are imperatives. The objectivity is that of a construction, not of a discovery. Ayer never considered such a possibility. For him, in line with positivist concerns, is-sues of objectivity and of (roughly) cognitivism were always the same.

Ayer insisted that his meta-ethical analysis had no implications for first-order moral thought. His argument for this was a standard prescriptivist

---

[1] 'On the Analysis of Moral Judgements', originally published in *Horizon* xx (1949), reprinted in *PE* [This is a reference to A. J. Ayer, *Philosophical Essays* (London: Macmillan, 1954).—Ed.]; this quotation is from pp. 237–238 in that reprint.

version of the fact/value distinction, together with the claim that meta-ethical analysis, because analysis, is descriptive. Ayer was concerned to emphasize the point that the subjectivist analysis does not lead to a nihilist conclusion that moral considerations are trivial or unimportant. This was as near as he came to meeting, though he did not share, Russell's worry, and he was perhaps encouraged to make the point by criticisms from Christians, Cyril Joad and others who tended to accuse positivism of moral frivolity or worse. Equally, Ayer did not suppose that the meta-ethical analysis had any implications in the opposite direction; he did not think that subjectivist considerations might be used to support some more positive conclusions, such as toleration. This is another difference from Russell, who—in entirely comprehensible conflict with his worry about his subjectivism and the strength of his convictions—was disposed to agree with J. S. Mill that bigots were fortified in their bigotry by cognitivism, at least of some varieties.

Of course, even granted Ayer's assumptions, we are not told what philosophy should do: the assumptions themselves show us why they cannot tell us that. If we are to conclude, as Ayer and many other partisans of the fact/value distinction concluded, that philosophy is not in the business of morality, we need a further premise, which Ayer accepted, to the effect that philosophy is confined to analysis. Moreover, the idea that philosophy could not support any distinctive moral conclusions was helped by the belief that 'supports' had to mean one of two things: either 'entails' or, alternatively, 'by a statistical law encourages people to think . . .' Ayer accepted this too, another positivist legacy. That left it open whether the profession of certain philosophical views might turn out, as a matter of statistical fact, to encourage certain moral or political attitudes, and in this empirical sense 'support' them. But Ayer also seemed to think that if this did turn out to be so, it would not follow that the philosopher who professed the views had any responsibility in that direction—the misunderstanding was, so to speak, the hearers' fault. There is something innocent, or (on a harsher view) conventionally academic, in this outlook. The content of moral utterances is boldly reduced to their force, and their force virtually reduced to their effects. But the remarks of philosophy, the results of analysis, remain secure in their conceptual content, and mean no more or less than they say. Any effects they may have are seen as firmly separated from them.

Granted these views, it was something of an aberration when, in the Eleanor Rathbone Lecture that he gave in 1965,[2] Ayer explained in historical and political terms the fact that French philosophers had offered more

---

[2] 'Philosophy and Politics', published 1967 by the Liverpool University Press, reprinted in *MCS* [This is a reference to A. J. Ayer, *Metaphysics and Common Sense* (London: Macmillan, 1969).—Ed.]; the quotation is from pp. 259–260 of the reprint.

(moral) views about politics than British philosophers had. He did not say simply, as he must have thought he was entitled to say, that British philosophers stuck to philosophy. Nevertheless, he remained faithful to the separation that he accepted between philosophy and first-order political views, and indeed enacted it with surrealistic exaggeration in this lecture. In the first part of it he ran through a well-known tutorial rehearsing thirteen reasons that have been given for why one should obey the law. He then moved to give, unphilosophically, an account of his own, somewhat muted, liberal views:

> In this matter I am like the rest; I have nothing new to offer. Only the old familiar liberal principles; old, but not so firmly established that we can afford to take them for granted. Representative government, universal suffrage, freedom of speech, freedom of the press, the right of collective bargaining, equality before the law, and all that goes with the so-called welfare state. It is not a heady brew. Such principles nowadays are a ground for excitement, a source of enthusiasm, only when they appear to be violated. For most of us participation in politics takes the form of protest; protest against war, against the aggressive actions of the major powers, against the maltreatment of political prisoners, against censorship, against capital or corporal punishment, against the persecution of homosexuals, against racial discrimination; there is still quite a lot to be against. It would be more romantic to be marching forward shoulder to shoulder under some bright new banner towards a brave new world. But I do not know: perhaps it is the effect of age. I do not really feel the need for anything to replace this mainly utilitarian, mainly tolerant, undramatic type of radicalism.

In this passage he is in more than one way unfair to himself. He is unfair to the vigour with which he indeed campaigned for these causes; he is unfair in the implication that aged 55, as he then was, he was anywhere near the end of his energies or his commitment to those campaigns. But perhaps the most touching implication of the lecture as a whole is its suggestion, contrary to the tenor of what he believed in philosophy, that if politics were more ideological, political philosophy would be livelier than it was—livelier, indeed, than the demonstration that he himself gave of it.

Another consequence that Ayer insisted did not follow from his metaethical view was relativism. In particular, the meta-ethical view cannot entail a particular kind of relativistic attitude, one that is marked by toleration of divergent moral practices. If in making moral utterances, I prescribe, then I indeed prescribe, and for everyone. There must be some truth in this; toleration is a substantive attitude, and it is certainly not going to spring out of an analysis of moral language. Yet, at the same time, many people have thought, as (I mentioned earlier) Russell thought, that subjectivism could have something to do with toleration: that there was something more general to be learned from the fact that some bigots are particularly vigorous objectivists. Perhaps if we relax the notion of a 'consequence' somewhat, and allow a rather broader kind of reflection than Ayer allowed, it may be a real question whether consciousness of subjectivism should not have some consequences for toleration and, in those terms, for liberalism. This is the question I shall consider for the rest of this paper.

Some cognitivist views certainly provide added motives to bigotry, for instance by holding out hopes of divine reward, suggesting divine encouragement of zeal, offering assurances that the benighted are being assisted and so on. A more sceptical philosophy might hope to clear away some of these inducements, a point that has been familiar at least since Montaigne, and which is standard in Enlightenment thought. Ayer did not make much of this line of argument, perhaps because he thought that if the cognitivist content were identifiably religious, then the views would be 'factual' and not moral. The only moral element, on his analysis, will be the prescription to obey God or whatever it may be. So this might be said, if rather narrowly, not to be a point about moral cognitivism as such. Moreover, it is of course true that there could be other cognitivist considerations, whether of a religious character or not, that had a more tolerant tendency. But the broadly positivist outlook of which Ayer's subjectivism was part was devoted, as a progressive view, to rejecting myths, and among the myths it rejected were some that institutionally or psychologically opposed toleration. This constitutes an *historical* association, at least, between subjectivism and toleration.

I said earlier that prescriptivist and similar theories do not fit altogether easily with the phenomenology of moral thought. In part, this is because one's moral beliefs do not seem to be things that one acquires by decision. More broadly, the subject of seeking to arrive at a moral conclusion is left out. Ayer himself always presents the moral subject as already holding views, opposed to some others' views; the subject is not represented as in doubt about what views to hold. This does not allow enough for the part that is played in moral experience by such thoughts as that other views are possible, that they might be more satisfactory, that someone else could be right, that there can be explanations of why they might be right. To some degree, these thoughts encourage cognitivist or other objectivist pictures: the thought that I might be wrong and someone else might be right invites the further thought that there must be something that we can be right or wrong about.

However, thoughts of this kind may equally encourage one to reflect in a different direction, about possible moralities other than the one that happens to be one's own, and those reflections do not uniquely favour objectivism: they may lead us to some broader associations between subjectivism and toleration. 'A possible morality' means here not just an empirically possible human phenomenon, but something that could be acknowledged on the basis of one's understanding of human life as an intelligible solution to the requirements of a human society in certain circumstances. The thought that there are various possible moralities is perhaps compatible with some forms of cognitivism, but those forms are likely to represent the moral 'facts' as very general or indeterminate. If, however, objectivism—and not merely cognitivism—is false, the class of possible moralities is open. This is opposed to an assumption of standard morality, identified by Nietzsche, that morality is unique, the only morality—an assumption which is oddly carried over into the structure of Ayer's prescriptivism, where it is used in the way I have already mentioned, in order to shout down relativism.

To accept that there are various possible moralities does not, certainly, lead directly to a relativism or to toleration. One reason for this is obvious, that the content of a morality must to some extent determine one's attitude to other, and conflicting, moralities. If I am opposed to what, on my view of things, is called the subjection of women, then this does not leave me indifferent to the merits of moralities that practise, as it seems to me, the subjection of women. Not being indifferent, it is likely, equally, that I shall not be tolerant. This does not mean that I will support the suppression of these practices by force, but I may campaign against them, urge legal restraints, and so forth. Since this is obviously so, it may well seem that the relations between subjectivism and toleration do not extend further than an historical association. It may well be true that the same movements of ideas have supported both, and this is very comprehensible, but it may still be difficult to find any deeper connection between them. It is simply that those who hold subjectivist views also hold distinctive moral opinions, some of which, on certain matters, are more tolerant.

Is this all there is to it? The connections, it seems to me, can be pressed rather further. First, there is the consideration that on a subjectivist account of the matter, the function of holding a moral outlook is basically to regulate and define one's relations to other people. To the extent that this is clearly understood, moral outlooks will have a tendency to lose impetus if their expressions are not directed to people with whom one's relations need to be regulated and defined: in particular, if they are directed to people remote in time. Subjectivism tends to support what I have elsewhere (1985)** called 'the relativism of distance'. Cognitivism is less likely to be

** This is a reference to Bernard Williams, *Ethics and the Limits of Philosophy* (London: Fontana).—Ed.

sympathetic to such an outlook: if the aim of moral speech is to set out how things stand with the moral, then distance in itself has no effect.

There are some results of this asymmetry, but they are not very spectacular. On the one hand, even robust forms of cognitivism can presumably embrace the thought that some moral truths are more worth announcing (by a given speaker at a given time) than others: addressing oneself at length to the merits of Brutus or the demerits of Caligula may seem just as pointless if you think that you are pointing out timeless truths of morality as it does if you think you are doing the things that Ayer thought you were doing. In fact, comments on the distant may come into question more with matters of general practice, concerning whole moral outlooks; but then it is very unlikely that *mere* distance will be the issue. There will be substantive social differences between the two situations, and then cognitivism can deploy familiar resources to explain why the same view need not be taken of two different situations.

It is true that there is a difference between thinking, as a subjectivist perhaps may, that moral opinions simply do not apply to the distant, and thinking, as a cognitivist can perhaps at most think, that judgments at a distance apply but may not be worth announcing. One difficulty in putting much weight on this is that the subjectivist may actually be reluctant to use his distinctive resources. As Ayer's own peculiar account of our relations to Brutus illustrates, once the question of the distant is raised, moral judgments seem to find it quite easy to work up the energy to reach the target. A sophisticated subjectivism will have no difficulty in explaining, in turn, that fact, but of course it cannot at the same time use the supposed asymmetry in support of its position: there will not be an asymmetry, but rather two different explanations of why there is not one.

In any case, a mere relativism of distance will not distinctively support toleration. The most that it could support would be a form of indifference, towards the distant. It can be said that indifference is actually inconsistent with toleration—if you are indifferent, you do not need to be tolerant. But that is true, if at all, only about tolerance as a personal virtue, not about toleration as a social and political practice. Indifference is no doubt one route to toleration as a practice; it can scarcely be denied that toleration of religious variation has increased with a decline of enthusiasm for religion and religious issues. But indifference *merely to the distant* is no route to toleration. Toleration essentially involves attitudes to those who are not at a distance, and the issues it raises are in the first instance issues for people living in the same social space.

Perhaps there is a different asymmetry between cognitivism (at least) and subjectivism, one that bears on the situation in which toleration may be called for. It may be expressed in terms of paternalism. On a cognitivist view, if X believes some moral P, and Y does not, X can have this thought: if Y were to come to believe P, not only would there be the advantages that follow merely from that change (among them, less conflict with me), but Y's views would be nearer to the truth. How much content there is to this thought depends on the type of cognitivism. But if there seems to be some content, this can (though it need not) provide X with reasons for making it more probable that Y acquire this belief, in ways perhaps offensive to liberalism. In particular, since Y can be credited with an interest in coming to know the truth, X can invoke paternalist reasons for helping to enlighten Y. If cognitivism is false, there can be no such reasons. Cognitivism adds a possible paternalist argument for altering others' beliefs.

This represents a real asymmetry, which is important as far as it goes. The additional paternalist consideration is no more than a possible addition, since cognitivism might have its own arguments for liberal toleration, such as an appeal to the virtues of people finding things out for themselves. This illustrates a general point which has come out already: subjectivism is unlikely to achieve any unique results in this area. For any consequence of subjectivism in favour of toleration, there will be some version of cognitivism or other forms of objectivism that can yield the same result. (This is one of the many phenomena that make it obscure, as these types of theories are progressively elaborated, how much distance is going to be left between them.) The only issue is whether there are features of subjectivism that make it natural, by more than an historical association, to expect it to support toleration.

It might be thought that this paternalism argument can be strongly generalized. Suppose a society in which there is a variety of conflicting beliefs about moral issues. Then, it might be argued, the subjectivist, on reflection, will see that an attempt to make the other parties agree with one's own view would be a mere act of will, whereas for the objectivist it would not. This is another application of the point made in the paternalism argument, that the objectivist has another description of what is going on when the other parties' beliefs change. But a mere act of will by one party against another must be inconsistent with the conditions of co-existing in a society at all: to curb such acts of will is a basic point of society's existence. Hence subjectivism yields, it may be claimed, from this obvious premise, an argument for toleration which is lacking to objectivism.

This argument cannot be sound as it stands. The sense in which any society is committed to curbing 'mere acts of will' is one in which such acts are contrasted with procedures that are supported by certain kinds of reason: 'I want it because it serves my interests' will not count as a justifying reason, while 'it must be stopped because it damages the interests of many' may serve as such a reason, and action done for that reason will not, correspondingly, count as a 'mere act of will'. But when the argument deploys from its account of subjectivism the notion of a 'mere act of will', this is a notion that applies to any act at all that is based on a moral reason; or, perhaps, to any act based on a moral reason which another party does not accept; or, at the very least, to any act which involves an imposition on another party and which is done for a moral reason that the other party does not accept. The idea of a mere act of will which is derived from a subjectivist account of what a moral judgment is, is not the same as the idea of a mere act of will as what is excluded by the basis of social arrangements. That is unsurprising, since the first is, as it were, a 'transcendental' idea, derived from the mere idea of a moral judgment, whereas the latter is based in a distinction between some kinds of reasons and others.

Can the argument be improved? It can be improved only if subjectivism, in some way or another, can make a contribution to the question of what reasons might, and what reasons might not, justify the suppression or other social discouragement of deviant moral belief and behaviour. If we ask what contribution might be made at that level of generality, it looks as though the only answer to be found would lie in the requirement that no justification could be offered that turned solely on the values of truth, or consisted simply in the consideration that it was better for a group to believe the moral truth rather than moral falsehood.

But this restriction, beyond the bounds of the paternalism argument itself, can exercise very little distinctive influence. In factual matters, after all, the claim that some theories rather than others should be taught in school, while it will be supported by the claim that those theories are true, will not be supported by that claim and no more; it will be supported by whatever reasons make one think that those theories are true. Similarly, the claim that some moral beliefs should prevail over others—at the limit, not permit the toleration of practices based on them—would be supported by the objectivist not with the simple claim that those beliefs are true, but by bringing forward whatever reasons supposedly support those beliefs; in the more drastic case, the further claim that the beliefs need to be enforced would have to be supported by reasons going beyond the mere claim that the beliefs were true. (If not, we are back in the territory of the paternalism argument.) An argument on the matter will be an argument about, and in terms of, the reasons: in the first instance, it will be an argument with the parties to be coerced, and if that argument breaks down, then reasons will have to be deployed among the other, dominant, parties to explain to themselves and to anyone else who may be interested why, in this case, they think coercion is justified.

None of those activities, in themselves, derives special strength or encouragement from either a subjectivist or an objectivist meta-ethic. These activities, of course, presuppose that the society is, broadly, in the business of giving reasons for its various moral beliefs and for its tolerant or intolerant practices. All societies must be to some degree in that business, though clearly they may differ a good deal in the extent to which that is so, in the range of groups between which reasons have to be given, and in the degree of specificity that is demanded for particular policies, as opposed to generalized appeals to legitimacy. If a meta-ethical theory is adequate to give an account of what it is for anyone to have a reason for any moral attitude, it seems plausible to suppose that it will have some materials in terms of which these issues can be discussed. If a version of subjectivism or objectivism can meet the more basic requirement of giving an account of reasons in moral discussion, then it should be able to give some account of the role of reason-giving in, in particular, a liberal society, and hence of the requirements and possibilities of toleration.

If this outline discussion is right, it looks as though, with the limited exception of the paternalism argument, there may be less intrinsic, as opposed to historical, connection between subjectivism and toleration than some have supposed. However, it must not be forgotten how important the historical connections themselves are. The mere fact that the question can now look like this, and adequately sophisticated versions of subjectivism and objectivism can now seem difficult to distinguish, is a tribute to the fact that more fanatical claims have been laid aside. It might well be claimed at this point, and Ayer might have claimed it, that the symmetries that seem now to extend over most of these matters are not themselves symmetrical in their implications, because it is various forms of objectivism, in particular religious forms, that have lost their fanatical impulse. It can be pointed out that it was traditionally objectivism that supposed so much to turn on the issue of the debate between objectivism and subjectivism, and if less now seems to turn on that debate, the significance of that fact is itself not symmetrical: it implies that objectivism, in particular, has lost some of its force.

No doubt paradoxes can be conjured from that statement of the situation. But Ayer himself, certainly, would have supposed that such paradoxes were a great deal less important than the fact that if fanatical religious intolerance (and with it, some particularly unrepentant forms of objectivism) is not prominent in philosophy, that is a point about philosophy, not yet one about the world. Ayer himself would have thought that this put these discussions into a correct perspective: he devoted a good deal more energy to the defence of toleration than to the discussion of meta-ethics.

NINE

The Actus Reus of Dr. Caligari

I

Michael Moore's book is subtitled "the philosophy of action and its implications for criminal law."[1] For much of his discussion, this formulation does express the way in which he proceeds: an account of action that is philosophically (as he often puts it, "metaphysically") motivated yields the kinds of distinctions and conclusions that are needed in order to support central principles of the criminal law, particularly as these have been formulated in the tradition reaching back to Jeremy Bentham and John Austin. In particular, three fundamental principles of the criminal law are defended, on the basis of philosophical considerations, from philosophical scepticism. These are the principles that Moore calls the voluntary act requirement, the actus reus requirement, and the double jeopardy requirement.[2] Moore's many subtle and interesting discussions succeed in showing that these principles can be defended against scepticism by philosophical argument.

However, there are areas in relation to which the subtitle seems to me to represent, as one might say, an exaggeration. In these areas, the best that one can do is to take some distinction or conclusion necessary to the criminal law and show that a theoretical account of it can be given that is at least not inconsistent with formulations motivated by the philosophy of action. It seems obvious, on reflection, that there must be areas about which this is true. The criminal law, after all, has special aims and purposes, and the requirements that it imposes on describing people's actions are unlikely to coincide throughout with distinctions that are motivated quite independently of those special purposes. I have argued elsewhere that any conception of responsibility involves the four elements of cause, intention, state, and response.[3] Responsibility is (with certain comprehensible exceptions) standardly ascribed to a person as the cause of a state

---

[1] MICHAEL S. MOORE, ACT AND CRIME: THE PHILOSOPHY OF ACTION AND ITS IMPLICATIONS FOR CRIMINAL LAW (1993). [Williams's essay first appeared in an issue of *University of Pennsylvania Law Review* that consisted of essays commissioned for a symposium on Moore's book: Moore's book is published by Oxford University Press.—Ed.]

[2] *See id.* at 4–5.

[3] *See* BERNARD WILLIAMS, SHAME AND NECESSITY 55–56 (1993).

of affairs; the questions will arise of what that person was trying to bring about and of what state of mind he or she was in at the time. Finally, an ascription is made with the aim of directing some response to that agent in this connection.

There is no one setting of these various factors, particularly those of intention and state of mind, that will suit every purpose, and this is manifestly so in contemporary law, where the setting of the requirements on intention is typically different in tort law from what it is in the criminal law. All the more, then, the various settings of these conditions in our everyday descriptions of action are unlikely to coincide already with those required by various branches of the law. There is no reason to believe that the various distinctions we use will provide, *ready-made*, what the criminal law needs, without taking account of special requirements within the criminal law.

Moore has no need to deny this point, and he often seems to accept it. He says, for example: "[T]he relevant question here is not: can any complex action be performed without the performance of a volitionally caused bodily movement? Rather, the question is: can any of the complex actions *prohibited by Anglo-American criminal law* be performed except by volitionally caused movement?"[4] This, in itself, does not require much modification or redirection of the philosophy of action by the concerns of the criminal law. The relevant question might collect its answer on purely philosophical grounds, and the only way in which the discussion will have been shaped by the interests of the criminal law will be the restriction of the question to a certain class of actions that are the law's concern. However, even this modest step does require the notion of the kind of actions that are the criminal law's concern, and that notion itself is not going to be generated by the philosophy of action.

A more significant consideration arises when the law demands answers (as, of course, it often does) which everyday users of action descriptions would not feel compelled to give—which, indeed, they might well feel disposed in common sense not to give. Consider the well-known questions of where and when A killed B.[5] If A squeezes the trigger in one jurisdiction and B is hit by the bullet in another, or if A administers the poison at one time and B dies as a result very much later, there is a notorious difficulty in answering questions of "where" or "when." The philosophy of action—more specifically, perhaps, the analysis of action descriptions—certainly shows why there is a difficulty, and indeed it is a condition on the adequacy of such a philosophy that it should be able to explain why there is a difficulty. However, there is no reason to suppose that philosophical

---

[4] MOORE, *supra* note 1, at 263.
[5] *See id.* at 280–92.

procedures themselves can answer that difficulty. This is because we need a special reason, such as the reasons provided by the demands of the criminal law, to want to answer the question at all.

The point is similar to those raised by indeterminacy through vagueness. It is a requirement on the philosophy of language that it should make plain what our difficulty is in saying when people become bald or (to take a more contentious case) in saying at what point a fertilized ovum becomes a human baby. But those explanations themselves should not be expected to answer the question. Aristotle was prepared to move the same point into metaphysics itself, when he said that it was sensible not to seek more precision than is allowed by the underlying subject matter.[6] But this absorption of the issue into metaphysics is, in relation to the present questions, slightly misleading. Aristotle's suggestion is that if the metaphysics of the situation (the underlying subject matter) does not in itself permit the distinction to be made, then the distinction should not be made. But this does not follow—all that follows is that the distinction should not be made if one is solely interested in metaphysics. If the distinction has to be made for some other reason, as when, for legal reasons, it must be determined where or when Smith was killed, then one has to go beyond metaphysics or the philosophy of action to make distinctions that one cannot get from those subjects if they are left to themselves.

II

Moore respects this point in a good deal of his practice. However, there is at least one area in which Moore tries to make the philosophy of action generate a determinate answer when it cannot do so and it is explicable that it cannot do so. He does this because of fairly obvious requirements of the criminal law. In this connection, we might perhaps say that Moore's subtitle represents more than an exaggeration. Here, it should rather read: "criminal law and its implications for the philosophy of action." The area in question is that of somnambulism or behaviour under hypnosis, and the rest of this Article will be devoted to this issue and to the lessons that it has for the general methodology. This is a matter on which Moore disagrees with a claim that I have made (in agreement with Herbert Hart[7]) that it is appropriate beyond dispute to describe somnambulistic and similar behaviour in the language, not just of action, but of purposive action; I have cited in this respect Shakespeare's wonderful description of the

---

[6] See ARISTOTLE, ETHICA NICHOMACHEA 1094 b 12.

[7] See H.L.A. HART, PUNISHMENT AND RESPONSIBILITY: ESSAYS IN THE PHILOSOPHY OF LAW 109 (1968).

actions of Lady Macbeth.[8] Moore claims that "the data of ordinary English usage"[9] do not provide us with any argument to show this at all.

Now if my argument had been, as Moore implies, simply that it was "idiomatic in ordinary English to describe (these happenings) with the ordinary verbs of action," this would not have been much of an argument, and Moore would be right in drawing our attention to the fact that active verbs can be ascribed to inanimate subjects, as when we say that sulphuric acid dissolves zinc. But this was not all there was to the argument. The claim was, rather, that Lady Macbeth acted purposively in various respects and that her movements had an intentional contour.[10] She had, for instance, gotten out of bed, recognized something as a light, picked it up, opened a door, and come downstairs. All of these were actions that she might have performed when fully awake, and in good part they are explained by the kinds of reasons by which they would be explained if she were awake. Thus she opened the door because she had the aim of getting out of her bedroom. One unusual thing she did was rub her hands as though she were washing them (when they were not actually in water). This is something that Shakespeare caught exactly:

> DOCTOR: Look how she rubs her hands . . . .
> GENTLEMAN: It is an accustomed action with her, to seem thus washing her hands.[11]

It is very important for the description of Lady Macbeth's case that, with the exception of the deviant handwashing performance, her actions are purposively the same as actions that she might have performed when awake, and the same with respect to the reasons that we could ascribe to her. It is thus not simply a matter of an inanimate object being in causal relations to its environment. The problem is set precisely by the fact that actions of this kind have an intentional or purposive aspect.

Now Moore has a way of acknowledging this point, when he says that the actions of a somnambulist are "metaphorical."[12] What is it for them to be "metaphorical actions" or, as he also puts it, "metaphorically actions?"[13] Moore is not referring to a metaphorical description of something that is certainly an action, as when we say the objector drove a horse and cart through the speaker's argument. What he means is that bodily movements of the agent are metaphorically described as actions. He ex-

---

[8] *See* Bernard Williams, *Voluntary Acts and Responsible Agents*, 10 OXFORD J. LEGAL STUD. 1, 1 (1990).

[9] MOORE, *supra* note 1, at 253.

[10] *See* Williams, *supra* note 8, at 1.

[11] WILLIAM SHAKESPEARE, MACBETH act 5, sc. 1.

[12] MOORE, *supra* note 1, at 254.

[13] *Id.*

plains this idea, moreover, in terms of a peculiar theory. He draws our attention to what he calls

> the often unnoticed ambiguity in the nouns and pronouns by which we refer to persons. I may say: 'I hit the ball,' and 'I am six feet tall,' yet the thing referred to in these two sentences is different. The first 'I' refers to me as a personal agent, the second, only to my body as inanimate object.[14]

The account of the metaphor, then, seems to be that there are two objects of reference, and we can use in a metaphorical way the verbs of action (which in their literal sense apply to the person) by applying them to a subject which is in fact the body.

In introducing this theory, Moore refers in a note to Peter Strawson's distinction between P-predicates and M-predicates, offered in Strawson's book *Individuals*.[15] It is rather ironic that Moore should make this reference, since Strawson's aim in using this distinction of predicates was precisely to avoid a distinction of subjects—his whole thesis was that the two supposed classes of predicate applied to one and the same subject, namely a person. In any case, the invocation of Strawson's distinction is not very helpful to Moore. We run into great difficulties when we try to sort predicates into the two kinds,[16] and Moore's idea involves an even more severe version of the same difficulty, when we attempt to determine where in a given statement the reference has changed.* "He became embarrassed, turned red, and broke out in a sweat" presumably refers to two different subjects, though it may be rather unclear which of them the second conjunct involves. "He dried himself with a towel" does not, as you might have thought, introduce a reflexive action, in the strict sense of an action that an agent does to himself. Again, a sentence such as "people who are very heavy have difficulty lifting themselves over a wall" will require considerable analysis in order to discover the various things that we are talking about.

Besides difficulties of this kind, there is the basic problem that we only know, on Moore's account, which of these objects of reference is being picked out by a given pronoun because we understand the predicate that is applied to it. We have been led to the distinction by Moore's use of the example "I am six feet tall." (This is the lead that I followed in con-

---

[14] *Id.*

[15] *See* P.F. Strawson, Individuals: An Essay in Descriptive Metaphysics 87–116 (1959).

[16] I have argued this previously. *See* Bernard Williams, *Are Persons Bodies?*, *in* Problems of the Self: Philosophical Papers 1956–1972 at 64–70 (1973).

* I have slightly recast the final clause of this sentence, which was garbled in the original. —Ed.

structing the difficult sentences above.) But at least "is six feet tall" is a kind of predicate that could be ascribed to something that was not a person—it belongs, to the extent that we can understand that distinction, with Strawson's M-predicates. However, "has just picked up a light, opened a door, and walked down the stairs" seemed to be paradigmatically the kind of predicate that is applied to a person. So even if we accepted Moore's quite implausible suggestion that apparent references to persons may really be references to a different object of reference, namely a body, we would be very unlikely to pick out the sentences that ascribe, as it seems, actions to somnambulists as introducing that bodily object of reference. It is only if we have *already* decided that there is something peculiar about these predications that we would start to look in that direction.

The idea of the two objects of reference does seem manifestly an unhelpful device. Indeed, it introduces a kind of dualism which is quite foreign to many things that Moore wants to say about actions and their relations to bodily movements. Why should he possibly be forced in this direction? Why should he say, further, that what somnambulists perform—or rather, on his dualistic view, what their "inanimate" bodies do—are "involuntary bodily movements"[17] which we mistake for actions? The movements of Lady Macbeth are not, in an easily recognizable sense, involuntary bodily movements. Moore admits that responsiveness to the environment and so forth, the adjustment of bodily motion to perceptual cues, are present, and these features, he says, "certainly make such movements look like actions."[18] This, he claims, is an illusion.

Except on extremely Cartesian views, there is something odd about discussing such cases and their relation to action in terms of *appearance and reality*. A set of movements can of course look like an action of a certain kind without being an example of an action of that kind; this is familiar enough from the stage. There could, indeed, be some reflex or similar movement of a limb that was not an action of any kind, which we took for an action of some particular kind. But the most obvious case in which this would be so would be one in which there was not the array of features to which Moore agrees, such as the shaping of behaviour to a purposive end and the responsiveness to perceptual cues—it is precisely the absence of such things that would lead one to say it was not after all an action, but something that we took for an action. But that, certainly, is not the problem with Lady Macbeth. There is no doubt that Lady Macbeth has picked up the light, found the door, undone its bolt, and carefully come down the stairs. Moreover, it is not a matter of a mechanically determined routine which merely looks as though it were responsive to percep-

---

[17] MOORE, *supra* note 1, at 255.
[18] *Id.*

tual cues; some somnambulists, at least, and we may suppose that they include Lady Macbeth, will walk around pieces of furniture that are not in their normal place. So why should we say that these movements only *look like* actions?

The reason must be, presumably, that they have no intentional aspect. I have already suggested that this is incorrect, since the movements that Lady Macbeth made in opening the door were done as movements that open the door, and indeed she has succeeded in opening the door. Relatedly, the somnambulist may try to do things that she fails in doing: she may try more than one way of getting the door open. Is there an argument, nevertheless, that the somnambulist does not act intentionally?

III

Here we may get some help from cases of hypnotic suggestion. The hypnotist tells the hypnotized subject to do various things, and quite often the subject does those very things, and may indeed, in the more spectacular cases, take various steps to do those things. Again, the hypnotist may tell the subject to do a certain thing when there is no way of doing that thing, but the hypnotist has made the subject believe that there is. In those cases, the subject may go through the appropriate movements without doing that thing. Now this subject is of course suffering from false belief, and is under some kind of illusion about her environment. If she has been instructed to lay a table and, in the embarrassing way that some stage hypnotists impose on their subjects, she is given quite inappropriate objects to lay out, she can rightly be said not to know what she is doing.

Now it might be argued that if the hypnotized subject is told to lay a table, and is given real knives and forks, she still does not know what she is doing, since she is in a state in which the hypnotist could just as well have persuaded her that she was handling knives and forks when she was not. The argument might then be generalized to suggest that hypnotized subjects never know what they are doing. This, in turn, might suggest that they do nothing intentionally, and hence (on Davidsonian principles, at least)[19] that they do not really do anything. This is the conclusion that Moore wants, for the hypnotized and for the somnambulist.

This is probably the best argument for Moore's conclusion, but it is not a very good one. First, there is a paradox in arriving at this conclusion from these premises, as what she is supposed not to know is *what she is*

---

[19] *See* DONALD DAVIDSON, *Agency, in* ESSAYS ON ACTIONS AND EVENTS 43–61 (1980). Davidson's view is that an event constitutes an action only if there is some description under which that action is intentional.

doing, and this certainly does not mean that she does not know what *her body* is doing. The implication, rather, is that she is doing certain things, but she does not know what they are.

This implication is surely correct. Even if we accept the argument to the effect that even when she is handling knives and forks she does not know what she is doing, and hence is not acting intentionally under the description *laying a table*,[20] this would give no reason to deny that her bodily movements are intentional; nor to deny that she does various other things intentionally, such as moving towards one piece of furniture while avoiding others, placing rather than dropping an object on to a surface, and so forth. Indeed, there is a large class of things that the hypnotized subject must be able to do if she is to do whatever it is she does do in supposedly carrying out the hypnotist's commands.

The state of the hypnotist's subject is that she acts under the hypnotist's suggestions. One aspect of this is that he can induce in her (something like) false beliefs. Another aspect is that, to some extent, he can get her to do things that she would not otherwise do in those circumstances. This second aspect is not simply an application of the first: in some cases, she would not do in those circumstances (in public, for instance, before an audience) the things that he has made her think that she is doing. The argument we have considered relies on the cognitive aspect in order to say that the agent does not really act, and I have denied that this can be generalized to everything that she does.

In Lady Macbeth's case, there is not even a controlling agent, except her own guilty self, and part of the reason for describing her activities, all the more, in terms of purpose and intention is that they are *her* purposes and intentions. She does share some cognitive failings with the hypnotized subject, and she may well not remember afterwards what she has been doing. There is no doubt more to be learned about these states psychologically, and the findings of further enquiries may properly affect our descriptions. But this is not the level at which Moore is working. Rather, he supposes that we can already be clear, for conceptual reasons, that the behaviour of the somnambulist or the hypnotized agent should not be classified as actions. But at this prescientific level it is, on the contrary, clear why we do describe this behaviour in terms of actions, and in so far as there are manifest differences from normal cases of action, it is not very

---

[20] I shall not engage with this argument here. It is important that it is stronger than a mere application of the argument from illusion. When the agent gets it right, she is in the same unusual cognitive state (subject to the hypnotist's suggestions) as she is when she gets it wrong. All the same, the argument still relies on disputable assumptions in the theory of knowledge.

difficult simply to register them.[21] We get into difficulties only if we embark on the essentially scholastic task of insisting that the criteria of what it is to be an action are such that there is no middle ground between actions with all their standard features, on the one hand, and, on the other, "involuntary" bodily movements—movements which on Moore's suggestion are not even ascribed to the same subject as the subject of actions.

IV

Why should anyone want to take that scholastic course? In this case the reason is extremely obvious; it lies in the demands of the criminal law. Even if the somnambulist does perform actions, he may very well not be criminally responsible for those actions or for what those actions bring about. Moreover, somebody else may be responsible. We can turn from the case of Lady Macbeth who, though not innocent, was at least innocent in her somnambulism, to another fictional case. This is the criminal figure of Dr. Caligari, who in Robert Wiene's 1919 film *The Cabinet of Dr. Caligari* controlled a figure called Cesare (memorably played by Conrad Veidt).[22] Cesare is kept in a box, and, when roused and instructed by Caligari, moves somnambulistically at his bidding. Among other crimes, he kills (as we would naturally put it) the town clerk with a dagger.

Cesare's behaviour is interestingly different from both Lady Macbeth's and that of the hypnotized subject. Unlike Lady Macbeth's, his behaviour is under someone else's control, but unlike the hypnotized subject's, it does not involve false beliefs. Caligari's control is over his objectives, and Cesare does whatever is needed, in the light of the situation, to achieve those objectives. His state is certainly peculiar; he is a sleepwalker. But the argument, such as it was, for saying that the hypnotized subject displays no intentions or purposes, gets even less grip on him than on the hypnotized subject.

However, this does not mean that Cesare is responsible. I take it that Caligari would be held guilty with respect to these deaths, and not Cesare. I assume that it is fairly obvious why the law can reasonably and justly take this line. Although it is not obvious what exactly is wrong with Cesare, it is obvious that Caligari, in this peculiar way, controls Cesare's

---

[21] This is not to deny that there is a substantive question of what exactly is wrong with such agents—the nature, for instance, of their dissociation. Such questions are discussed by Stephen Morse in his contribution to this volume. *See generally* Stephen J. Morse, *Culpability and Control*, 142 U. Pa. L. Rev. 1587 (1994). [This is a reference to the *University of Pennsylvania Law Review*.—Ed.]

[22] I shall follow the story that most of the film presents. It turns out at the end of the film that this story is actually a fantasy of the psychotic young man who has been narrating it.

objectives. I want to insist that the conclusions about responsibility should not be based on supposing that the reason why Caligari, and not Cesare, is the murderer is simply that the killing of the town clerk was Caligari's action and not Cesare's.

The town clerk was killed with a dagger, so, if Caligari killed him (and no one else), he killed him with a dagger. Perhaps he did, and our slight resistance to this may be attributed to an everyday implication of saying that Caligari killed him with a dagger, namely that Caligari drove the dagger into the victim with his own hand; an implication which in these peculiar circumstances is false.[23] This implication, however, seems to be an *entailment* of the description "he stabbed him"; so Caligari did not stab him. But if anyone stabbed him, then (on Moore's line) it was Caligari, so we shall have to deny that the town clerk was stabbed. Perhaps, then, we should deny this implication. But there will always be more difficulties of the same sort. Cesare has been instructed in a repertoire of killing techniques, and some other victim may have met her death by suffocation, a pillow held over her face. Caligari must have killed her, too. And while (I take it) he did not suffocate her, any more than he stabbed the town clerk, he must at least have brought about her death by suffocation, since that was certainly how she was killed. But he did not do that by holding a pillow over her face; yet, surely, she was suffocated because a pillow was held over her face.

We should not have to struggle with these difficulties. Cesare suffocated her, as he stabbed the town clerk. But he did it when he was asleep. He did these things as a result of a very peculiar relation he had to Dr. Caligari, one that enabled Dr. Caligari to bring it about that he did those things without his agreeing to do them. For suppose Caligari had said, "You agree to do it?" and Cesare, in his somnambulistic state, had said "Yes, I agree to do it." Cesare would not have actually agreed to do it: *that* is not an act that in this state he can perform. The explanation is to be found in his dissociation from considerations that essentially bear on his doing so. In this state, he cannot summon up, for instance, thoughts that would relate the killing to the rest of his life. This helps to explain why he is not responsible, but lends no support to the idea that he does not do the killings. We cannot say that he was forced to do them; he put up no resistance, and had no consciousness of a price. We cannot naturally say that he was induced to do them. We can best say, perhaps, that he was instructed to do them, though we would have to add that he received the instructions in a peculiar state. Whatever the best description,

---

[23] Moore gives this kind of interpretation. *See* MOORE, *supra* note 1, at 236. The appeal to what he calls "individual nuances," however, will surely not do for "stab" and "suffocate".

we can see how it is on these facts that Caligari is guilty with respect to these deaths and Cesare is not, but that is not because no stabbing or suffocating was done by Cesare.

Recalling that "instructions" can be given to a computer, someone may say on Moore's behalf that Cesare might as well have been a robot. It is not clear exactly what that means, but I think it is not true. What is true is that Caligari, for his murderous purposes, might as well have used a robot.[24] There is, certainly, a spectrum of possibilities from Cesare to a robot. But this tells us less than Moore's supporter might hope for. It tells us virtually nothing, in fact, unless we know what a robot can do. More significantly, if there is a slope from Cesare to a robot (however exactly a robot is to be described), there is equally a slope, in the opposite direction, from Cesare to Lady Macbeth, to actual somnambulist and hypnotic subjects, to people who are for various reasons in extremely suggestible states in general or in relation to a particular dominating person. It must be a scholastic illusion to suppose that somewhere on those slopes, uphill from Cesare, real, full-blown action is suddenly to be found as opposed to mere bodily movement.

We already have quite good ways of describing various dimensions in which what is done may fall short of the paradigm of fully voluntary action, and philosophy can help us to understand and to develop those ways. But it must be a mistake to suppose that it can yield by itself everything that the ascription of responsibility, in particular criminal responsibility, requires.

I have said that with respect to these deaths, Caligari is guilty and Cesare is not. Nevertheless, Cesare killed both victims, by stabbing one and suffocating the other. So what is Caligari guilty of? Certainly, of causing or bringing about these deaths. In terms of the four-fold structure that I mentioned earlier,[25] what Cesare does is a cause of death, but so is what Caligari does—which we are to assume consists in saying something to Cesare. Caligari in the fullest sense intends that death and has it as an objective. Cesare intends it just to the extent that he brings it about intentionally, rather than (for instance) by mistake—though it is significant that he might conceivably have done that, in circumstances that would have made it his, and not Caligari's, mistake. Did Caligari kill the victims? On Moore's own view, Caligari certainly did, because Moore defends the principle that "X caused Y's death" entails "X killed Y."[26] Moore, however, takes a different view from mine with respect to Cesare's role, one

---

[24] But not, in terms of the film, for his overriding purpose: he was researching somnambulism.

[25] See *supra* note 3 and accompanying text.

[26] MOORE, *supra* note 1, at 226–32.

that makes it easier for him to accept "Caligari caused their deaths" and hence (on his understanding of the entailment) "Caligari killed them." I am not clear whether on my view of Cesare's involvement—that Cesare killed them—Moore would say that Caligari killed them. As I have said, it does seem hard to deny that Caligari at least caused their deaths. I also think that he killed them; he killed the suffocated victim, for instance, not by suffocating her, but by bringing it about that Cesare suffocated her.

Of course, there is the further point relevant to responsibility, that if Caligari is a killer, he is a pathological but self-conscious and intelligent killer, a state which indeed raises some questions about the response that might be appropriate to such a person. These are questions, however, that would arise even if he had not used a somnambulistic agent. In short, the questions of responsibility, in the sense of what the law's response should be to these happenings, are questions about the state and the intentions of Caligari and of Cesare, and of the relations between those people. It is not a question that can be answered by ascribing to one of them and not to the other actions and intentions which are the cause of death.

TEN

Values, Reasons, and the Theory of Persuasion

1. Internal and External Reasons

The distinction that I shall discuss under this title is not, strictly speaking, a distinction between two kinds of reason, but rather a distinction between two kinds of claim that can be made about what an agent A has reason to do. The statement 'A has reason to X' receives an internal interpretation if it is taken to mean 'A could arrive at a decision to X by sound deliberation from his existing S', where S is A's existing set of desires, preferences, evaluations, and other psychological states in virtue of which he can be motivated to act. An external interpretation does not carry this implication. (Throughout the discussion I adopt the simplifying assumption that 'A has reason to X' means 'A has more reason to X than to do anything else'; additional qualifications would in fact enable one to drop this restriction.) A view that I have expressed elsewhere (Williams 1980; 1989; 1995b), and will defend here, is that if 'A has reason to X' has a distinctive sense, then it must receive the internal interpretation; in simplified form, the only reasons for action are internal reasons. I do not deny that 'A has reason to X' can entirely intelligibly be asserted without this implication. The claim is merely that when it is so asserted, it means something that could be expressed by a different kind of sentence, for instance to the effect that it is desirable that A should do the thing in question, or that we have reason to desire that A should do it. Only the internal interpretation represents the statement as distinctively a statement about A's reasons. Relatedly, if a statement of this kind is true, and A declines to do the thing in question, what is called in question is A's capacity in this connection to act rationally or reasonably. It would be too strong, for more than one reason, to say that in such circumstances A acts irrationally, but the line of criticism that will be appropriate in these circumstances will address itself to A's performance as a rational or reasonable agent rather than to other deficiencies that he may have.

It is important to emphasize the variety of elements that are, on this view, to be included in the agent's S. It does not contain merely inclinations or, again, egoistic motivations, and it can certainly contain dispositions associated with the agent's recognition of various kinds of values. Moreover, it is not the case that everything in the agent's S has already to be formed into preferences; and in so far as it is formed into preferences, those preferences do not necessarily have to satisfy formal conditions of completeness. There is no naturalistic reason, based on considerations of psychology or the philosophy of mind, to suppose that these indeterminacies are radically reducible, in particular to preference orderings that can be handled by Bayesian techniques. If there is a demand for such a reduction, it is of a normative, rather than an explanatory, character or, perhaps, the kind that is a fusion of the two, namely a demand that the phenomena should be such that a particular kind of explanation should be possible.

It is not an objection to the internalist account, interpreted in this broad way, that it involves vagueness and indeterminacy. This merely mirrors the truth that statements to the effect that A has a reason to do a certain thing are themselves vague and in various ways indeterminate. It would, of course, be an objection if the indeterminacy were such that there were no constraints on statements of this kind; if, for instance, there were no distinction between a situation in which someone, advising an agent, helped that agent to discover what he had reason to do, and the situation in which the adviser made a difference to the agent's S and gave him a reason for action which he did not have before. This question of vacuity will come up later in this chapter.

There is another difficulty, which concerns the form of the internalist account. In referring to what the agent would arrive at by a sound deliberative route, it can be taken to imply a claim to the effect that if the agent were to deliberate, and were to deliberate soundly, then he would arrive at this conclusion. This cannot be quite right, since deliberation is itself a psychological process, which has effects.

This means that we cannot necessarily equate 'A could arrive by a sound deliberative route at the decision to X' with 'A would arrive at that conclusion if he deliberated and did so soundly'. Someone may, indeed, do what he has most reason to do without deliberating and, perhaps, because he did not deliberate. We must not assume that thinking about the question of what to do, rehearsing considerations, and so forth, are simply like perception of an external reality. There is a dynamic process involved. Because of this, the internalist account's reference to arriving at a conclusion by a sound deliberative route has to be taken in an idealized or abstract form, which leaves out distinctive psychological effects of the actual process of deliberation. It is to be conceived in terms of a relation between the agent's S, the action in question, and the agent's principles of deliberation in so far as those principles are sound.

This raises the question of what count as sound principles, and of what counts as a sound deliberative route. It is essential to any adequate account of 'A has reason to X' that it should be normative, and should admit the possibility of A's being shown that he is mistaken in thinking that he has a reason for a certain course of action. The internalist account does leave room for normative correction; it allows, for instance, for the agent to be shown that his deliberation is unsound because it is based upon false information. It may be asked why the agent's deliberative route can, on the internalist account, be shown to be unsound by reference to factual mistakes, while claims that what the agent is doing is immoral or imprudent do not necessarily count as showing that the deliberative route is unsound. The answer to this is, crudely, that an agent is committed in general to acting in the light of sound information, simply by being a rational agent; included in the S of every rational agent is a desire not to fail through error. (There are of course complex exceptions to the general working of this desire, but they are necessarily exceptions.) Now it may be claimed that prudential, or again moral, policies are similarly involved in what it is to be a fully rational agent, and some philosophers have claimed conclusions of this kind. It may, indeed, to some extent be true, particularly with regard to a modest amount of prudence; if an agent is totally devoid of a concern for the effects of his actions on himself, we may indeed have problems in understanding what could count for him as a sound deliberative route at all. But to the extent that these things are true, then we are being told something about the necessary contents of the S of any rational agent.

If the claim is that those contents must include, for instance, moral elements, then we need an argument to that effect, an argument that the philosophers who have made these claims have in some cases tried to provide. When Kant, for instance, claimed that a rational agent as such is committed to seeing himself as acting impartially, he constructed an entire philosophy with the intention of delivering that conclusion. It is important that the internalist account in itself does not rule out a conclusion of that kind. It merely demands that the conclusion should be argued, and that it cannot be acquired on the cheap, for instance by pointing out the obvious truth that people often describe unfair conduct as 'unreasonable'. It takes more than ordinary language to deliver large Platonic, Aristotelian, or Kantian conclusions to the effect that virtue and reason will coincide.

2. RATIONALITY: INTERPRETATION AND VALUE

What then are the criteria of deliberative rationality, in which a rational agent presumably does necessarily have an interest? How far do they go beyond the general desire for true information, and minimal constraints of consistency? In particular, how far do they include the kinds of demands that rational decision theory has tended to place on them? I shall not try to answer this extremely large question, but there is an important aspect of it that I shall discuss, because a consideration in this area may seem to undermine the internalist view. It has been convincingly argued (Hurley 1989; Broome 1991a; 1991b) that in general we cannot disambiguate an agent's preferences and hence, in particular, assess the coherence of those preferences, without taking the agent to have values, values which must be intelligible to us. This might be thought to undermine the thesis of the internalism of reasons, by requiring that at least at some point 'there is reason to X' is prior to 'A has reason to X'.

The argument starts from the familiar point that there are prima-facie counter-examples to even very elementary principles of rational decision theory, and that while it is very easy to save the theory by re-describing these cases, some further constraints are needed if this process is not simply going to render the theory trivial. We may take an example of Broome's (1991b: ch. 5), about transitivity. Maurice, when offered the choice between going to Rome and going to the mountains, prefers visiting Rome, because he is frightened by mountaineering. Faced with the choice between staying at home and going to Rome, he prefers to stay at home, because he is anti-culture. Compatibly with these two choices, he can prefer going to the mountains to staying at home.* The solution to this failure of transitivity lies in a finer individuation of alternatives: we can distinguish between the option of staying at home when Rome is the only alternative and the option of staying at home when mountaineering is the only alternative. (The first of these, Broome claims, Maurice does actually prefer to mountaineering but this is not a practical preference, that is to say, one that is expressed in actual choice. I am not sure that this is an altogether satisfactory solution, and some re-description will be needed if it is rejected; but the general principle of such methods is what concerns us here.) Similar problems, and similar solutions, are familiar from Allais's paradox and the Sure Thing Principle.

The problem now is that such differentiation may seem to be entirely arbitrary, with the result that the theory will be trivialized. Broome's

---

* Given that Williams's description of this case omits, somewhat bemusingly, any reason Maurice might have for preferring going to the mountains to staying at home, and given that what Broome says about this belies Williams's characterization of Maurice as "anti-culture," I thought that it would be helpful to cite, in full, Broome's own description of the case (1991b, p. 101): "Mountaineering frightens [Maurice], so he prefers visiting Rome. Sightseeing bores him, so he prefers staying at home. But to stay at home when he could have gone mountaineering would, he believes, be cowardly. That is why, if he had the choice between staying at home and going mountaineering, he would choose to go mountaineering. (To visit Rome when he could have gone mountaineering seems to him cultured rather than cowardly.)"—Ed.

solution is that Maurice is rational in these circumstances if and only if he is justified in having a preference between the two subdivided options that involve his staying at home; this implies that there is no rational principle requiring him to be indifferent between them. This introduces the notion of a 'justifying difference', which Broome interprets in terms of a differentiation with regard to good and bad. This may seem to lead to a rejection of internalism. The alternative, it seems, to there being no rational constraints on what will count as deliberative preference, is that discriminations of the agent should be rationally intelligible in terms of values, considerations that we can understand as intelligibly related to questions of value.

I agree with Broome that there is a need for substantive constraints on the interpretations of preference, but I do not agree that this leads to the rejection of internalism. We need in the first place to distinguish two possible aims that can be ascribed to a rational agent as such:

(i)   to arrive at conclusions about what to do by procedures that cannot be faulted for irrationality;
(ii) to do what he has most reason to do.

(i) is neither a sufficient nor a necessary condition of (ii). It is not a sufficient condition for the simple reason that he may do everything that could conceivably be demanded of a rational agent, but fail through bad luck, in particular through non-culpable ignorance, and in that sense he will not have done what he actually has most reason to do. (This is the sense in which 'a sound deliberative route', if it is to provide a sufficient condition of what the agent has most reason to do, must consist of more than simply the agent's deliberating as best he can in the circumstances.) Equally, (i) is not a necessary condition of (ii), for the reason already mentioned, that the application of any deliberative methods may itself, in certain circumstances, have psychological effects that get in the way of the agent doing what he has most reason to do. Now the rational agent's aim must be more basically (ii), rather than (i): the idea that (i) is more fundamentally the aim of the exercise than (ii) is, in effect, the notorious defensive civil servant syndrome.

What may mislead one about this is that, as a general policy, we can achieve (ii) only because the thing in question is the rational thing for us to do, and that consideration seems to imply (i). It is not a contingent fact that (i) helps in achieving (ii) but, even so, as we have already seen, (i) does not always need to be pursued in pursuing (ii). Now, suppose an agent seems to be failing in pursuing (ii) because of some deviant relation of his choice to his S, for instance through failure of transitivity. (Here, of course, we encounter the familiar problem of what is the ground of irrationality in such a case, for instance whether it is enough to say that a Dutch book could be made against him. It is an important consideration here, and one not always recognized by economic theory, that taking on a bet is always an additional step; it is always a relevant question to ask 'would you make a Dutch book with this man?'.) The agent's interest is in achieving (ii): he is not passing an examination in practical rationality. So what he has to do is to see whether he can make sense of himself, whether he can understand his *S* in terms that will rationalize his choices to himself. Some fine individuations between objects of preferences are just given, but when there is a real issue of interpretation, we can agree with Broome that further reasons, and indeed further values, may be needed at this point. But they are the agent's values, and not the assessor's. It is those values, moreover, that an external interpreter will invoke if he is making sense of the agent's conduct as rational.

Is this an anti-Humean conclusion? In one sense, perhaps it is, inasmuch as some values have to be invoked in order to make sense of preferences,[1] but it is not anti-internalist, even when we grant a further point, that what counts as an intelligible invocation of a value is a shared matter of interpretation. To some extent, it may well be the case that we can interpret another agent's *S*, and, in particular, values that he may invoke in discriminating his own objects of preference, only by ascribing to him some values that we share ourselves. This indeed leaves untouched the internalist claim that what he has reason to do is a function of his *S*—it merely says something about what it is to understand his *S*.

However, internalist doctrine would be pointless if everyone's values, and everyone's *S*, were the same; in those circumstances, anyone's deliberation could be anyone else's, and the distinction between externalism and internalism would fade away. But clearly this is not how it is. We need to invoke some values, no doubt, in interpreting other people's preferences and in construing their rationality, but the values that we have to invoke are their values rather than ours. This will be true even if, to a limited extent, we can understand their values only by relating them to ours.

3. How Much Does the Internalist Account Exclude?

As we have seen, the internalist account is generous with what counts as a sound deliberative route. It rejects the picture by which a determinate and fixed set of preferences is expressed simply in terms of its decision-theoretical rational extensions, and deliberation is construed simply as discovering what these are. The difficulty is that if, in abandoning this

---

[1] Susan Hurley (1989), perhaps misleadingly, describes any position that concedes this as 'objectivist'.

false picture, we allow any extension whatsoever of the agent's S to count, we have lost hold of the notion of what the agent has reason to do in virtue of his S. The problem can be modelled in terms of a shared deliberation, in the sense of a deliberation about what A is to do in which B takes part, typically by seeing the situation so far as possible from the point of view of A's S. (Some of the same considerations will apply also to a shared deliberation in the sense of a deliberation by A and B about what they should collectively do, but this is not the case most relevant to the present issue.) The questions of the limitations on what counts as a sound deliberative expression of the agent's S can be put in terms of a distinction between B's helping A to arrive at such an expression and B's acting in such a way as to change A's S. If we give up the idea that there is** a determinate set of rational deliberative procedures (it is often called an 'algorithmic' conception of deliberation), the danger is, once more, that the idea of 'a sound deliberative route' will have no constraining effect, and any resolution that the agent can psychologically reach 'from' his present S— that is simply to say, setting out from his present S—will equally count.

The traditional account assumed a highly determinate S, and a highly constrained set of procedures for arriving at new decisions on the basis of that S. In terms of this, one could supposedly determine what procedures of an adviser or fellow deliberator would count as assisting the agent to discover what he had reason to do, as opposed to giving the agent new reasons or persuading him to do something he originally had no reason to do. To the extent that we lose hold of determinate constraints on 'a sound deliberative route', we shall have problems, too, with these derived descriptions: it will be unclear what counts as deliberative assistance in finding what one has reason to do, as opposed to interventions that come closer to conversion.

A possible suggestion at this point is to reverse the order of explanation, and, in some part, place the constraints on the procedures that are to count as deliberative assistance in contrast to these other interventions. What someone has reason to do will be what he can arrive at by a sound deliberative route; and he can arrive at a conclusion or resolution by a sound deliberative route, perhaps, only if he could be led to it by deliberative assistance that operated within those constraints.

What might those constraints be? What will the helpful deliberative assistant be like? Two necessary conditions perhaps are the following.

(i) The assistant will be truthful, in the sense both of telling the truth and of helping the agent to discover the truth. An application of

---

** I have inserted both the word "up" and the phrase "the idea that there is" into the original text because that seems to me to make better sense of the text. The original essay this is that the assistant will be truthful about his own procedures and motives, with the result that these can be transparent to the agent; the assistant has no hidden agenda in his dealings with the agent.

(ii) The assistant will try to make the best sense of the agent's S, and, in particular, if there is a conflict between the assistant's and the agent's interpretations of the agent's S, the assistant will have some suitable explanation of the agent's misinterpretation. (This condition is not circular: it does not say that the assistant has to make the best sense of what the agent's reasons are.)

If an assistant acting in this way gets the agent to agree that what he has most reason to do is to X, may we say that this is indeed what the agent had most reason to do, in virtue of his original S? Not necessarily. Just as, in the purely first-personal construction, we had to allow for new psychological effects of the agent's actually deliberating, so in the two-person situation we have to factor out extraneous effects of the advisory situation itself. Thus the assistant might operate scrupulously within the constraints, and the agent fall in love with her, something which radically modifies his S. He is led to new courses of action as a result of shared deliberation within the constraints, but the outcome cannot count as what he originally had reason to do.

In the light of this, it is clear that we cannot leave out altogether retro-spective interpretation of the ways in which the decision is related to the agent's original S. We still need the notion of the decision being the expres-sion, even if an indirect one, of motivations that the agent had in the first place, and not of motivations which he has acquired in the process, unless those motivations themselves are expressions of what there was before. We cannot put all the weight on the procedural criterion in terms of the way in which an assistant has led, or might lead him to the conclusion. But have we now put any weight on it at all? Do we need the idea of the assistant? I suggest that we do. One reason is that the conception of what such an assistant might do itself plays a part (though only one part) in the interpretation of the way in which the decision is related to the agent's S.

The traditional account of rational deliberation leaves no room for the deliberation's introducing radically new material. As one might expect from the picture's resemblance to standard accounts of formal inference, it does not allow for a creative step in deliberation, in the sense of the agent's thinking of a course of action which does not already figure in the beliefs or motivations that he has. The traditional account might be

---

contained a large number of typographical errors, and I think it is more than possible that some such expressions had been lost from Williams's own manuscript.—Ed.

extended from this in what, very loosely, could be called a Popperian way: it might allow new material, but be interested only in its relation to the original base, and not in where it came from—it would regard that as a purely psychological question. But we can hardly leave the matter there. Once we admit the truth that the relation of the decision to the original base cannot be algorithmic, or even very tightly constrained, the question of how the new material got into the deliberation becomes important, and the fact that it was suggested favourably by someone else may itself be thought (at least if it is not related in the most obvious and direct ways to the original base) to count in favour of saying that this is a case of the agent's being given a new motivation by persuasion rather than one of the agent's discovering what he already had reason to do. Constraints on the nature of the other person's intervention can play an important part in overcoming this assumption.

If we reflect on the advice and deliberative assistance, it will help us to see not only what counts as the agent's being helped to discover what he has reason to do, but also why this should not in fact be contrasted with persuasion.

The kinds of constraint that are in question here do not imply that the adviser's activity may not be a form of persuasion: it can be a form of persuasion, one that is truthful and addresses the question from the adviser's best understanding of the wants and interests of the agent. It is therefore not manipulative. But it is still pointful to call it 'persuasion', to remind us that it need not be free from emotional effects, it may work by seizing the agent's imagination, and it may be an expression of a power that could be used for other purposes.

A contrast between reason and persuasion, at both an individual and a political level, goes back at least to Plato, and it is still with us. We have to learn, against this, that the operations of reason, above all in its practical applications, cannot be recognized on formal grounds; and equally, a procedural account that tries to eliminate the dimension of persuasion is certain to be empty. (This point applies, obviously enough, to Habermas's 'ideal speech situation', a topic which is very relevant to the present subject but which I am unable to take up here.) Even when the reasons in question are those of an individual, and hence, on the account I have given, grounded in that agent's *S*, we can see why the two ideas, of the agent's discovering what he has reason to do, and of a sympathetic adviser operating within particular kinds of constraint, are connected. If we pursue such connections, we may be able to see more clearly why even internal individual reasons call for discussion with other people; why also, in hoping that public political discussion should be moderately rational and should address the reasons of individuals and groups, we are not committed to the nonsense of supposing that it could be transcendentally airlifted out of the world of persuasion and power. Indeed, the internal account of individual reasons particularly brings out the importance of linking the discussion of reason with the theory of persuasion: the failings of an externalist account come out all the more clearly when we reflect on the kind of discussion that might be needed to convince an agent that such a reason applied to him, and how that discussion could hardly fail to be coercive.

REFERENCES

Allais, M. (1979), 'The so-called Allais Paradox and Rational Decision under Uncertainty', in Allais and Hagen (1979).
—— and Hagen, O. (1979) (eds.), *Expected Utility Hypotheses and the Allais Paradox* (Dordrecht: Reidel).
Broome, J. (1991a), 'Rationality and the Sure-Thing Principle', in Meeks (1991).
—— (1991b), *Weighing Goods* (Oxford: Basil Blackwell).
Harrison, R. (1980) (ed.), *Rational Action* (Cambridge: Cambridge University Press).
Hurley, S. L. (1989), *Natural Reasons* (Oxford: Oxford University Press).
Meeks, G. (1991) (ed.), *Thoughtful Economic Man* (Cambridge: Cambridge University Press).
Williams, B. (1980), 'Internal and External Reasons', in Harrison (1980) (reprinted in B. Williams (1991), *Moral Luck* (Cambridge: Cambridge University Press)).
—— (1989), 'Internal Reasons and the Obscurity of Blame', *Logos* 10 (Santa Clara, Calif.) (reprinted in B. Williams (1995a), *Making Sense of Humanity* (Cambridge: Cambridge University Press).
—— (1995a), *Making Sense of Humanity* (Cambridge: Cambridge University Press).
—— (1995b), 'Replies', in J. E. J. Altham and R. Harrison (eds.), *World, Mind, and Morality: Essays on the Ethical Philosophy of Bernard Williams* (Cambridge: Cambridge University Press).

ELEVEN

Moral Responsibility and Political Freedom[1]

In the phrase "moral responsibility", the term "moral" can register two different ideas. On the one hand, it may introduce a particular field of application and a corresponding class of consequences, which are informal and social rather than formal and supported by force. Used in this way, "moral responsibility" is distinguished from legal responsibility. A quite different use of the term is involved when "moral" is introduced to imply a certain basis of assessment, one that places particular emphasis on the voluntary. In this sense, moral responsibility can be proposed as a basis of assessment even when what is in question is legal responsibility, for instance in relation to the criminal law.

When the first idea is dominant, and a contrast is being stressed with (in particular) the legal, there need be no special emphasis on voluntary agency. Someone may be said to be morally, but not legally, responsible for an omission, or for the consequences of having carelessly led someone to form a particular expectation. However, when, in the second sense, it is urged that moral responsibility should be the basis of assessing responsibility in the criminal law, the stress is on voluntariness. This will be the principal concern of this paper.

I have argued elsewhere[2] that any conception of responsibility involves four elements: cause, intention, state, and response.

If a conception that is brought to bear on an agent with respect to a given outcome is to count as *responsibility*, as opposed to other notions such as that of a scapegoat, the agent must, basically, be regarded as the *cause* of the outcome. There are exceptions to this, when under legal arrangements responsibility is transferred, ascribed, assumed, etc., and responsibility can be undertaken at one remove, as in most situations of strict liability. The present discussion is confined to the basic case, personal responsibility in which the agent is the cause of the outcome in question.

The distinction between *intention* and *state* is one between what an agent means to do (and whether he means to do a certain thing at all) and

---

[1] The Aquinas Lecture of the International Society of Criminology, delivered in Cambridge on 5 May 1994, and hosted by the University of Cambridge Institute of Criminology.

[2] Williams, *Shame and Necessity* (Berkeley 1993), chapter 3.

what state of mind he is in when he means to do it and does it.[3] The distinction is important, though it can be indeterminate in particular cases whether we are concerned with intention, or state, or both. A man who in a fit of rage destroys a vital and irreplaceable document may, for that moment, not have realised what he was doing, or he may have known what he was doing and for that moment not have cared; or there may be no reason to say one of these things rather than the other. In certain states, intentional action is not possible at all. Michael Moore[4] has claimed this for all somnambulistic and hypnotic states, but this is surely an exaggeration; the significance of such states for the criminal law is not so much that agents in those states can do nothing intentionally but rather that the intentional acts that they do in those states do not bear a regular relation to their plans or character.

Response means what is expected, demanded, or required of the agent, or is imposed on him. In some cases, notably under the criminal law, this is identified as punishment. The present discussion will concentrate on this example, but it is important that it is not the only response recognised in relation to responsibility, or indeed to moral responsibility.

A conception of criminal responsibility in terms of moral responsibility sets requirements on the *intention* and the *state* of the agent which together mean that the action has to be voluntary. "A does X voluntarily" is equivalent to "A does X intentionally in a normal state of mind". The inherent vagueness of this will be of concern later.

It is a significant question, well known in relation to no-fault divorce, car insurance and so forth, whether in a given area we should be using a conception of responsibility at all. However, those who lay emphasis on the notion of moral responsibility do not typically see things in this way. Moral responsibility is thought, as it were, to apply itself. The consequence of this attitude is that if the causality, the intention and the state are of a certain kind—if the agent is voluntarily the cause of certain kinds of outcome—then this in itself is thought to attract the appropriate response. Where the response is punishment, this is a version[5] of the retributive theory of punishment. This "internalism" or criterial self-sufficiency

---

[3] It is illustrated in *Shame and Necessity* by the contrast between two agents in Homer: Telemachus, who carelessly left a door open, and Agamemnon, who look Briseis away from Achilles, and indeed meant to do so, but was (he later claims) in a strange state of mind when he did so.

[4] Moore, *Act and Crime: The Philosophy of Action and Its Implications for Criminal Law* (Oxford 1993), pp. 253 *seq.* For a discussion of this and related views of Moore's see the symposium in 142 *University of Pennsylvania Law Review* (1994), pp. 1443–1840. [This is the source of Essay 9 above.—Ed.]

[5] The voluntaristic version. Retribution is not necessarily confined to the voluntary: see below. p. 123.

is a general feature of conceptions associated with the moral. Here, as with moral judgement and moral merit, the morality system tries to sustain the idea that there is no relevant external point of view from which its determinations can be assessed.

This idea cannot entirely be sustained; we need a reasonable external perspective on the practices and provisions of moral responsibility. Moral responsibility gets some support from the fact that the principal candidate as an alternative to it in the criminal law is a direct Utilitarian treatment of particular cases, and this is much more unattractive than moral responsibility. As Hart[6] pointed out, however, consequentialist arguments can be applied at a more general level. Bentham's own higher-level Utilitarian argument for restricting punishment to voluntary offences—that only voluntary offences can be deterred—is unsound, since a practice of punishing the involuntary might in fact help to deter voluntary offences, through a chilling effect. However, Hart offered a better argument, which invokes not just welfare but freedom. This is based on the principle that citizens should be able to conduct their affairs so far as possible without the state's power being unpredictably directed against them. This rationalises other things as well, such as a ban on retrospective legislation and the requirements that the laws should be comprehensible and as far as possible well-known.

This argument relates very directly to the value of *political* freedom: that is to say, to the citizen's freedom with respect to intentionally directed uses of state power. It is not an argument simply in terms of maximising freedom across society. One of the effects of undeterred crime is to decrease people's freedom, and a straightforwardly maximising calculation would have to weigh these effects of crime against the limitations of freedom imposed by the law's willingness to punish the non-voluntary.[7] The argument implies, rather, a particular responsibility of the state with respect to the use of its own power, a responsibility which, I take it, will be claimed by any version of liberalism. This is not the place to set out a political theory of liberalism; the point is only that it is political theory that grounds this aspect of moral responsibility.

The argument is thus specially concerned with state power, as opposed to other power that might curtail a citizen's freedom; but it is also, more specifically, concerned with the intentionally directed use of state power. It may be said that citizens anyway suffer to an indefinite degree from side-effects of state power. This is true, but the distinction between being

---

[6] Hart, *Punishment and Responsibility: Essays in the Philosophy of Law* (Oxford 1968), esp. ch. 2.

[7] I am grateful to Antony Duff for making this point in the discussion of the Aquinas Lecture.

the object of someone's power and being affected incidentally by someone's activities is in general significant with respect to freedom, as emerges in the very primitive connections between lacking freedom, being in someone else's power, and being subject to that person's will. The condition of being politically free in a certain regard is not, in the first instance, that of being unaffected by what the state does; it is, rather, a condition in which the state's intention does not forcibly become one's own intention. Why this distinction also should be important is once again a matter of political theory.

It is an argument in political philosophy, then, that will provide external considerations to support the criteria of moral responsibility. The argument applies specially to criminal punishment, with regard to which there cannot be such things as no-fault insurance. You cannot insure to compensate the victims of your criminal acts, and although the state can do so, there are severe limits to this; there is also a limit in political justice, since it is likely to represent an arbitrary transfer of resources via the insurance fund at the criminal's will, if not to the criminal.

The argument for moral responsibility in relation to legal punishment will be: granted a justification for punishment such as deterrence, demands of transparency imply a system of public punishment applied to criminal agents; political freedom implies, further, that it should be applied to voluntary agents.

It is clear, however, that punishment is not explained entirely in terms of deterrence. Much of it represents the expression of anger, and when it is properly conducted it is regarded as the rightful expression of rightful anger. This truth can presumably be said to yield a "retributive theory" of punishment. It is less clear that it yields a retributive justification of punishment. It may rather be that if one accepts the retributive theory, one stops looking for a justification of punishment as such, although one may well look for justifications of particular practices: one may, for instance, be opposed to long intervals between act and punishment. A serious difficulty is that it may turn out that no just procedure in a modern state can adequately express retribution, and this is a point that will concern us later.

What are called "retributive justifications" of punishment often make it seem as though there were some illuminating description of what is done by punishment under retribution, as when it is said that punishment will "show him" or "teach him a lesson."[8] These are consequentialist

---

[8] "Turn him round with regard to values" is Robert Nozick's phrase in Nozick, *Philosophical Explanations* (Harvard 1984), at pp. 363 *seq.* For further comment on the present lines, see "Nietzsche's minimalist moral psychology", *European Journal of Philosophy* 1.1 (1993), reprinted in Williams, *Making Sense of Humanity* (Cambridge 1995). [This is now

misdescriptions of what is in fact, on the retributive account, an intransitive process. On the retributive understanding of it, nothing is essentially *done* by punishment except to hurt the recipient. He is, it is claimed, rightfully hurt, but the criterion of that is not what punishment does, but what he has done.

It is worth saying that a purely denunciatory theory of punishment seems not to be a theory of punishment, unless denunciation is in itself sufficiently painful to be the punishment. The idea that traditional, painful, punishments are simply denunciations is incoherent, because it does not explain, without begging the question, why denunciations have to take the form of what Nietzsche identified as the constant of punishment, "the ceremony of pain".

With a retributive understanding of punishment, the argument for moral responsibility, grounded in political freedom, still goes through. (There is a difference in the argument when it is expressed in terms of retribution rather than deterrence. When the justification is deterrence, we need an extra premiss about transparency, since social mechanisms such as deterrence (as Utilitarians often remind us) do not have to be declared to be effective; legal retribution, on the other hand, is essentially public.)

The argument from political freedom for the criteria of moral responsibility is still available under a retributivist understanding of punishment; more important, it is still necessary. This is not because we still need an argument for punishment. On a retributivist view, we already have all the argument for punishment (in principle) that we are going to get—though there remains the important question whether defensible legal procedures can adequately express retribution. The reason why we still need the argument for moral responsibility is that retribution does not have to be directed to voluntary acts. This is easily overlooked, because the presence of intention on the part of the agent is important to the psychology of retribution. Yet voluntariness cannot be strictly necessary, since retributive feelings easily extend to a reckless agent with respect to the actual outcome, and not simply to the recklessness itself.

Moreover, even when the agent had the relevant harmful intention, retribution is less sensitive than moral responsibility is to his psychological *state*. One aspect of "heinousness" is the awfulness of the act, and with awful actions retributive considerations can be fairly insensitive to state. Another aspect of heinousness, however, is premeditation, and some of the considerations associated with this are on the borders of state and intention, as are questions about impulsive acts: was the agent's state such

also reprinted in Bernard Williams, *The Sense of the Past: Essays in the History of Philosophy*, ed. Myles Burnyeat (Princeton: Princeton University Press, 2006).—Ed.]

that he did not know what he was doing, or such that he momentarily did not care that he was knowingly doing that thing?

If we think that retributive punishment should be constrained by attention to moral responsibility, this does not simply follow from what retribution is (at least so far as many questions about the agent's state are concerned), but rather from the argument already used in relation to deterrence, the argument that relies on political freedom.

As I have already mentioned, there is a serious issue about the operation of retributive punishment in a modern society. A partial truth contained in expressive or denunciatory accounts of punishment is that retribution has to be seen as such if it is to have any point at all. But if judicial process requires opportunities of appeal that take a long time, and if, relatedly, limitations are set on the forms that punishment can take, it is very unclear that what actually happens can match anyone's idea of retribution. In a sense, the paradigm of retributive punishment is a lynching, under the condition that the right person is being hanged. It was, notoriously, never easy to make sure of meeting that condition. Under modern demands on what counts as being sure of meeting that and other conditions, even an execution, if executions are allowed at all, is not going to reach the expressive standard of a lynching. But there is no road back from modern demands on justice in their general outlines, even if particular practices can be modified. The point here is not that retribution is inherently evil or primitive or irrational. It is simply that no punishment under modern conditions can really be retribution. Those who think that punishment has a lot to do with retribution should, correspondingly, ask whether anything done to an offender under modern conditions can really be punishment.

Even if we have a general argument for moral responsibility we must recognise that its effects are severely restricted by the limitations of the concept of the voluntary itself. That concept is effective up to a point, but it is both vague and superficial. These are two different considerations. There is great indeterminacy and vagueness about the agent's psychological state and the soundness of associated counterfactuals, as in the case of "irresistible impulse" and other areas of obscurity lying between state and intention. There are unanswerable questions about what is "normal" for a given agent, and disputes about the degree to which this should count.

The concept of the voluntary is also superficial, because even if it is established that the agent's action was intentional in a normal state (e.g. highly premeditated), there is a further question of why he is someone who can want to do such things, whether it is in his control that he is such a person, and so on. It is clear that if voluntariness is to do its work such questions cannot be pressed beyond a certain point. It is not that they get a favourable answer, as free-will libertarians suppose, nor that they get an unfavourable answer which puts moral responsibility out of business. Nor again is it, as some reconcilers perhaps suppose, that there is a transparent rationale for construing the voluntary within certain limits that exclude those questions. It is simply that the voluntary is an inherently superficial concept which should not be asked to do too much.

I do not suppose that this fact makes punishment under these shallow conditions of voluntariness in itself unjust. But there is a real question about what punishment can mean, and whether it can mean what most people want it to mean. It is with negative desert as Nozick rightly said it was with positive desert: it does not go all the way down.[9] We can draw some lessons from this for moral responsibility. We can use the notion; we should not push questions associated with it too far; we should not insist on its merits in cases where its weaknesses come under pressure, if there is something else that will meet our needs better; and above all, we should not make a grandiose mystery out of it.

Of course, in that last recommendation, there is a significant judgement. It is perfectly possible for people to agree with most of what I have said, and disagree with this judgement, because they think that the only way of keeping moral responsibility going is by making a grandiose mystery out of it. I do not believe this, both in the sense that I do not think that in the modern world one can get away with it, and also because I think that certain values that make it impossible to get away with it also make it a bad thing to want to get away with. Both I and my hypothetical opponent reject traditional, in particular traditional enlightenment, attempts to rationalise moral responsibility thoroughly, but one's attitude to the enlightenment, here as elsewhere, is finally a matter of one's attitude to political honesty.

Moral responsibility has a function, and there is much to be said for its doing some of the work of ascriptions of responsibility and dealing with our responses to offences, so long as one does not take it too seriously. But if one accepts the idea of moral responsibility, this is often taken to imply that moral responsibility is self-applying and does not need or permit any external justification or assessment; that it is profound, or can be made so; and that it is the ideal in terms of which other institutions are to be judged and to which they should try to approximate. All of these further conceptions are false. If moral responsibility necessarily involved these conceptions, it would have to be abandoned.

[9] Nozick, *Anarchy, State and Utopia* (Basic Books 1974), p. 225.

TWELVE

Tolerating the Intolerable

The difficulty with toleration is that it seems to be at once necessary and impossible. It is necessary where different groups have conflicting beliefs—moral, political or religious—and realise that there is no alternative to their living together; no alternative, that is to say, except armed conflict, which will not resolve their disagreements and will impose continuous suffering. These are the circumstances in which toleration is necessary. Yet in those same circumstances it may well seem impossible.

If violence and the breakdown of social co-operation are threatened in these circumstances, it is because people find others' beliefs or ways of life deeply unacceptable. In matters of religion, for instance (which, historically, was the first area in which the idea of toleration was used), the need for toleration arises because one of the groups, at least, thinks that the other is blasphemously, disastrously, obscenely wrong. The members of one group may also think, very often, that the leaders or elders of the other group are keeping the young, or perhaps the women, from enlightenment and liberation. In this case, they see it as not merely in their own group's interest, but in the interest of some in the other group, that the true religion (as they believe it to be) should prevail. It is because the disagreement goes this deep that the parties to it think that they cannot accept the existence of each other. We need to tolerate other people and their ways of life only in situations that make it very difficult to do so. Toleration, we may say, is required only for the intolerable. That is its basic problem.

We may think of toleration as an attitude that a more powerful group, or a majority, may have (or may fail to have) towards a less powerful group or a minority. In a country where there are many Christians and few Muslims, there may be a question whether the Christians tolerate the Muslims; the Muslims do not get the choice, so to speak, whether to tolerate the Christians or not. If the proportions of Christians and Muslims are reversed, so will be the direction of toleration. This is how we usually think of toleration, and it is natural to do so, because discussions of toleration have often been discussions of what laws should exist—in particular, laws permitting or forbidding various kinds of religious practice—and the laws have been determined by the attitudes of the more powerful group. But more basically, toleration is a matter of the attitudes of any group to another, and does not concern only the relations of the more powerful to the less powerful. It is certainly not just a question of what laws there should be. A group or a creed can rightly be said to be 'intolerant' if it would like to suppress or drive out others even if, as a matter of fact, it has no power to do so. The problems of toleration are to be first found at the level of human relations and of the attitude of one way of life towards another. It is not only a question of how the power of the state is to be used, though of course it supports and feeds a problem about that—a problem of political philosophy. However, we should be careful about making the assumption that what underlies a *practice* of toleration must be a personal *virtue* of toleration. All toleration involves serious difficulties, but it is the virtue that most drastically threatens to involve conceptual impossibility.

If there is to be a question of toleration, it is necessary that there should be *something to be tolerated*; there has to be some belief or practice or way of life that one group may think (however fanatically or unreasonably) to be wrong, or mistaken, or undesirable. If one group simply hates another, as with a clan vendetta or cases of sheer racism, it is not really toleration that is needed: the people involved need rather to lose their hatred, their prejudice, or their implacable memories. If we are asking people to be tolerant, we are asking for something more complicated than this. They will indeed have to lose something, their desire to suppress or drive out the rival belief; but they will also keep something, their commitment to their own beliefs, which is what gave them that desire in the first place. There is a tension here between one's own commitments and the acceptance that other people may have other and perhaps quite distasteful commitments. This is the tension that is typical of toleration, and the tension which makes it so difficult.

Just because it involves this tension between commitment to one's own outlook and acceptance of the other's, toleration is supposed to be more than mere weariness or indifference. After the European wars of religion in the sixteenth and seventeenth centuries had raged for years, people began to think that it must be better for the different Christian churches to co-exist. Various attitudes went with this development. Some people became sceptical about the distinctive claims of any church, and began to think that there was no truth, or at least no truth discoverable by human beings, about the validity of one church's creed as opposed to another's. Other people began to think that the struggles had helped them to understand God's purposes better: that He did not mind how people worshipped, so long as they did so in good faith within certain broad Christian limits. And in more recent times, a similar ecumenical spirit has extended beyond the boundaries of Christianity.

These two lines of thought in a certain sense went in opposite directions. One of them, the sceptical, claimed that there was less to be known about God's designs than the warring parties, each with its particular fanaticism, had supposed. The other line of thought, the broad church view, claimed to have a better insight into God's designs than the warring parties had. But in their relation to the battles of faith, the two lines of thought did nevertheless end up in the same position, with the idea that precise questions of Christian belief did not matter as much as people had supposed; that less was at stake. This leads to toleration as a matter of political *practice*, and that is an extremely important result. However, as an attitude, it is less than toleration. If you do not care all that much what anyone believes, you do not need the attitude of toleration, any more than you do with regard to other people's tastes in food.

In many matters, attitudes that are more tolerant in practice do arise for this reason, that people cease to think that a certain kind of behaviour is a matter for disapproval or negative judgement at all. This is what is happening, in many parts of the world, with regard to kinds of sexual behaviour that were previously discouraged and in some cases legally punished. An extra-marital relationship or a homosexual ménage may arouse no hostile comment or reaction, as such things did in the past, but once again, though this is toleration as a matter of practice, the attitude it relies on is indifference rather than, strictly speaking, toleration. Indeed, if I and others in the neighbourhood said that we were *tolerating* the homosexual relations of the couple next door, our attitude would be thought to be less than liberal.

There are no doubt many conflicts and areas of intolerance for which the solution should indeed be found in this direction—in the increase of indifference. Matters of sexual and social behaviour which in smaller and more traditional societies are of great public concern will come to seem more a private matter, raising in themselves no question of right or wrong. The slide towards indifference may also provide, as it did in Europe, the only solution to some religious disputes. Not all religions, of course, have any desire to convert, let alone coerce, others. They no doubt have some opinion or other (perhaps of the 'broad church' type) about the state of truth or error of those who do not share their faith, but they are content to leave those other people alone. Other creeds, however, are less willing to allow error, as they see it, to flourish, and it may be that with them there is no solution except that which Europe discovered (in religion, at least, if not in politics)—a decline in enthusiasm. It is important that a decline of enthusiasm need not take the form of a movement's merely running out of steam. As the various sects of Christianity discovered, a religion may have its own resources for rethinking its relations to others. One relevant idea, which had considerable influence in Europe, is that an expansive religion really wants people to believe in it, but it must recognise that this is not a result that can be achieved by force. The most that force can achieve is acquiescence and outer conformity. As Hegel said of the slave's master, the fanatic is always disappointed: what he wanted was acknowledgement, but all he can get is conformity.

Scepticism, indifference or broad church views are not the only source of what I am calling toleration as a practice. It can also be secured in a Hobbesian equilibrium, under which the acceptance of one group by the other is the best that either of them can get. This is not, of course, in itself a principled solution, as opposed to the sceptical outlook which is, in its own way, principled. The Hobbesian solution is also notoriously unstable. A sect which could, just about, enforce conformity may be deterred by the thought of what things would be like if the other party took over. But for this to be a Hobbesian thought, as opposed to a role reversal argument which, for instance, refers to rights, some instability must be in the offing. The parties who are conscious of such a situation are likely to go in for pre-emptive strikes, and this is all the more so if the parties involved reflect that even if they can hope only for acquiescence and outer conformity in one generation, they may conceivably hope for more in later generations. As a matter of fact, in the modern world the imposition by force of political creeds and ideologies has not been very effective over time: one lesson that was already obvious in the year 1984 was the falsity in this respect of Orwell's *1984*. However, the imposition of ideology over time has certainly worked in the past, and the qualification in the previous statement, 'in the modern world', is extremely important. This is something I shall come back to.

So far, then, toleration as a *value* has barely emerged from the argument. We can have practices of toleration underlaid by scepticism or indifference, or, again, by an understood balance of power. Toleration as a value seems to demand more than this, something that can be expressed in a certain political philosophy, a certain conception of the state.

To some degree, it is possible for people to belong to communities bound together by shared convictions (religious convictions, for instance), and for toleration to be sustained by a distinction between those communities and the state. The state is not identified with any set of such beliefs, and does not enforce any of them; equally, it does not allow any of the groups to impose its beliefs on the others, though each of them may of course advocate what it believes. In the United States, for instance, there is a wide consensus that supports the Constitution in allowing no law that enforces or even encourages any particular religion. There are many religious groups, and no doubt many of them have deep convictions, but none of them wants the state to suppress others, or to allow any of them to suppress others.

Many people have hoped that this can serve as a general model of the way in which a modern society can resolve the tensions of toleration. On the one hand, there are deeply held and differing convictions about moral or religious matters, held by various groups within the society. On the other hand, there is a supposedly impartial state, which affirms the rights of every citizen to equal consideration, including an equal right to form and express his or her convictions. This is the model of *liberal pluralism*. It can be seen as enacting toleration. It expresses toleration's peculiar combination of conviction and acceptance, by finding a home for people's various convictions in groups or communities less than the state, while the acceptance of diversity is located in the structure of the state itself.

This is not to say that there is no need of any shared beliefs. Clearly there must be a shared belief in the system itself. The model of a society that is held together by a framework of rights and an aspiration towards equal respect, rather than by a shared body of more specific substantive convictions, demands an ideal of citizenship that will be adequate to bear such a weight. The most impressive version of that ideal is perhaps that offered by the tradition of liberal philosophy flowing from Kant, which identifies the dignity of the human being with autonomy. A free person is one who makes his or her own life and determines his or her own convictions, and power must be used to make this possible, not to frustrate it by imposing a given set of convictions.

This is not a purely negative or sceptical ideal. If it were, it could not even hope to have the power to bind together into one society people with strongly differing convictions. Nor could it provide the motive power that all tolerant societies need in order to fight, when other means fail, the intolerant. This is an ideal associated with many contemporary liberal thinkers such as John Rawls, Thomas Nagel and Ronald Dworkin.[1]

Under the philosophy of liberal pluralism, toleration does emerge as a principled doctrine, and is represented as a value; more exactly, perhaps, it emerges as very closely related to a certain more fundamental value, that of autonomy. Because this value is taken to be understood and shared, this account of the role of toleration in liberal pluralism implies a picture of justification. It should provide an argument that could be accepted by those who do find *prima facie* intolerable outlooks that obtain in the society, and which liberalism refuses to deploy the power of the state to suppress. Thomas Nagel has expressed the matter well:

> Liberalism purports to be a view that justifies religious toleration not
> only to religious sceptics but to the devout, and sexual toleration not

---

[1] See John Rawls, *A Theory of Justice*, Oxford, Oxford University Press, 1971; John Rawls, *Political Liberalism*, New York, Columbia University Press, 1993; Thomas Nagel,

only to libertines but to those who believe extramarital sex is sinful. It distinguishes between the values a person can appeal to in conducting his own life and those he can appeal to in justifying the exercise of political power.[2]

No one, including Nagel himself, believes that this will be possible in every case. There must be, on any showing, limits to the extent to which the liberal state can be disengaged on matters of ethical disagreement. There are some questions, such as that of abortion, on which the state will fail to be neutral whatever it does. Its laws may draw distinctions between different circumstances of abortion, but in the end it cannot escape the fact that some people will believe with the deepest conviction that a certain class of acts should be permitted, while other people will believe with equal conviction that those acts should be forbidden. Equally intractable questions will arise with regard to education, where the autonomy of some fundamentalist religious groups, for instance, to bring up their children in their own beliefs will be seen by liberals as standing in conflict with the autonomy of those children to choose what beliefs they will have. No society can avoid collective and substantive choices on matters of that kind, and in that sense, on those issues, there are limits to toleration, even if people continue to respect one another's opinions.

The fact that there will be some cases that will be impossible in such a way does not necessarily wreck liberal toleration, unless there are too many of them. There is no argument of principle to show that if A thinks a certain practice is wrong and B thinks that practice is right, A has to think that the state should suppress that practice or B has to think that the state should promote that practice. These are considerations at different levels. Nevertheless, there is a famous argument to the effect that the liberal ideal is in principle impossible. Some critics of liberalism claim that the liberal pluralist state, as the supposed enactment of toleration, does not really exist. What is happening, they say, is that the state is subtly enforcing one set of principles (roughly, principles which favour individual choice, social co-operation and business efficiency) while the convictions that people previously deeply held, on matters of religion or sexual behaviour or the significance of cultural experience, dwindle into private tastes. On this showing, liberalism will be 'just another sectarian doctrine': the phrase that Rawls used precisely in explaining what liberalism had to avoid being.

What is the critic's justification for saying that the liberal state is 'subtly enforcing' one set of attitudes rather than another? Nagel distinguishes

Equality and Impartiality, Oxford, Oxford University Press, 1991; Ronald Dworkin, 'What is Equality?', *Philosophy and Public Affairs*, 10, 1981.

[2] Nagel, *Equality and Impartiality*, p. 156.

sharply between *enforcing* something like individualism, on the one hand, and the practices of liberal toleration, on the other, though he honestly and correctly admits that the educational practices, for instance, of the liberal state are not 'equal in their effects'. This is an important distinction, and it can make some significant difference in practice. It is not the same thing to be proselytised or coerced by militant individualism, and merely to see one's traditional religious surroundings eroded by a modern liberal society. The liberal's opponents must concede that there is something in the distinction, but this does not mean that they will be convinced by the use that the liberal makes of it, because it is not a distinction that is neutral in its inspiration. It is asymmetrically skewed in the liberal direction, because it makes a lot out of a difference of procedure, whereas what matters to a non-liberal believer is the difference of outcome. I doubt whether we can find an argument of principle that satisfies the purest and strongest aims of the value of liberal toleration, in the sense that it does not rely on scepticism or on the contingencies of power, and also could in principle explain to rational people whose deepest convictions were not in favour of individual autonomy and related values that they should think a state better which let their values decay in preference to enforcing them.

If toleration as a practice is to be defended in terms of its being a value, then it will have to appeal to substantive opinions about the good, in particular the good of individual autonomy, and these opinions will extend to the value and the meaning of personal characteristics and virtues associated with toleration, just as they will to the political activities of imposing or refusing to impose various substantive outlooks. This is not to say that the substantive values of individual autonomy are misguided or baseless. The point is that these values, like others, may be rejected, and to the extent that toleration rests on those values, then toleration will also be rejected. The practice of toleration cannot be based on a value such as that of individual autonomy, and also hope to escape from substantive disagreements about the good. This really is a contradiction because it is only a substantive view of goods such as autonomy that could yield the value that is expressed by the practices of toleration.

In the light of this, we can now better understand the impossibility or extreme difficulty that was seemingly presented by the personal virtue or attitude of toleration. It appeared impossible because it seemingly required someone to think that a certain belief or practice was thoroughly wrong or bad, and at the same time that there was some intrinsic good to be found in its being allowed to flourish. This does not involve a contradiction, if the other good is found not in that belief's continuing, but in the other believer's autonomy. People can coherently think that a certain outlook or attitude is deeply wrong, and that the flourishing of such an attitude should be tolerated, if they also hold another substantive value in favour of the autonomy or independence of other believers. The belief in toleration as a value, then, does not necessarily involve a contradiction, but rather that familiar thing, a conflict of goods. However, this in turn gives rise to the familiar problem that others may not share the liberal's view of those goods; in particular, the people that the liberal is particularly required to tolerate are unlikely to share the liberal's view of the good of autonomy, which is the basis of his toleration, to the extent that this expresses a value.

Granted this, it is perhaps as well that, as we saw earlier, the practice of toleration does not necessarily rest on any such value at all. It may be supported by Hobbesian considerations about what is possible or desirable in the matter of enforcement, or again by scepticism about the issues of disagreement and their eventual resolution—though with scepticism, of course, the point will be reached where nobody is sufficiently interested in the question for toleration even to be necessary. It is important, too, that these attitudes do not exist in a context in which there are no other values at all. Appeals to the misery and cruelty involved in intolerance may, in favourable circumstances, have some effect even with those who are not dedicated to toleration as an intrinsic virtue.

It may be that the best hopes for toleration are to be found not so much in the abstract principle which challenges one to combine the maximum of the pure spirit of toleration with one's detestation of what has to be tolerated. It may lie rather in modernity itself, or what is left of it, and in its principal creation, international commercial society. Despite unnerving outbreaks of fanaticism in many different directions, it is still possible to think that the structures of this international order will encourage scepticism about religious and other claims to exclusivity, and about the motives of those who impose such claims. Indeed, it can encourage such outlooks within religions themselves. When such scepticism is set against the manifest and immediate human harms generated by intolerance, there is a basis for the practice of toleration—a basis that is indeed allied to liberalism, but is less ambitious than the pure principle of liberal pluralism, which rests on autonomy. It is closer to the tradition that may be traced to Montesquieu and to Constant, which the late Judith Shklar called 'the Liberalism of Fear.'[3]

It may be that liberal societies can preserve, in an atmosphere of toleration, a variety of strong convictions on important matters. Only the future will show whether that is so, and also how much it matters to humanity whether that variety, and so all but a few convictions, will fade away.

[3] Judith Shklar, 'The Liberalism of Fear' in Nancy Rosenblum (ed.), *Liberalism and Moral Life*, Cambridge, Mass., Harvard University Press, 1989, pp. 21–38.

Perhaps toleration will prove to have been an interim value, serving a period between a past when no one had heard of it and a future in which no one will need it. For the present, it is very obvious that the time has not yet come when we can do without the awkward practices of toleration. But those practices have to be sustained not so much by a very pure principle as by all the resources that we can put together. Besides the belief in autonomy, those resources consist of scepticism against fanaticism and the pretensions of its advocates; conviction about the manifest evils of toleration's absence; and, quite certainly, power.

THIRTEEN

The Human Prejudice

Once upon a time there was an outlook called "humanism." In one sense there still is: it is a name given these days to a movement of organized, sometimes militant, opposition to religious belief, in particular to Christianity. What was more or less the same movement used to go under a name equally inherited from the past of philosophy, which was "Rationalism." In Britain atheist organizations under these different names have existed at the same time, and I believe that one man, who wrote indefatigably to the newspapers, may once have been secretary of them both.

It is not "humanism" in any such sense that I shall be concerned with, but I will make one point about it, because it is relevant to questions about our ethical outlook and the role played in it by the idea of humanity, which are the questions that I do want to discuss. Humanism in the sense of militant atheism encounters an immediate and very obvious paradox. Its speciality lies not just in being atheist—there are all sorts of ways of being that—but in its faith in humanity to flourish without religion; moreover, in the idea that religion itself is peculiarly the enemy of human flourishing. The general idea is that if the last remnants of religion could be abolished, humankind would be set free and would do a great deal better. But the outlook is stuck with the fact that on its own submission this evil, corrupting, and pervasive thing, religion, is itself a *human* invention: it certainly did not come from anywhere else. So humanists in this atheist sense should ask themselves: if humanity has invented something as awful as they take religion to be, what should that tell them about humanity? In particular, can humanity really be expected to do much better without it?

However, that is not the subject. When I said that once upon a time there was an outlook called "humanism," I meant rather the time of the Renaissance. The term applied in the first place to new schemes of education, emphasizing the Latin classics and a tradition of rhetoric, but came to apply more broadly to a variety of philosophical movements. There was an increased and intensified interest in human nature.[1] One form of this was a new tradition inaugurated by Petrarch, of writings about the dignity and excellence of human beings (or, as the tradition inevitably put

---

[1] I am indebted here to Jill Kraye, "Moral Philosophy," in *The Cambridge History of Renaissance Philosophy*, ed. C. B. Schmitt (Cambridge: Cambridge University Press, 1988), esp. pp. 306–16.

it, of man). These ideas were certainly not original with the Renaissance. Many of the arguments were already familiar, for instance the Christian argument that the superiority of man was shown by the choice of a human being to be the vehicle of the Incarnation; or the older idea, which goes back at least to Protagoras as he is presented by Plato, that humans have fewer natural advantages—fewer defences, for instance—than other animals, but that they are more than compensated for this by the gifts of reason and cognition.

Others of course took a gloomier view of human powers and potentialities. Montaigne wondered how peculiar human beings were, and was a lot less enthusiastic about the peculiarities they had. But whether the views were positive and celebratory, or more sceptical or pessimistic, there was one characteristic that almost all the views shared with one another. They shared it, too, with traditional Christianity, and this was hardly surprising, since virtually everyone in the Renaissance influenced by humanism was some sort of Christian. For a start, almost everyone believed that human beings were literally at the centre of the universe (with the exceptions perhaps of Nicolas of Cusa and Giordano Bruno, who thought that there was no centre to the universe). Besides that purely topographical belief, however, there was a more basic assumption, that in cosmic terms human beings had a definite measure of importance. In most of these outlooks, the assumption was that the measure was high, that humans were particularly important in relation to the scheme of things. This is most obviously true of the more celebratory versions of humanism, according to which human beings are the most perfect beings in creation. But it is also present in outlooks that assign human beings a wretched and imperfect condition—Luther's vision, for instance, in which man is hideously fallen and can do nothing about it simply by his own efforts. The assumption is still there—indeed, it is hardly an assumption, but a central belief in the structure—that that fact itself is of absolute importance. The cosmos may not be looking at human beings, in their fallen state, with much admiration, but it is certainly looking at them. The human condition is a central concern to God, so central, in fact, that it led to the Incarnation, which in the Reformation context too plays its traditional role as signalling man's special role in the scheme of things. If man's fate is a very special concern to God, there is nothing more absolute than that: it is a central concern, period.

Overtly anthropocentric views of the cosmos are certainly less common today than they were then. Leaving aside the distribution of concerns on earth itself, which I shall come back to, people for a long time now have been impressed by the mere topographical rearrangement of the universe, by which we are not in the centre of anything interesting: our location in the galaxy, just for starters, seems almost extravagantly non-committal.

Moreover, many people suppose that there are other living creatures on planets in this galaxy, in other galaxies, perhaps in other universes. It seems hubristic or merely silly to suppose that this enterprise has any special interest in us. Even Christians, or many of them, are less impressed by the idea that God must be *more* concerned with human beings than he is with any other creature (I'm afraid I don't know what the current state of thought is about the Incarnation). The idea of the absolute importance of human beings seems firmly dead or at least well on the way out.

However, we need to go a little carefully here. The assumption I am considering, as I put it, is that in cosmic terms human beings have a definite measure of importance. The most common application of that assumption, naturally enough, has been that they have a high degree of importance; and I have suggested that that itself can take two different forms: the Petrarchan or celebratory form, in which man is splendidly important, and what we may call the Lutheran form, that what is of ultimate significance is the fact that man is wretchedly fallen. But there is another and less obvious application of the same assumption: that human beings do have a definite measure of importance in the scheme of things, but that it is very low. On this view, there is a significance of human beings to the cosmos, but it is vanishingly small. This may not be a very exciting truth about the cosmos, as contrasted with those other outlooks I mentioned, but it is still meant to be a truth about the cosmos; moreover, it is meant to be an exciting, or at least significant, truth about human beings. I think that this may have been what Bertrand Russell was thinking when, for instance in an essay significantly called *A Free Man's Worship*, he went on about the transitoriness of human beings, the tininess of the earth, the vast and pitiless expanses of the universe and so on, in a style of self-pitying and at the same time self-glorifying rhetoric that made Frank Ramsey remark that he himself was much less impressed than some of his friends were by the size of the universe, perhaps because he weighed 240 pounds.

This outlook can make people feel that human activities are absurd, because we invest them with an importance which they do not really possess. If someone feels about human activities in this way, there is never much point, it must be said, in telling him that his feelings involve a muddle: the feelings probably come from some place which that comment will not reach. All the same, they do involve a muddle. It is a muddle between thinking that our activities fail some test of cosmic significance, and (as contrasted with that) recognizing that there is no such test. If there is no such thing as the cosmic point of view, if the idea of absolute importance in the scheme of things is an illusion, a relic of a world not yet thoroughly disenchanted, then there is no other point of view except ours in which our activities can have or lack a significance. Perhaps, in a way, that is what Russell wanted to say, but his journey through the pathos of loneliness and insignificance as experienced from a non-existent point of view could only generate the kind of muddle that is called sentimentality. Nietzsche by contrast got it right when he said that once upon a time there was a star in a corner of the universe, and a planet circling that star, and on it some clever creatures who invented knowledge; and then they died, and the star went out, and it was as though nothing had happened.[2]

Of course, there is in principle a third possibility, between a cosmic point of view and our point of view, a possibility familiar from science fiction: that one day, we might encounter other creatures who would have a point of view on our activities—a point of view which, it is quite vital to add, we could respect. Perhaps science fiction has not made very interesting use of this fantasy, but there may be something to learn from it, and I shall come back to it at the end of these remarks.

Suppose we accept that there is no question of human beings and their activities being important or failing to be so from a cosmic point of view. That does not mean that there is no point of view from which they are important. There is certainly one point of view from which they are important, namely ours: unsurprisingly so, since the "we" in question, the "we" who raise this question and discuss with others who we hope will listen and reply, are indeed human beings. It is just as unsurprising that this "we" often shows up within the *content* of our values. Whether a creature is a human being or not makes a large difference, a lot of the time, to the ways in which we treat that creature or at least think that we should treat it. Let us leave aside for the moment distinctions of this kind that are strongly contested by some people, such as the matter of what we are prepared to eat. Less contentiously, we speak, for instance, of "human rights," and that means rights that are possessed by certain creatures because they are human beings, in virtue of their being human. We speak of "human values." Indeed, at Princeton there is a Center for Human Values. Of course, that phrase could mean no more than that the values in question are possessed by human beings, but in that purely possessive sense the term would hardly be adding much, since on this planet at least there isn't any other creature that has any values, or, certainly, a Center to study and promote them. Human values are not just values that we have, but values that express our humanity, and to study them is to study what we value inasmuch as we are what we are, that is to say, human beings.

---

[2] Friedrich Nietzsche, "On Truth and Lies in a Nonmoral Sense," in *Philosophy and Truth: Selections from Nietzsche's Notebooks of the Early 1870s*, trans. and ed. Daniel Breazeale (Brighton: Harvester Press, 1979), opening paragraph.

Now there are some people who suppose that if in any way we privilege human beings in our ethical thought, if we think that what happens to human beings is more important than what happens to other creatures, if we think that human beings as such have a claim on our attention and care in all sorts of situations in which other animals have less or no claim on us, we are implicitly reverting to a belief in the absolute importance of human beings. They suppose that we are in effect saying, when we exercise these distinctions between human beings and other creatures, that human beings are more important, period, than those other creatures. That objection is simply a mistake. We do not have to be saying anything of that sort at all. These actions and attitudes need express no more than the fact that human beings are more important *to us*, a fact which is hardly surprising.

That, mistaken, objection takes the form of claiming that in privileging human beings in our ethical thought we are saying *more* than we should: we are claiming their absolute importance. There is a different objection, which one might put by claiming that we are saying *less* than we need to say: that we need a reason for these preferences. Without a reason, the objection goes, the preference will just be a prejudice. If we have given any reason at all so far for these preferences, it is simply the one we express by saying "it's a human being" or "they're human" or "she's one of us," and that, the objectors say, is not a reason. They will remind us of the paradigm prejudices, racism and sexism. "Because he's white," "because he's male" are no good in themselves as reasons, though they can be relevant in very special circumstances (gender in the case of employing a bathroom attendant, for example, though even that might be thought in some circles to involve a further prejudice). If the supposed reasons of race or gender are offered without support, the answer they elicit is "*What's that got to do with it?*" Those supposed reasons are equally of the form "he's one of us," for a narrower "us." The human privilege is itself just another prejudice, these objectors say, and they have a suitably unlovely name for it, "speciesism."

How good is this objection? How exactly does it work? It will take a little while to answer those questions, because they require us to try to get a bit clearer about the relations between our humanity, on the one hand, and our giving and understanding reasons, on the other, and the route to that involves several stops. A good place to start, I think, is this: not many racists or sexists have actually supposed that a bare appeal to race or gender—merely saying "he's black" or "she's a woman"—did constitute a reason. They were, so to speak, at a stage either earlier or later than that. It was earlier if they simply had a barely articulated practice of discrimination: they just went on like that and did not need to say anything to their like-minded companions in the way of justification of the practice. The day came when they did have to say something in justification: to those discriminated against, if they could not simply tell them to shut up, to outsiders or to radicals, or to themselves in those moments when they wondered how defensible it might be, and *then* they had to say *more*. Mere references to race or gender would not meet what was by then the need; equally, references to supernatural sources which said the same thing would not hold up for long. Something which at least seemed relevant to the matter at hand—job opportunities, the franchise, or whatever it might be—would then be brought out, about the supposed intellectual and moral weakness of blacks or women. These were reasons in the sense that they were at least to some degree of the right shape to be reasons, though they were of course very bad reasons, both because they were untrue and because they were the products of false consciousness, working to hold up the system, and it did not need any very elaborate social or psychological theory to show that they were.[3]

With the case of the supposed human prejudice, it does not seem to be quite like this. On the one hand, it is not simply a matter of inarticulate or unexpressed discrimination: it is no secret that we are in favour of human rights, for instance. On the other hand, "it's a human being" does seem to operate as a reason, but it does not seem to be helped out by some further reach of supposedly more relevant reasons, of the kind which in the other cases of prejudice turned out to be rationalizations. We are all aware of some notable differences between human beings and other creatures on earth, but there is a whole range of cases in which we cite or rely on the fact that a certain creature is a human being, but where those differences do not seem to figure in our thought as *justifications* for going on as we do. In fact, in many cases it is hard to see how they could. Uniquely on earth, human beings use highly articulated languages; they have developed to an unparalleled extent non-genetic learning through culture, possess literatures and historically cumulative technologies, and so on. There is of course a lot of dispute about the exact nature and extent of these differences between our own and other species. There are discussions, for instance, of how far some other primates transmit learned skills, and whether they have local traditions in this. But this is not the point: there is, on any showing, a sharp and spectacular behavioural gap between us and our nearest primate relatives. This is no doubt because other hominid species have disappeared, probably with our assistance. But why should considerations about these differences, true as they are, play any role in an argument about vegetarianism, for instance? What has

[3] For a theoretically unambitious version of a "critical theory" test which applies to such situations, see my *Truth and Truthfulness: An Essay in Genealogy* (Princeton: Princeton University Press, 2002), chapter 9, sections 4 and 5.

all that got to do with human beings' eating some other animals, but not human beings? It is hard to see any argument in that direction which will not turn out to say something like this, that it is *simply better* that culture, intelligence, technology should flourish—as opposed, presumably, to all those other amazing things that are done by other species which are on the menu. Or consider, not the case of meat eating, but of insecticides: if we have reason to use them, must we claim that it is simply better that we should flourish at the expense of the insects? If any evolutionary development is spectacular and amazing, it is the proliferation and diversification of insects. Some of them are harmful to human beings, their food, or their artifacts; but they are truly wonderful.[4] What these last points show is that even if we could get hold of the idea that it was *just better* that one sort of animal should flourish rather than another, it is not in the least clear why it should be us. But the basic point, of course, is that we can't get hold of that idea at all. This is simply another recurrence of the notion we saw off a while ago, absolute importance, that last relic of the still enchanted world. Of course, we can say, rightly, that we are in favour of cultural development and so on, and think it very important; but that itself is just another expression of the human prejudice we are supposed to be wrestling with.

So there is something obscure about the relations between the moral consideration "it's a human being" and the characteristics that distinguish human beings from other creatures. If there is a human prejudice, it is structurally different from those other prejudices, racism and sexism. This doesn't necessarily show that it isn't a prejudice. Some critics will say, on the contrary, that it shows what a deep prejudice it is, to the extent that we cannot even articulate reasons that might be supposed to support it. And if, as I said, we seem very ready to profess it, the critic will say that this shows how shamelessly prejudiced we are, or that we can profess it because, very significantly, there is no one we have to justify it to, except a few reformers who are fellow human beings. That is certainly significant. Other animals are good at many things, but not at asking for or understanding justifications. Oppressed human groups come of age in the search for emancipation when they speak for themselves, and no longer through reforming members of the oppressive group, but the other animals will never come of age: human beings will always act as their trustees. This is connected to the point, which I shall come back to, that in relation to them the only moral question for us is how we should *treat* them.

[4] Cf. in this connection the late Stephen J. Gould's point about the false impression of "progress" given by the standard old representation of the evolutionary tree.

Someone who speaks vigorously against speciesism and the human prejudice is of course Professor Peter Singer. (Incidentally, he holds his chair at the Center for Human Values at Princeton, which I have already mentioned, and I have wondered what he makes of that name. In the purely possessive, limp, sense of the expression it is presumably all right, but in the richer sense which must surely be its intention, I should have thought it would have sounded to him rather like a Center for Aryan Values.) Whatever exactly may be the structure of the human prejudice, if it is a prejudice, Singer's work has brought out clearly some consequences of rejecting it as a prejudice, consequences which he has been prepared to advocate in a very robust style.

A central idea involved in the supposed human prejudice is that there are certain respects in which creatures are treated in one way rather than another simply because they belong to a certain category, the human species. We do not, at this basic initial level, need to know any more about them. Told that there are human beings trapped in a burning building, on the strength of that fact alone we mobilize as many resources as we can to rescue them. When the human prejudice is rejected, two things follow, as Singer has made clear. One is that some more substantial set of properties, supposedly better fitted to give a reason, are substituted. The second is that the criteria based on these properties, the criteria which determine what you can properly do to a creature, are applied to examples one at a time: it is always a question whether this particular individual satisfies the criteria.

Consider the question, not of protecting, but of killing. Singer thinks that our reasons for being less ready to kill human beings than we are to kill other animals—the "greater seriousness" of killing them, as he puts it—are based on

> our superior mental powers—our self-awareness, our rationality, our moral sense, our autonomy, or some combination of these. They are the kinds of thing, we are inclined to say, which make us "uniquely human". To be more precise, they are the kinds of thing that make us persons.[5]

Elsewhere, he cites with approval Michael Tooley's definition of persons as "those beings who are capable of seeing themselves as continuing selves—that is, as self-aware beings existing over time."[6] It is these characteristics that we should refer to, when we are deciding what to do, and

[5] Peter Singer, *Unsanctifying Human Life: Essays on Ethics* [UHL], ed. Helga Kuhse (Oxford: Blackwell, 2002), p. 193. [This quotation is from an article entitled "Individuals, Humans, and Persons: The Issue of Moral Status," co-authored by Helga Kuhse.—Ed.]

[6] UHL, p. 239. [This quotation is from an article entitled "Should All Seriously Disabled Infants Live?", co-authored by Helga Kuhse.—Ed.]

in principle we should refer to them on a case-by-case basis. "If we are considering whether it is wrong to destroy something, surely we must look at its actual characteristics, not just the species to which it belongs," and "actual" here is taken in a way that leaves no room for potentiality. You can't say that an embryo gets special protection because it is potentially a person; it is not yet a person, and therefore it is a non-person, just as (in Tooley's terminology) someone suffering from acute senile dementia is an ex-person.[7]

As I have said, Singer brings out very clearly these two consequences of his view and relies on them in arriving at various controversial conclusions. I am concerned with the view itself, the rejection of the human prejudice, rather than particular details of Singer's own position, but there is one point I should mention in order to make clear what is at issue. What Singer rejects is not quite the form of the human prejudice to which I and many other people are attached. Singer considers the following familiar syllogism:

Every human being has a right to life.
A human embryo is a human being.
Therefore the human embryo has a right to life.[8]

We had all better agree that the conclusion follows from the premises. Those who oppose abortion and destructive embryo research typically think that both the premisses are true. Those who, under certain circumstances, support these things must reject the argument, and they typically deny the second premiss. Singer denies the first. More strictly, he thinks that the first is correct only if "human being" is taken to mean "person," but in *that* sense the second premiss is false, because the embryo is not yet a person. There is a sense in which the second premiss is true (the embryo belongs to the species), but in that sense of "human being" it is not true that every human being has a right to life. I mention this because it distinguishes Singer from those, such as most moderate pro-choice campaigners, who accept, obviously enough, that the embryo is human in the sense that it is *a human embryo*, but who do not accept that it is yet a human being, any more than a bovine embryo is a cow. Jonathan Glover once caused nearly terminal fury in a distinguished "pro-life" advocate by what seemed to me the entirely reasonable remark that if this gentleman had been promised a chicken dinner, and was served with an omelette made of fertilized eggs, he would have a complaint. The point is an important one. The standard view, the view which Singer attacks, is that "human being" is a morally relevant notion, where "human being" in-

---

[7] *UHL*, p. 194. [See above, n. 5.—Ed.] For potentiality, see Peter Singer and Karen Dawson, "IVF Technology and the Argument from Potential," in *UHL*, pp. 199–214.

[8] *UHL*, p. 192. [See above, n. 5.—Ed.]

deed means an animal belonging to a particular species, our species; but those who hold this view are not committed to thinking that a fertilized ovum is already such an animal, any more so than in the case of other species.

I think that this and some other peculiarities of Singer's position come in part from his concern with one kind of controversy: he is trying to combat conservative policies based on a particular notion, the sanctity of human life. This helps to explain why his position on abortion and infanticide is the same as the pro-life position, but the other way up: he and the pro-lifers both argue "if abortion, then infanticide," but they take it as an objection, and he takes it as an encouragement. Against this, it is very important to say that one can believe that the notion of a human being is central to our moral thought without being committed to the entire set of traditional rules that go under the label "the sanctity of human life."[9]

The most basic question, however, is that raised by the general structure of Singer's position, and it is the same kind of question that we have encountered already. *Why* are the fancy properties which are grouped under the label of personhood "morally relevant" to issues of destroying a certain kind of animal, while the property of being a human being is not? One answer might be: we favour and esteem these properties, we encourage their development, and we hate and resent it if they are frustrated, and this is hardly surprising, since our whole life, and not only our values but our having any values at all, involve our having these properties ourselves. Fine answer, but it doesn't answer this question, since we also, and in complex relation to all that, use the idea of a human being in our moral thought, and draw a line round the class of human beings with regard to various things that we are ethically prepared to do. A different answer would be that it is *simply better* that the world should instantiate the fancy properties of personhood, and not *simply better* that human beings as such should flourish. But that is once more our now familiar friend, absolute importance, that survivor from the enchanted world, bringing with it the equally familiar and encouraging thought that the properties we possess—well, most of us, not counting the infants, the Alzheimer's patients, and some others—are being cheered on by the universe.

I should say at once that this is not Singer's own answer to the question. He is a Utilitarian, and he thinks (very roughly speaking) that the only thing that ultimately matters is how much suffering there is. To the extent

---

[9] Ronald Dworkin, in *Life's Dominion: Argument about Abortion and Euthanasia* (London: Harper Collins, 1993), tries to recruit "life is sacred" in favour of radical policies. I doubt that this works any better.

that we should give special attention to persons, this is supposedly explained by the fact that persons are capable of suffering in some special ways. I do not want to argue over the familiar territory of whether that is a reasonable or helpful explanation of all the things we care about in relation to persons. I want to ask something else, which leads us back to my central question of our moral conception of ourselves as human beings living among other creatures. My question is not: does the Utilitarian view make sense of our other concerns in terms of our concern with suffering? My question is rather: how far does their view make sense of our concern with suffering itself?

Many Utilitarians, including Singer, are happy to use the model of an Ideal or Impartial Observer. A philosopher proposing one version of such a model fifty years ago memorably described this figure as "omniscient, disinterested, dispassionate, but otherwise normal."[10] The model comes in various versions, in many of which the figure is not exactly dispassionate: rather, he is benevolent. This can mean several different things, in terms of there being a positive value to preference-satisfaction, and so on, but let us concentrate on the simplest application of the idea—that the Ideal Observer (IO) is against suffering and wants there to be as little of it as possible. With his omniscience and impartiality he, so to speak, *takes on* all suffering, however exactly we are to conceive of that, and takes it all on equally. He does look, of course, a lot like a slimmed-down surrogate of the Christian God, and this may well suggest that he represents yet another re-enactment of the cosmic point of view: suffering or its absence is what has absolute importance. But I assume that Utilitarians such as Singer hope that the model can be spelled out in more disenchanted terms.

They deploy the model against what they see as prejudice, in particular the human prejudice, and the idea behind this is that there is a sentiment or disposition or conviction which we do have, namely compassion or sympathy or the belief that suffering is a bad thing, but we express these sentiments in irrationally restricted ways: in ways governed by the notorious inverse square law, where the distances involved can be of all kinds, spatial, familial, national, racial, or governed by species-membership. The model of the IO is supposed to be a corrective; if we could take on all suffering as he does, we would not be liable to these parochial biasses and would feel and act in better ways. No doubt the history of the device does lie in fact in a kind of secularized *imitatio Christi*, and I suspect that some of the sentiments it mobilizes are connected with that, but the Utilitarians hope to present it as independent of that, as a device expressing an extensive rational correction of something we indeed feel.

---

[10] Roderick Firth, "Ethical Absolutism and the Ideal Observer," *Philosophy and Phenomenological Research* 12 (1952): 317–45.

So I want to take the model seriously: perhaps more seriously, from a certain point of view, than those who use it. I have two problems with it. One is very familiar, and concerns the relations between the model and human action. Even if we thought that the IO's outlook were a reliable guide to what would be a *better state of affairs*, how is that connected to what we—each of us—should be trying to do? With regard to animal suffering, a form of the problem (a form that goes back to the nineteenth century) is the question of policing nature. Even though much suffering to animals is caused, directly or indirectly, by human beings, a lot of it is caused by other animals. This must form a significant part of what is on the IO's screen. We are certainly in the business of reducing the harm caused by other animals to ourselves; we seek in some degree to reduce the harm we cause to other animals. The question arises, whether we should not be in the business of reducing the harm that other animals cause one another, and generally the suffering that goes on in nature. Utilitarians do offer some arguments to suggest that we should not bother with that, arguments which invoke the most efficient use of our time and energies and so on, but I find it hard to avoid the feeling that those answers are pallid and unconvincing rationalizations of a more basic reaction, that there is something altogether crazy about the idea, that it misrepresents our relations to nature. Some environmentalists of course think that we should not try to improve nature in this respect because nature is sacred and we should interfere with it as little as possible anyway, but they, certainly, are not governed simply by the model of the IO and his concern for suffering.

This leads to a second and more fundamental point. Those who see our selective sympathies as a biassed and prejudiced filtering of the suffering in the world; who think in terms of our shadowing, so far as we can, the consciousness of the IO, and guiding our actions by reflection on what the IO takes on: I wonder whether they ever consider what it would really be like to take on what the IO supposedly takes on. Whatever exactly "takes on" may mean, it is supposed to imply this—that the sufferings of other people and of all other creatures should be as vividly present to us, in some sense, as closely connected with our reasons for action, as our own sufferings or those of people we care for or who are immediately at hand. This is how the model is supposed to correct for bias. But what would it conceivably be like for this to be so, even for a few seconds? What would it be like to take on every piece of suffering that at a given moment any creature is undergoing? It would be an ultimate horror, an unendurable nightmare. And what would the connection of that nightmare to our actions be? In the model, the IO is supposed just to be an Observer: he can't do anything. But our actions, the idea is, are supposed to shadow or be guided by reflection on what he in his omniscience and impartiality is taking on, and if for a moment we got anything like an adequate idea of what that is, and we really guided our actions by it, then surely we would annihilate the planet, if we could; and if other planets containing conscious creatures are similar to ours in the suffering they contain, we would annihilate them as well.

The model has things entirely inside out. We indeed have reasons to listen to our sympathies and extend them, not only to wider groups of human beings, but into a concern for other animals, so far as they are in our power. This is already a human disposition. The *OED* definition of the word "humane" reads:

> Marked by sympathy with and consideration for the needs and distresses of others; feeling or showing compassion and tenderness towards human beings and the lower animals. . . .

We can act intelligibly from these concerns only if we see them as aspects of human life. It is not an accident or a limitation or a prejudice that we cannot care equally about all the suffering in the world: it is a condition of our existence and our sanity. Equally, it is not that the demands of the moral consciousness require us to leave human life altogether and then come back to regulate the distribution of concerns, including our own, by criteria derived from nowhere. We are surrounded by a world which we can regard with a very large range of reactions: wonder, joy, sympathy, disgust, horror. We can, being as we are, reflect on these reactions and modify them to some extent. We can think about how this human estate or settlement should be run, and about its impact on its surroundings. But it is a total illusion to think that this enterprise can be licensed in some respects and condemned in others by credentials that come from another source, a source that is not already involved in the peculiarities of the human enterprise. It is an irony that this illusion, even when it takes the form of rejecting so-called speciesism and the human prejudice, actually shares a structure with older illusions about there being a cosmic scale of importance in terms of which human beings should understand themselves.

If we look at it in the light of those old illusions, this outlook—namely, the opposition to the human prejudice—will be closer in spirit to what I called the Lutheran version than to the celebratory versions, in virtue of its insistence that human beings are twisted by their selfishness. It is unlike the Lutheran outlook, of course, precisely in its anti-humanism: Luther thought that it did matter to the universe what happened to mankind, but this view thinks that all that matters to the universe is, roughly speaking, how much suffering it contains. But there is another difference as well. Luther thought that human beings could not redeem themselves unaided, but the opponents of the human prejudice typically think that with the help of rationality and these theories, they may be able to do so. (Here there is a resemblance to the so-called humanists with whom I started, the strangely optimistic advocates of atheism.)

I have said that it is itself part of a human, or humane, outlook to be concerned with how animals should be treated, and there is nothing in what I have said to suggest that we should not be concerned with that. But I do want to repeat something that I have said elsewhere, that, very significantly, the only question for us is how those animals should be treated.[11] This is not true of our relations to other human beings, and this already shows that we are not dealing with a prejudice like racism or sexism. Some white male who thinks that the only question about the relations between "us," as he puts it, and other human beings such as women or people of colour is how "we" should treat "them" is already prejudiced, but in the case of other animals that is the only question there could be.

That is how it is here, on this planet, now; it is a consequence of the fact I mentioned earlier, that in terms of a range of abilities that control action, we happen to live on an evolutionary plateau. Human beings do not have to deal with any creature that in terms of argument, principle, worldview, or whatever, can answer back. But it might be otherwise; and it may be helpful, in closing, to imagine something different. Suppose that, in the well-known way of science fiction, creatures arrive with whom to some extent we can communicate, who are intelligent and technologically advanced (they got here, after all), who have relations with one another that are mediated by understood rules, and so on and so forth. Now there is an altogether new sort of question for the human prejudice. If these culturally ordered creatures arrived, a human being who thought that it was just a question of how *we* should treat *them* has seriously underestimated the problem, both ethically and, probably, prudentially.

The late Robert Nozick once gave it as an argument for vegetarianism that if we claimed the right to eat animals less smart than ourselves, we would have to concede the right to such visitors to eat us, if they were smarter than us to the degree that we are smarter than the animals we eat.[12] In fact, I don't think that it is an argument for vegetarianism, but rather an objection to one argument for meat eating, and I am not too sure how good it is even in that role (because the point of the meat-eater may not be the distance of the animals from our level of understanding, but the absolute level of the animals' understanding). But the main point

[11] *Ethics and the Limits of Philosophy* (London: Fontana, 1985), pp. 118–19.

[12] Robert Nozick, *Anarchy, State, and Utopia* (New York: Basic Books, 1974), pp. 45–47. [Williams originally referenced Nozick's *Philosophical Explanations*, but I think this passage from *Anarchy, State, and Utopia* must have been what he had in mind.—Ed.]

is that if they proposed to eat us, it would be quite crazy to debate their *rights* at all. The nineteenth-century egoist philosopher Max Stirner said, "The tiger that assails me is in the right, and I who strike him down am also in the right. I defend against him not my *right*, but *myself.*"[13]

But Stirner's remark concerns a tiger, and it is a matter of life and death. Much science fiction, such as the puerile movie *Independence Day*, defines the issue in those terms from the beginning and so makes the issues fairly easy. It is fairly easy, too, if the aliens are just here to help, in terms that we can recognize as help. The standard codings of science fiction, particularly in movies, are designed to make such questions simple. The hostile and nasty tend to be either slimy and disgusting, or rigid and metallic (in one brilliant literary example, Wells's *War of the Worlds*, they are both). The nice and co-operative are furry like the co-pilot in *Star Wars*, or cute like ET, or ethereal fairies like those little things in the bright light at the end of *Close Encounters of the Third Kind*. However, we can imagine situations in which things would be harder. The arrivals might be very disgusting indeed: their faces, for instance, if those are faces, are seething with what seem to be worms, but if we wait long enough to find out what they are at, we may gather that they are quite benevolent. They just want to live with us—rather closely with us. What should we make of that proposal? Some philosophers may be at hand to remind us about distinguishing between moral and non-moral values, and to tell us that their benevolence and helpfulness are morally significant whereas the fact that they are unforgettably disgusting is not. But suppose their aim, in their unaggressive way, is to make the world more, as we would put it, disgusting? And what if their disgustingness is really, truly, unforgettable?

Or turn things round in a different direction. The aliens are, in terms of our preferences, moderately good-looking, and they are, again, extremely benevolent and reasonable; but they have had much more successful experience than we have in running peaceable societies, and they have found that they do need to *run* them, and that too much species-self-assertion or indeed cultural autonomy proves destabilizing and destructive. So, painlessly, they will rid us, certainly of our prejudices, and, to the required extent, of some of our cultural and other peculiarities. What should we make of that? Would the opponents of speciesism want us to join them—join them, indeed, not on the ground that we could not beat them (which might be sensible if not very heroic), but on principle?

The situation that this fantasy presents is in some ways familiar. It is like that of a human group defending its cultural, possibly ethnic, identity against some other human group which claims to dominate or assimilate

[13] *Der Einziger und sein Eigenthum*, translated by S. T. Byington as *The Ego and His Own*, ed. James J. Martin (Sun City, Calif.: West World Press, 1982), p. 128.

them: with this very large difference, however, that since we are dealing here with another and indeed extra-terrestrial species, there is no question of cultural or ethnic variation being eroded by sexual fusion. (From the perspective of sex, it must be said, the idea that so-called speciesism, racism, and yet again gender prejudice are all alike, already looks very peculiar.)

Anyway, the fantasy situation with the aliens will resemble the familiar political situation in some ways. For one thing, there may well be a disagreement among the threatened group, in part an ethical disagreement, between those we may call the collaborators, and others who are resisters. (It looks as though the Utilitarians will join the collaborators.) In the fantasy case, the resisters will be organizing under the banner "Defend humanity" or "Stand up for human beings." This is an ethical appeal in an ethical dispute. Of course this does not make "human being" into an ethical concept, any more than the cause of Basque separatism—an ethical cause, as Basque separatists see it—makes "Basque" into an ethical concept. The relevant ethical concept is something like: loyalty to, or identity with, one's ethnic or cultural grouping; and in the fantasy case, the ethical concept is: loyalty to, or identity with, one's species. Moreover—and this is the main lesson of this fantasy—this is an ethical concept we already have. This is the ethical concept that is at work when, to the puzzlement of the critics, we afford special consideration to human beings because they are human beings. The fact that we implicitly use this concept all the time explains why there is not some other set of criteria which we apply to individuals one by one. It is merely that as things are in actual life we have no call to spell this concept out, because there is no other creature in our life who could use or be motivated by the same consideration but with a different application: that is to say, no creature belonging to some other species can articulate, reflect on, or be motivated by reasons appealing to their species membership.

So the idea of there being an ethical concept that appeals to our species membership is entirely coherent. Of course, there may be ethical arguments about the merits or value of any concept that appeals to something like loyalty to group membership or identity with it. Some people, in the spirit of those who would be principled collaborators in the fantasy case, are against such ideas. In the political morality of the present time, the standing of such attitudes is strikingly ambiguous. Many people, perhaps most people of a critical disposition, seem to be opposed to such attitudes in dominant groups and in favour of them, up to a point, for subordinate groups. (It is a good question, why this is so, but I shall not try to pursue it here.) Others, again, may be respectful of the energizing power of such conceptions, and of the sense they can give of a life that has a rich and particular character, as contrasted, at the extreme, with the Utilitarian ideal of the itinerant welfare-worker who, with his bad line to the IO, goes round turning on and off the taps of benevolence. At the same time, however, those who respect these conceptions of loyalty and identity may be rightly sceptical about the coercive rhetoric, the lies about differences, and the sheer violence that are often associated with such ideas and with the movements that express them. Some of these objections carry over to the ways in which we express species identity as things are, and that is why the opponents of so-called speciesism and the human prejudice quite often have a point about particular policies toward other animals, even though they are mistaken about the framework of ideas within which such things should be condemned.

It is a good question whether the human prejudice, if one wants to call it that, must for us be ultimately inescapable. Let us go back once more to the fantasy of the arrival of the benevolent managerial aliens, and the consequent debate among human beings between the collaborators and the resisters. In that debate, even the collaborators have to use a humanly intelligible discourse, arguments which their fellow human beings can recognize. But does that imply that their arguments would have to be *peculiar* to human beings? If so, their situation would indeed be paradoxical. It would be as though, in the similar political discussions about, say, the cultural identity of the Basques, even the assimilationists had to use only arguments peculiar to Basque culture. So let us suppose that it does not imply this. The relevant alternative in the fantasy case will be that collaborators use arguments which they share not only with their fellow human beings but with the aliens. These arguments presumably provide the basis of their colloboration.

Of course, some moral philosophers think that the correct moral principles are ones that could be shared with any rational and reflective agents, whatever they were otherwise like. But even if this were so, it is important that it would not necessarily favour the collaborators. This is because those principles would not necessarily tell us and the aliens how to share a life together.[14] Maybe we and they would be too different in other respects for that to be possible—remember the disgusting aliens—and the best we could do is to establish a non-aggression pact and co-exist at a distance. That would leave our peculiarities—our prejudices, if that is what they are—where they were. But suppose we are to live together. There is no reason to suppose that the universal principles we share with the aliens will justify our prejudices. We cannot even be sure that they will justify our being allowed to have our prejudices, as a matter of toleration; as I said in setting up the fantasy, the long experience and benevolent

---

[14] Perhaps we might consider in this perspective the fact that Kant, despite his central emphasis on the application of the moral law to rational agents as such, expresses the third formulation of the Categorical Imperative in terms of how we must always treat *humanity*.

understanding of the aliens may enable them to see that tolerating our kinds of prejudice leads to instability and injustice, and they will want to usher our prejudices out, and on these assumptions we should agree. The collaborators must then be right, because the moral conceptions they share with the aliens transcend the local peculiarities.

But if this is so, doesn't something stronger follow? I said, in setting up these fantasies, that the *Independence Day* scenario, in which the aliens are manifestly hostile and want to destroy us, is, for us, an ethically easy case: we try to defend ourselves. But should we? Perhaps this is just another irrational, visceral, human reaction. The benevolent and fair-minded and farsighted aliens may know a great deal about us and our history, and understand that our prejudices are unreformable: that things will never be better in this part of the universe until we are removed. I am not saying that this is necessarily what the informed and benevolent aliens would think. Even if they did think it, I am not saying that the universal moralists, the potential collaborators, would have to agree with them. But they might agree with them, and if they were reluctant to do so, I do not see how they could be sure that they were not the victims of what in their terms would be just another self-serving prejudice. This, it seems to me, is a place at which the project of trying to transcend altogether the ways in which human beings understand themselves and make sense of their practices could end up. And at this point there seems to be only one question left to ask: Which side are you on?

In many, more limited, connections hopes for self-improvement can lie dangerously close to the risk of self-hatred. When the hope is to improve humanity to the point at which every aspect of its hold on the world can be justified before a higher court, the result is likely to be either self-deception, if you think you have succeeded, or self-hatred and self-contempt when you recognize that you will always fail. The self-hatred, in this case, is a hatred of humanity. Personally I think that there are many things to loathe about human beings, but their sense of their ethical identity as a species is not one of them.

PART THREE

The Scope and Limits of Philosophy

FOURTEEN

Political Philosophy and the Analytical Tradition

There was a time, not very long ago, when analytical philosophy had more or less given up on political philosophy. The introductions to successive volumes of *Politics, Philosophy and Society* expressed anxiety about whether the subject could continue to exist, or amazement that it still did; at least one international symposium had as its title "La philosophie politique, existe-t-elle?" and many others had the same theme. There is no need to stress that that time is now past. I do not intend to spend time myself worrying exactly what philosophy is analytical, nor in encouraging discussion on that unrewarding topic, but I take it that for instance *A Theory of Justice* is in the analytical tradition, as are Nozick's *Anarchy, State, and Utopia* and most contributions to *Philosophy and Public Affairs*. Clearly, the predicted funeral has been indefinitely postponed.

In part, I take the change to be traceable simply to a law—which is so far as I know exceptionless, but not for all that transparent—that living political philosophy arises only in a context of political urgency. The somnolence of political philosophy was to that extent a phenomenon of the period which prematurely saluted the end of ideology. But if so, this already tells us something about political philosophy's uneasy relation to the analytical tradition. For political philosophy's habitual, and it seems ineliminable, dependence on the urgency of political questions which are not in the first place philosophical is of a piece with its insistence, when at all interesting, on being both normative and impure. It is normative at least in the sense that first-order moral and political disagreement with the author can relevantly motivate disagreement with his philosophy, and impure in the sense that materials from non-philosophical sources—an involvement with history or the social sciences, for instance—are likely to play a more than illustrative part in the argument.

Analytical philosophy at that time wanted, and tried hard, to be neither normative nor impure. The distinction of fact and value (or rather, in this sort of case, of theory and value) supposedly served to segregate the philosophical from the normative, while the companion distinction of analytic and synthetic served to segregate the philosophical from the historical or social-scientific. Granted this program, and granted the hereditary characteristics of political philosophy, analytical philosophy was bound not to do much for it. So explanation of the torpor of political philosophy at that time cannot just settle back on the characteristics of the time; it must, further, explain why political philosophy is peculiarly resistant to being made pure and non-normative, and why analytical philosophy at that point had those negative ambitions.

The first question I shall discuss, rather obliquely, below. The second question I shall not try to answer at all, but I will outline what an answer would have to explain. It is often suggested that the negative ambitions of analytical philosophy followed solely from its acceptance, in strong forms, of the two distinctions which I have mentioned, in particular the fact-value distinction. But this must be wrong. For even granted a sharp distinction between fact and value, one has to add a doctrine about the proper role of philosophy in order to determine that philosophy will concern itself with the one but not the other. This point is well illustrated by the work of one of the modern fathers of the fact-value distinction in analytical philosophy, G. E. Moore. Moore, having announced in *Principia Ethica* (Cambridge: Cambridge University Press, 1903) the existence of the so-called "naturalistic fallacy" and its consequence that no purely logical process could get one from metaphysical propositions to value judgments, was not at all deterred from giving up much of his book to reports of what, in his view, was good. Of course, granted the naturalistic fallacy, these remarks must be in effect additional to his metaphysical and logical claims, but he does not mind making them. He differs from his successors not in views about the relationship of metaphysics or logic to statements of value, but on whether books written by philosophers should confine themselves to metaphysics and logic.

In part this difference can be traced to a difference about the epistemology of value judgments. There might be some reason, if an obscure one, to suppose that if the discovery of what was good rested, as Moore supposed, on the intuition of non-natural properties, then a philosopher would have some appropriate skill of holding relevant intellectual items in transparent suspension in his mind—a skill not peculiar to philosophy but at least favored by it. But once the later developments of fact-value theory led to non-cognitive accounts of the holding of value judgments, then indeed there was a difficulty about the philosopher's claim, so far as value judgments are concerned, on anyone's attention. In particular, the tendency to regard value judgments (or rather, their overt utterance) as primarily protreptic, as seeking to exhort or command their hearers, leaves a special darkness about the relation between the philosopher who says such things and his audience.

There has been a real problem about the relation of the modern moral or political philosopher to his audience, of what claim he has on anyone's attention, and I shall come back to it, briefly, at the end of this paper—though in a context, I hope, less flatly discouraging than that presented by the sort of view I have just mentioned. But in the present connection, it is important that the limitations on analytical philosophy could not possibly have been imposed merely by the fact-value distinction in itself. They required also a special view of the responsibilities of philosophy. It is important, too, that the limitations on philosophy, and the associated drying-up of political philosophy, were not uniquely encouraged by the belief, no doubt important to many "end of ideology" views, that serious value disagreement was at an end and substantial consensus obtained. On the contrary, it was precisely a sense of the contrast between the plurality of values, and their unresolvable conflict, as opposed to the supposed universality of logic and science, that helped to motivate the fact-value distinction.

The fact-value distinction and how to see it in 3-D. I mentioned the question of why political philosophy could not throw off its hereditary involvement with the normative and the impure and form a pure but productive alliance with the chastely limited ambitions of analytical philosophy. The short answer is that the peculiarly two-dimensional operation of the fact-value distinction as then employed offered all it had to offer about ethics or about value *in general*, and left nothing interesting to be said about the distinctively political issues. The distinction imposed a contrast between those elements of language which registered the state of the world, and those that expressed policies, principles, or decisions to change it—or at any rate, in another version, affective reactions which related to desires to change it. Many of our most interesting value concepts evidently combined both these functions, serving both to register some complex set of facts and to express an evaluation. But the evaluation had to be logically separable from the facts, or a certain way of describing the world would itself import evaluations. Fact would entail value, and, most basically, a certain kind of freedom which this view demands—that an individual's values should not be dictated to him by the world—would have been abrogated.

If this were right, then it would follow that nothing of a very interesting philosophical character could be said about these complex value concepts. Philosophy would make its general point about the separateness of the value element, and the question of why the descriptive elements should be grouped together, and how the evaluations related to a broader context of beliefs, would be left to the social sciences and thus, by the purity requirement, definitively outside philosophy. From this point of view, the complex value concept cannot invite the question of how those facts involve those values. That presumably would be a philosophical question, were it possible, but from this perspective it is not possible. No fact involves value. We, or other societies, apply values to some facts; and the questions invited by the complex value concept can only be how, and when, and to what facts we or they apply value, and that is seen as a question for the social sciences. But now the distinctive subject matter of political philosophy must certainly involve complex value concepts, for it is not any old right and wrong, but those imported by lawfulness, or justice, or equality, or liberty, which are its concerns. Hence the two-dimensional fact-value theory could find nothing of interest for political philosophy, and it is not an accident that political philosophy should have preserved its old recalcitrance in that respect.

Nor, equally, that it should remain impure. For if there is to be a philosophical way of doing better respect to the complexity of these value concepts and their relations to a wider background, it will not be one which totally leaves behind the interests of the social sciences, but rather one which cooperates with them. I certainly do not want to try to give here any extensive suggestions about the fact-value distinction and what should happen to it. But it is worth mentioning one possibility which curiously did not attract as much interest from fact-value theorists as it might have done: namely that there is no compulsion to use a given value concept at all. Two-dimensional fact-value theory implied that for any mixed concept C it was always possible to have a concept C' which had all and only the descriptive content of C but lacked its evaluative force; and that it would be a non-philosophical question whether C' had a use. But we can take it as itself a philosophical consideration that C could lose both its identity and its point without its evaluative force; and that its identity, further, can be involved in its relations to a wider range of concepts. By emphasizing this consideration, one might hope to recognize that evaluations can be more intimately bound up with ways of describing the world than the earlier analytical account would allow, so that, for instance, the selection of certain kinds of conduct for evaluation itself makes sense only in terms of a general framework of beliefs; and yet one could at the same time preserve the truth that moral beliefs cannot just be a record of what the world is like, and even, with a certain difference, preserve that ultimate value-freedom which the fact-value theorist wanted.

The concept of *sin*, for instance, relates in itself fact and value, and relates them in a complex way so that they are not merely external to each other—one could not merely have all those beliefs and abandon those values—but, as modern life reveals, there is no necessity for human beings to use the concept of sin. On this way of looking at it, one can regain the three-dimensional sense that it is in the context of a set of beliefs about the world and society that values have a meaning; one can examine the detailed structure of a set of values of this kind without supposing that it is the only possible one; one can approach the value systems of other times and places with a more realistic and flexible set of categories;

and one will need to, and be able to, make better use of the social sciences than to regard them as the repository of the non-philosophical.[1]

It is only with a certain difference that this preserves the requirement of ultimate value-freedom. The idea that one could, so to speak, withdraw one's value commitment from a complex value term presumably would mean, if it meant anything, that one had a peculiarly individual kind of freedom; but with the recognition that values are more deeply incorporated in systems of belief, the freedom in question becomes more ultimate and less available, since the reconstruction of an entire outlook has less the appearance of being to hand. The freedom becomes the freedom of man rather than of men. But it was only the extreme abstraction of the earlier view which gave the impression of anything else. It is interesting that the purest exponent of the earlier kind of analytical view I have been discussing, R. M. Hare, has now moved to a much more normative stance, but it is one, of utilitarian type, which precisely preserves the individualism implicit in the earlier view, and, at the same time, the opinion that substantive complex value concepts are in principle redundant or uninteresting.

Reflexive social understanding. It is possible to see that type of element in analytical philosophy as ideological—not, perhaps, in the sense that its propagation serves an interest, but at least in the sense that its direction and presuppositions are formed in ways not evident from its surface, and perhaps not evident to the writers themselves, and which admit of social explanation. I do not want to discuss the question of which, if any, such explanations are true: they tend in fact to wander between the vague and the anecdotal. But I should like to suggest that at any rate analytical philosophy up to now has been notably ill-equipped among philosophies for considering whether such things might be true, for reflexively raising questions of its own relations to social reality. The extreme abstraction I have already referred to, and the conceptual character of its subject matter, not only in an obvious way set it apart from considerations of this kind, but actually logically exclude them. An epistemological reflexion, in purely conceptual terms, on the status of theses of analytical philosophy is of course available and has taken up only too much attention: but reflexion in concrete historical terms was excluded by the ban on the empirical.

Insofar as the purely conceptual stance helps this immunity to social reflexion, one might hope that a greater openness to the impurities of the social sciences might help. Indeed it might, in an obvious and immediate sense, in that much social science at this moment is obsessed with such

---

[1] This is to imply that the study of the conceptual interrelations of a group's outlook forms part of the social scientific study of that group. It does not imply that it forms more than part. The idea that social science is, more than everything else, conceptual investigation (cf. Winch) is a quite different, and to me unacceptable, position.

issues, and some sociology gives the appearance of having collapsed into pure social epistemology. But if, in general terms, one were to believe that the mere presence of the social sciences were to encourage such reflexion, one would clearly be very optimistic, since some branches of the social sciences, in particular some types of political science, are the very subjects which have most emphatically invited complaints of lacking such reflexive self-criticism. It might be said that that criticism would be avoided if the idea of social understanding were joined to philosophy, since philosophy is essentially reflexive. But it is a marriage broker's optimism to suppose that the mating of reflexive philosophy with the consciousness of social reality gives reflexive social consciousness: as Bernard Shaw said to the actress, "suppose it has your brains and my looks?" To take a particular example, Winch's theory of the social sciences blends an openness to anthropological data with a philosophical method; indeed it obviously represents an over-close assimilation of social to conceptual understanding. But it is certainly not better blessed with reflexive consciousness than was either analytical philosophy or positivist social science.

There is in fact no mechanical way of ensuring that political and moral philosophers are more sensitive to these issues—as they should be, although the sensitivity should be prepared to take the form, on occasion, of looking the difficulty in the face and passing on (just as one's recognition of other traditions in philosophy should often take the form of looking them in the face and getting on with something one actually believes in). The lesson I draw from that is that the education of political philosophers should include such epistemological materials as will help them to get some measure of the varying claims of the sociology of knowledge. As it has been said that metaphysicians and philosophers of language should not be verificationists, but should have a verificationist conscience, so political philosophers should have a readiness to be embarrassed by the possibility of reflexion on the formation and direction of their views.

Bit-by-bit or systematic? The question of how systematic philosophy should be, and the related, if not identical, question of how far it should consist of theories, is one that has been the subject of much disagreement within analytical philosophy; with, extremely roughly, a British tradition of piecemeal improvisation (with the conspicuous exception of Russell) being opposed to a theory-directed Teutono-American tradition. The present state of this question largely corresponds to the present political and economic fortunes of these two groupings, and it can hardly be doubted that the more systematic and theory-based approach has, in central areas of philosophy, simply won. In the philosophy of language, notably, the point has established itself that an isolated distinction or analysis lacks both sense and point: Austin's professed view, that one collects linguistic distinctions like types of beetles, can be seen to be absurd about linguistic distinctions, and not very clever about beetles.

In a theory of meaning such as Davidson's, as also in Quine's, the notion of theory itself plays a quite central role: for the notion of meaning is introduced (insofar as it *is* introduced—the point will do just as well with regard to the surrogates for meaning in these theories) essentially in terms of what conditions are associated with a given expression by the theory which optimally fits all observed utterances. Now what is being referred to here is of course an empirical theory, a theory which a linguist might form about a given language which he was trying to understand, but the point has further ramifications into philosophy itself: for the philosopher will try systematically to give analyses or elucidations of expressions of our own language which will be of a type to fit in, at least, with such an empirical theory, and without some such constraint the choice between possible analyses or elucidations of expressions becomes indeterminate and pointless. This is a strong example, but the same point can be argued to hold more generally; it is only in terms of what could be said about a lot of cases, or expressions, or areas, that the choice of what to say about *this* case becomes determinate. It is the absence of such constraints that makes a lot of Wittgensteinian philosophy so empty. The original view was that what made the choice of an elucidation or a philosophical remark determinately appropriate was a *concern*, and what makes a lot of Wittgenstein's later work impressive is the presence of a recognizable such concern—his own. But many of his followers seem to be addressing postulated or type-concerns, which represent at best only a very weak constraint on what is in fact very inexplicit theory.

The systematic constraints on the philosophy of language hold for other very general areas of philosophy: metaphysics, theory of knowledge, philosophy of mind; in some part, because they *do* hold for the philosophy of language. Without some such constraints—and I do not want to exaggerate the degree to which they are yet clear or agreed—it is hard to see why one philosophical remark should be more relevant than another, or what might count as an explanation. In this sense, vaguely as I have pointed to it, I should want to claim that philosophy should be systematic. Moral and political philosophy are also parts of philosophy. But it does not follow from that that we should necessarily have systematic moral and political philosophy; or at least, if it does follow, it follows only in the weak sense, which I accept, that these branches of philosophy should be responsive to systematic demands from elsewhere: for one thing, the grammar of moral and political sentences—literal grammar, not Wittgensteinian—is the same as that of other sentences. What does not follow is that moral and political philosophy should have their own systems, or that to supply system should be a primary demand on philosophers in these areas.

The reason is that an important aim, and certain consequence, of systematizing in these areas is to reduce or eliminate conflict among our ideas and sentiments; and before we set out doing that, and while we are doing it, we should reflect on the significance of conflict. Conflict in our moral sentiments and beliefs is, first, a historically, socially, and probably psychologically conditioned phenomenon, the product of such things as pluralistic societies and rapid cultural change as well as, perhaps, more generally distributed psychological needs which tend to conflict. We can, to some extent, understand *why* we have conflicting sentiments, but that does not mean, or should not mean, that we therefore withdraw our loyalty from them. Second, it is not true that any situation in which there is no such conflict is better than one in which there is, or even—what is perhaps more plausible—that conflict reduction is an aim which always has a very strong priority. In the case of belief-conflict and of explanatory theories, conflict-reduction is an undoubted aim: whether it be for the pragmatist reason, that conflict-elimination itself defines the aim of the explanatory endeavor, or for the realist reason that conflicting beliefs cannot both, in some more substantial sense, be true. But the articulation of our moral sentiments does not necessarily obey these constraints, and to demand that they be schooled by the requirement of system is to alter our moral perception of the world, not just to make it in some incontestable sense more rational.

This is what makes Rawls' model so misleading, which assimilates moral "intuitions" to the intuitions of a native speaker such as are the input to a linguistic theory. It is not merely that more is involved in schooling the moral responses, in "reflective equilibrium," to theory than there is in finally writing off some marginal utterances as deviant. It is that the role of theory is different. It is the role of linguistic theory to explain and predict acceptable utterances, and it is *the* theory for doing that. But in the case of moral sentiments, a Rawlsian theory, that is to say a set of principles or moral notions which unifies our moral opinions and in that sense predicts the reflective reaction to a possible or imaginary case, is not alone in the field: for we can understand equally an external theory, e.g. of social explanation, which predicts that no one set of such principles or notions will do the job. Thus we may have systematically conflicting sentiments, for instance, about the value of character and the value of particular actions and intentions; or of the value of particular, non-moral, sentiments and the value of moral, impersonal sentiments of justice. We can feel the force of both utilitarian and anti-utilitarian arguments. Moreover, we can see perhaps why we have these conflicting sentiments; and if so, we cannot agree that there must be a unified theory which "predicts" the response to various situations, in the Rawlsian way, or else that some of our responses are to be jettisoned.

There are in fact two different points to be made here. First, the mere fact of the possibility of external explanation of value-conflict means that the Rawlsian question parallel to the question in the philosophy of language, "What unified and systematic set of principles will 'predict' these reactions?" is a question which need not necessarily have an answer. The unity of a language—even the unity of *my* language—is given in relation to the explanatory theory itself: whereas the unity of my values or sentiments is not so given, and in relation to the external explanations of how I came by them, they may emerge as not unified. (A man between two cultures is not like an effective speaker of a Creole language.)

The second point is that when these conflicts become clear to a man, there is still a question of to what extent and how he should reduce them. Thus many of us now have two kinds of sentiments about questions of people being killed: utilitarian sentiments on the one hand, and on the other sentiments which have a complex articulation but which involve such notions as that with regard to who is to get killed, no choice is better than choice, and that if a choice has to be made, structural considerations (such as fewer rather than more, the already dying rather than those not already dying, etc.) take precedence. This conjunction of sentiments leads to conflict; and utilitarians in particular (a) argue for a rationalization of our outlook and (b) argue for its rationalization in the utilitarian direction, diagnosing the second set of sentiments as the residue of some earlier non-utilitarian outlook. But there are at least three levels at which this pressure for rationalization can be resisted.

First—and this is one which utilitarians themselves can recognize—the consequences involved in the actual social realization may be more extensive and more harmful than expected. Second, at a psychological level, the rationalized values may be harder to live with and to handle. And third—removed now from utilitarian concerns—it may be the case that these sentiments are metaphysically involved with more of our view of what people are than appears on the surface. That requires exploration, and that exploration requires patience with our apparent irrationalities. And perhaps more than patience—at least, indefinite patience.

It is an open, and I think difficult, question how far it is an unquestionable ideal that even ultimately, moral responses should be harmoniously integrated, in ways in which ours now are for the most part certainly not. (A related, and equally difficult, question is how far an analogous demand holds on first-personal rationality: it is certainly a far from self-evident demand, made by Rawls, Nagel, and many other writers, that one should rationally plan for one's life *as a whole*, as though it were a given rectangle to be optimally filled in.) But whatever the answer to those questions, it is certain that such an ideal end is not to be taken as realized in the deep structure of our existing sentiments, nor to be approached by the direct route of setting out to school them in accordance with system. First they have to be understood, which, while it must be done in the context of a systematic philosophy in general, is likely to be a patient and untidy business.

It may be said that morality requires action, and action requires decision—one hopes, on rational principles. It is true that we have to act, but it is only the view that action exhausts the point and content of moral thought that could lead anyone to think that that is the end of this matter. What follow rather are such familiar facts as that sometimes we act, and necessarily act, with less than 100 percent conviction; or again—less familiar, this, than the well-known liberal lack of conviction, and perhaps more invigorating—that it is possible to act with 100 percent conviction on one occasion while quite conscious that on another occasion, only obscurely different from that first one, conviction might not have arrived. The relations between action, conviction, and rationality constitute an area in which moral philosophy, the philosophy of mind, and metaphysics most significantly meet.

But however that may be, politics, it may reasonably be said, is a different matter: for while individual persons can to varying extents go round with conflicting moral sentiments, there is a demand of rational consistency and principle in public positions (quite apart from what is legally enacted). There is obvious truth in this; but among many further things that should be said about it are two which, in terms of a program for political philosophy, qualify its effect. First, the requirement of consistency in principle which obtains on a series of public decisions by an enduring authority in a rational state (idealized as that may be), or on the program of one party (even more idealized though that may be), obviously does not extend to political life as a whole, which precisely can embody not only conflicts of interests, and of straightforwardly opposed principles, but of conflicting values, and of conflicting interpretations of the same values (consider here the conflicts of equality of opportunity with equality of esteem; or of justice as equality with justice as entitlement). The philosopher's thoughts do not have to be directed to solving these differences; he may do his best work, in fact, in sharpening them, by making it clear in what ways both have a foot in our sentiments. This may not be, in the short term at least, an altogether helpful activity, but it can be a good one.

Second, even insofar as a philosopher's efforts are directed to assisting rationality in political practice, they may helpfully take the form of providing structures in which it can be recognized how much conflict of value that process can and should absorb. In particular I have in mind here the philosophical study of decision theory, with particular emphasis on structures more complex than the linear, often utilitarian, models, with an emphasis on direct comparability of values, which have often prevailed. It is admitted that actual structures of decision in political bodies lie a long way from these idealizations; but it is also probable that very simple models of what practical rationality is can feed into and affect decision processes. A combination of a mastery of the appropriate formal skills and a steady sense of the existence of genuinely competing and only partially reconcilable goods—something which distinguishes the work of Amartya Sen in this field—is something which political philosophy needs to provide.

History. I am not going to say anything, except by implication, about genuine historical understanding. I suppose, for reasons which are obvious and would be tedious to rehearse, that genuine historical understanding is of the first importance in the understanding of politics and political thought; that diachronic distancing is one very important form of the distancing we need to secure from our own society; and that that gains another importance when the society is an ancestor of our own. Further, it seems to me that to read Plato only as in last week's *Mind* is to lose an important part of reading Plato.

About what genuine historical understanding of a text is, understanding of what it *meant*, I agree with Quentin Skinner that if it is recoverable at all, it must be in the kind of terms which he has detailed, of those contemporary expectations in terms of which a communicative intention could be realized. Moreover, it is clear beyond doubt that the fundamental sense of the question, asked of a historical text, "What does it mean?" is "What *did* it mean?"

However, there is another sort of question, which can be expressed in such forms as "What does it mean to me?" or "What do I get out of it?" This question, I would rather say, is not so much asked *of* the text, as asked *about* it; and that is asked about a book, a set of words, which maximally resemble the words written in the past. These questions, and the answers we give to them, seem to me only rather loosely connected with history, in the sense of the past which gave rise to the book, but they have quite a lot to do with the *history of the book*—in particular, the more interesting among these questions may continue that history. The book's *Nachleben* is not only itself studied, it is lived.

When we treat these books in this way, and for instance represent arguments in them in our own terms, supply modern questions which are like what we take these questions to be, and so on, we are doing something which is indeed conventionally called "history of philosophy," but is really a sort of philosophy—we might call it "history-of-philosophy philosophy." In particular, we should beware of two misleading impressions that may be created by calling it "history of philosophy." One is that the pursuit of the maximally consistent interpretation—a basic rule of this kind of exercise—is a genuine principle of historical reconstruction. We may think it is, for instance, because of its resemblance to a type of principle that plays a genuine role in the sort of linguistic theory I discussed earlier: the principle of charity, by which one interprets an alien language so that what should be evidently true to native speakers comes out as true, and they don't simply contradict themselves. But that principle, at that level of generality, plays a different role: it is not just a contingent assumption, for we have no independent control over the idea that in general they might be evidently mistaken or contradicting themselves (really). In the case of a particular author and a particular text, however, there is in principle more control over this idea, and some conclusions about it can even be reached *a priori*. Thus people spend enormous time (I have spent some myself) on trying to find interpretations of Plato's *Sophist* which make Plato's theories consistent. But if Plato's *Sophist* is about what we think it is about (and granted his theories about these very difficult subjects came when they did) it is wildly improbable that his theories on those subjects would succeed in being consistent. Of course, the rejection of the principle of consistent interpretation leaves the whole question in a very boring state, since then there are no unique solutions and there are indeterminately many ways in which it might be inconsistent. But to count boringness as a criticism—of answers, I mean, not of questions—just shows that one is doing philosophy, or at any rate, not history.

The second misleading consequence of taking the history of philosophy, in the usual sense, as history, is that we think we have a rationale for doing it; for instance, in the sense of providing ourselves with the historical background of our own ideas. But if the study is not genuinely history, then it doesn't provide us with the historical background to anything. These texts, of ancient provenance, bearing some largely indeterminate relation in our understanding to what they meant, are complex but ambiguous objects on which we project sets of philosophical ideas rather different in content from those we would be exercising in our own person. It may be interesting, helpful, instructive, even in some ways tell us about the past, but our justification for doing it, if there is one, can only very complexly be related to the fact that these men said what they said with certain meanings in the past. History of philosophy, and in particular, history of political philosophy, can, in principle, be made into history; but as it is most often done, especially in the spirit of analytical philosophy, it must be defended, if it is defensible, as a funny kind of philosophy with archaizing elements (something in the style of Stravinsky's *Pulcinella*), rather than as irresponsible history.

CONCLUSION

I have touched, broadly, on a number of themes. I have implied, without saying, that the political philosopher must be in touch with moral philosophy, and have said that, freed from the narrower preoccupations of the fact-value distinction, he will have the opportunity and the need to study substantial complex value notions, not merely in their conceptual interrelations, narrowly conceived, but in the background of beliefs and non-moral conceptions which give them sense; and that in this, his work must certainly interrelate closely with that of the social sciences. I have suggested that his work may require now a particular kind of reflexive sensitivity which is likely to be assisted by a study of epistemological issues in relation to the social sciences; and one may add, the natural sciences, too. He should have a sense of the systematic demands of philosophy without demanding a system within moral or political philosophy themselves; and he should help in some respects to keep alive the sense of genuine moral conflicts, the origins of which we may well understand, but which are prone to be prematurely rationalized out of existence. One area in which he may usefully be able to do this is the development of more complex and realistic structures in decision theory.

This leaves the question which so bothered many analytical philosophers of the fact-value persuasion: By what right can a philosopher claim the attention of an audience on these themes, especially if—as I, certainly, have taken for granted—his concerns will be in some part normative? It seems to me an encouraging sign of how far philosophy has come in the past fifteen or even ten years, that this question, which seemed so honestly pressing at one time, should seem so boring now. For its answer clearly is that he has whatever claim any adult and reflective person may have on the attention of others if he has thoughts about some important subject. He can sacrifice that claim, or fail to deliver on it, in as many ways as there are of writing words which are dead, unimaginative, stupid, ill-informed, and so forth. Since he is a philosopher, his claim to attention is more likely to be, as always, weighted towards the end of subtle analysis and the fact that some of his claims follow from others than, for instance, to lie in a wide and seasoned experience of men and events; but to suppose that that is all and only what should be asked of him, is from all points of view idiotic.

In saying that, and throughout, I have in mind still one who is doing analytical philosophy. I have spoken critically of some earlier limitations of the genre, but as I said at the beginning, I do not think that reform has changed or will change it out of all recognition. It would be pointless and unhelpful now, any more than at the beginning, to say what I take its defining characteristics to be, if indeed it has definite bounds. I take a generous view of it, but certainly much which is called philosophy is excluded. It is cheering that in political philosophy it has survived its regeneration into something interesting, with its undoubted virtues intact. In its insistence, at its best, on the values of unambiguous statement and recognizable argument; its patience; its lack of contempt for the familiar; its willingness to meet with the formal and natural sciences; its capacity for genuine and discussable progress—in all this, and despite its many and often catalogued limitations, it remains the only real philosophy there is.

FIFTEEN

Philosophy and the Understanding of Ignorance

Our subject is what we do not know; and this is a meeting under the auspices of philosophy—a meeting, indeed, designed to advance UNESCO's programme in philosophy. The conjunction of this subject and these auspices already confronts us with certain questions. How is philosophy related to ignorance?

One question I shall not pursue is whether philosophy itself just is a kind of ignorance, and whether there is such a thing as philosophical knowledge at all. It has often been said, particularly by positivists, that philosophy is virtually by definition a home of ignorance, that it consists of questions which we do not know how to answer by established forms of enquiry. On this account, questions that have previously been part of philosophy may mature into questions for the sciences or for other disciplines capable of accumulating knowledge. Thus some questions that have belonged to philosophy have moved into physics, others into linguistics, others into psychology. At the present time, questions about mind and body, perpetual concerns of philosophy, are (some would say) moving into the realm of cognitive science.

The processes presented in this picture do have to be distinguished from something else, namely the fact that, at least in the English language, the *word* "philosophy" has a more restricted reference than it used to have. Newton's great book was a contribution to a subject then called "natural philosophy," but those who practised the subject under that name were capable of drawing distinctions between that subject and the kind of enquiry that we would now call "philosophy," and drawing it on lines broadly familiar today. It is not this verbal point that I have in mind, but rather processes by which questions develop from a status in which we do not know how to answer them, and they belong to what is indisputably philosophy, to a status in which they have become a proper subject for systematic, and perhaps scientific, enquiry. The picture that emphasizes these processes might, then, suggest that not only does philosophy contain no knowledge, but it is virtually defined as not doing so. As I said, this is not a question that I want to take much further, since in general I believe that philosophy is not at its most interesting when it is talking about itself. But it perhaps can at least be said in leaving this topic that there is a certain paradox in thinking that what these processes demonstrate is that

philosophy offers no knowledge of any kind. There certainly are developments in which—to put it very roughly—questions move out of philosophy into other fields of enquiry. But these developments do not leave philosophy entirely passive in relation to them; it is not merely the wine cellar
in which a question matures until it reaches the state in which it can be
put on the market of science. Nor is it a place in which questions wait
until other sciences have developed, by their own processes, to a point at
which they are capable of picking them up. Philosophy itself contributes
to these processes, and indeed it can contribute so much that it is very
artificial to say that precisely the same question has graduated from philosophy to science. Questions are reformulated and redefined under such
processes, and those refinements and redefinitions, whatever precisely
their status, are certainly a product of philosophy.

What we should consider for rather longer is the subject, not of philosophy as ignorance, but of what, rather, philosophy might conceivably tell
us about ignorance more generally. This is a subject on which philosophy
has over the centuries shown a remarkably high degree of ambition: from
the ancient world through early modern philosophy to contemporary
studies, philosophers have been keen to suggest that we know little or
nothing. I do not want to deny the philosophical importance of these
skeptical arguments, but their importance seems to me to lie much more
in what they may be able to tell us about the nature or the basis of knowledge, than in any actual determination of what it is that we do not know.
The reason for this lies in their extreme generality: typically, they try to
show us that we know nothing, or know only the contents of immediate
experience, or know only some simple necessary truths. Such conclusions
do not make the boundary between what is known and what is not known
at all interesting, in particular because they do not represent it as a boundary that could in principle move. So while the possibility of skepticism
remains a challenge that a theory of knowledge has to deal with in one
way or another—if only, in the manner of some contemporary theories,
by turning their back on it—it does not, by its very nature, shed any very
interesting light on the question of what we know as opposed to what we
do not know.

This is perhaps only an example of a more general point that skepticism
is more interesting and more disquieting if it is based on more particular
kinds of consideration. What is often called skepticism "about other
minds" does, once again, represent an important area of philosophical
reflection, but when it is conducted at a level of very high generality, it
does not offer us any very anxious ground of concern. Someone who is
genuinely worried whether he or she knows that another person is in pain,
even if that person is writhing on the floor with a knife in his leg, is someone who should be referred for clinical treatment. This, like serious skepti-

cism about the external world, is a kind of skepticism which, as Descartes himself insisted, should be reserved for a reflective philosophical exercise. But this is not the only type of skepticism about other minds, and to insist upon skepticism at such a high level of generality actually serves to disguise the disquieting force of more particular manifestations of skepticism about other minds. While it is absurd, at a practical rather than a purely theoretical level, to wonder whether other people have any emotions, feelings or sensations at all, it is not at all absurd to entertain real doubt about what the character of their feelings is, or to raise the question of how much we know or ever could know about someone else's inner life once one gets beyond the familiar features of it that are, as a matter of mutual human understanding, genuinely given to us.

The same point applies to skepticism about our knowledge of the past, and also skepticism about the physical world. To raise the question of whether we know anything about the past *at all* is indeed a pathological state if it is considered as more than a device for investigating such knowledge. But, once again, to insist on simply this kind of skepticism, and hence, in reaction to that on a straightforward rejection of it, is to obscure the extent and depth of skepticism—a skepticism that may be entirely justified—that one may experience with regard to historical narratives. There is indeed a deep and structural problem about the credentials of such narratives, and one fails to grasp the force of that problem if one raises only the absolutely general problem of skepticism about the past; or if, as is often the case, one extends the skepticism appropriate to historical narrative even to the least ambitiously reported elements of a chronicle. It is certainly true that an earthquake struck Los Angeles in January 1994, and that Julius Caesar was killed in Rome in March 44 BC, and it is only if that level of affirmation about the past is acceptable that one can get on to raise the really interesting questions of how much we do not know, as opposed to what we do know, about the past.

Our concerns about what we do not know can get a real and compelling grip on us only if there are some things that we do know. This is why traditional philosophical skepticism, suggesting as it does that we may know nothing at all (or nothing about other minds, or nothing about the past) is not compelling, in the sense, at least, of attacking our assurance about those things. Still more, we should not be compelled—we cannot be compelled—by very general reflections directed not simply against knowledge but against truth. Recent forms of skepticism, drawing in many cases on a very partial reading of Nietzsche, have tried to discredit the notion of truth altogether. In doing this, they typically take on a tone of mild heroism about their project of uncovering our illusions (as they are inevitably, but on their own account misguidedly, tempted to call them).

What is disquieting about such positions is not so much their self-refutation, as their false promise of discomfort. What casts suspicion on everything casts suspicion on nothing: even the common or garden paranoiac needs his exercise book of carefully researched facts. Our suspect assurances will be undermined, as they are in Nietzsche's own practice, only by an interpretative attention which is selectively directed, and which accepts the materials that are needed if its direction of attention is to be intelligible. In the case of history, we can have doubts about our understanding of the past only if we have a past, and we have a past (as Wittgenstein emphasized) only if there are some things that certainly happened in it. It is only because we can accept large numbers of facts about the past, many of them in themselves very boring, that we can confront the genuinely disturbing suggestion that historical understanding requires narrative, and narrative demands closure, and closure in history is always a fiction and often a lie.

In the case of the physical world as such, the boundary between compelling versions of skepticism and noncompelling versions of it takes a different shape. A blank skepticism about the external world does not constitute a compelling skepticism, in the sense that it gives one any reason to worry whether everything we think we know about the external world might not be false. Equally, there can be no reason to suppose that we do not know a very large number of truths based on observation, whether the observation involves scientific apparatus, or is unassisted by apparatus. The interesting question arises with regard to our theoretical statements about nature, and the theoretical entities that are typically introduced by those theories. It is still very much a live issue in the philosophy of science, to what extent our theoretical understandings of nature constitute knowledge, but there are two different levels at which such concerns arise. On the one hand, there is the kind of question often expressed in terms of the choice between instrumentalism and realism, and this asks us whether *any* theory could constitute knowledge, or whether our real access to knowledge about nature is confined simply to the level of what is observable (where what is "observable" is itself an issue that involves some extremely pressing difficulties). On the other hand, we may ask whether some such theories *rather than others* constitute knowledge. At this level, it is no longer a question of whether there is something inherent in such theories that prevents them (as opposed to observations) from constituting knowledge; it is a question, rather, of whether some scientific theories make a better claim to that status than others.

It may be thought that this latter kind of question is not itself philosophical, but rather is precisely the kind of question that forms the substance of scientific practice, which is concerned with advancing and preferring some theories to others. However, I think it is a mistake to associate the term "philosophical" always with the most general kinds of question that can arise with regard to theories or hypotheses. To put it another way, there are areas of science in which the boundaries between the philosophy of science and science itself are pretty arbitrarily drawn. A notable example of this is quantum mechanics, in which a major concern precisely is the conceptual constraints that may be appropriate to the descriptions and explanations that it offers. While no-one can discuss these matters without being well informed about the contemporary currency of such physical theory, it becomes beyond that point fairly arbitrary in many cases to determine whether somebody is discussing the philosophical theory of quantum mechanics, or is doing quantum mechanics at a very highly theoretical level.

Some of the philosophical issues that I have mentioned themselves constitute questions to which, as it seems to me, we do not know the answers, but of which we might have hopes, if not of acquiring answers, of at least advancing our understanding in the coming years. This seems to me true with regard to the issues that I have just mentioned of the relation between observation and theory in the philosophy of science, and also with regard to the structure of a historical narrative and its relations to what I have called the materials of chronicle. We may reasonably be said not at present to know how best to discuss these subjects, and it does not seem to me foolish to suppose that we might come to understand these things better. These subjects are philosophical subjects, so if it is correct that we can hope to make progress with them, these will be examples of questions *within* philosophy to which we might come to have better answers than we have at present. For that very reason, we should not, as I have already suggested, pay too much attention to arguments that are designed to show that we can never come to know anything in philosophy. The phrase *philosophia perennis*, one might say, expresses pessimism. Nor is the relevance of philosophy to our topic to be found principally in its old invitation to suppose that we do not know anything at all.

There is, however, a quite different kind of philosophical argument that bears upon our theme, and which I think is more interestingly relevant to it. This kind of argument suggests that, while we can no doubt state some things that we do not know, we cannot in general state with confidence what it is that we do not know. There are limits in principle to the extent that we can know what we do not know. The point can be demonstrated, in a rather restricted way, by the following argument.[1] Suppose that I am looking at a room with a large number of people in it. I do not know how many people there are in the room and I am not in a position to count

---

[1] I owe this argument to T. Williamson, who develops it in a more precise and richer form in his book *Vagueness*, London, 1995.

them. But I do know (for instance) that there are fewer than a thousand people, and more generally, for various numbers n, I know that there are fewer than n people. When n gets rather smaller (closer to what is in fact the actual number of people), it ceases to be the case that I know that there are fewer than n people present. However, it is obvious that there is no particular number n such that I know that there are fewer than n people present but don't know that there are fewer than $(n-1)$ people present: so, for some numbers, it must be the case that I don't know whether I don't know that there are fewer than that number of persons present.

Now this is of course an extremely artificial and regimented example, but it illustrates a much more general point about the knowledge of ignorance. In general there are important limits to the knowledge of ignorance, and this point is implicit in the notion of a margin of error, a notion which is itself involved in the concept of knowledge. If I do not know in every case what I do not know, it is also true that, even if I do know something, I do not necessarily know that I know it: the principle so beloved of certain philosophers, that if I know, I must know that I know (the so-called "KK principle"), is certainly false. This has important consequences for any enquiry of the kind that we are addressing. We may indeed be able to mention some things that we do not know; I have already mentioned one or two such things, and I shall go on to mention one or two others. In some cases, it is possible to specify what it is that one does not know in such a way that one can know that one does not know it: so, in the previous example, I do know that I do not know *the exact number of people in the room*. Similarly, I, personally, express knowledge if I say that I do not know the name of the present Archbishop of Milan, or of Leonardo da Vinci's father. But we do not always know that we do not know certain things, and, as has already been argued, it can be shown that it is impossible that in every case of our not knowing something, we know that that is the situation.

There are other and less formal kinds of argument that lead to the same conclusion. Among the things that we do not know are things that people used to know, and also things that people might in the future come to know. There are some important asymmetries between these two. One asymmetry is that, with regard to things that people used to know but which we do not know, we suppose in general that we possess the terms in which such knowledge might be expressed. We know, or know of, the terms in which past people would have expressed their knowledge, terms which we might at some level be able to understand. This is because our picture of knowledge that has got lost is a picture of knowledge expressed (very broadly speaking) in terms which themselves have not got lost.

With regard to knowledge that people may acquire in the future, however, we do not necessarily have any such conception. It was a positivist error, to which no-one now is attached, to suppose that the fundamental vocabulary or conceptual resources of science are fixed, and that what will be discovered in the future can only be new facts or theories expressible in that same vocabulary. On the contrary, we believe that theoretical advances typically consist of introducing new concepts, and that those concepts may not be strictly commensurable with concepts that we presently have. I do not think that this need lead to a radical relativism; but it does mean that future science may contain theoretical innovations which, as things are, we could not understand at all. It is a disputed issue whether there might be such innovations which we could not in principle come to understand. Perhaps, as some have suggested, our idea of a possible language must be the idea of a language which we could in principle come to understand. But we need not engage with that issue; our present question merely concerns the possibility that future discoveries may be expressible only in a language which we now as a matter of fact cannot understand, and that certainly could not be ruled out by any argument of principle. Such future discoveries, we are assuming, would be *discoveries*, which is to say that they could constitute knowledge. But we cannot know what that knowledge would be, for the radical reason that we have no ways of expressing it; consequently we cannot know what it is exactly that, in lacking that knowledge, we do not know. We can in various degrees locate it, and we must locate it if we are to identify it as a possible scientific discovery—we must locate it in a space of problems, for instance. But this is a long way from our knowing in any exact terms what it is that we do not know.

This consideration, that one cannot foresee the terms in which future discoveries might be expressed, applies particularly to certain areas of scientific enquiry which presently invite the thought that there is not only a great deal that we do not know—that is obviously true of every area— but that there might be a certain insecurity to the knowledge that we hope we may already possess. I cannot pretend to any expertise at all in theoretical physics, and what I have to say about such subjects is of the most unprofessional kind. But the expert opinion of others who are better placed to understand the current situation can lead one to think that with regard both to scientific cosmology and to particle physics (fields closely allied to each other) the structures of theory that we have are in more than one way rather perilously related to what we definitely know. In the case of cosmology, the current conclusions or speculations may be rather extensively cantilevered out from observations and interpretations of those observations, to such an extent that the alteration of an assumption near the start of the argument might lead to radical readjustments of the theoretical picture as a whole. Among these conclusions, perhaps, are the orders of magnitude of time and distance that are invoked in the theory, and it may be reasonable to think that in these and in other respects some radical revision of current theory may await us.

The situation is in this respect different from that in other areas of science, which are themselves just as theoretical. (This illustrates the point I mentioned earlier, that philosophical distinctions between theory and observation do not coincide with the questions that interest us most in this discussion.) I think it is generally agreed that there is no question that our understanding of the structure of DNA and the mechanics of the transmission of genetic information could turn out to be other than fundamentally correct. Our understanding of this seems now to have attained the point at which much of it constitutes part of the data of any future theory rather than part of the content that could be replaced by future theory.

The case of particle physics, to the (again, very limited) extent that I understand the situation, is in some ways similar to that of cosmology, but here even those who are very confident that present theory is basically sound are conscious of a definite limitation on the increase of knowledge, which lies in financial and practical limits to controlled experimentation. I suppose that it is possible that the European super-collider, if indeed it is finally built, may be the last such machine ever to be built on earth, and we know already that not every question that can be raised within the present structure of particle physics, even supposing that structure to continue without radical revision, can be answered by that machine. This is an area in which theory has far outrun any foreseeable experiment. If this is so, then our knowledge of our ignorance will have a special structure; it will reflect the fact that, even if our questions are well posed, the amount of energy (and hence the resources) that would be needed to conduct experiments that might answer them simply outruns anything that we could bring to bear on the question. Such high energies are of course at work in the universe, and the ultimate laboratories of particle physics are in the stars; but we cannot conduct controlled experiments with the stars, and the gap between what we can sensibly construct for the purposes of experiment, and the energies required by experiments that could answer our questions, may be forever unbridgeable.

These speculations about the sciences have, as I have said, very little authority. However, they may at least illustrate a general point which is perhaps likely to be overlooked by philosophy, that it is possible to gain from inside a science itself some idea of the questions that it might or might not be able to answer, even though we grant the point that the terms in which an answer might be given may be to varying degrees not known to us. This apparent paradox can be resolved because to some extent we can form an idea of the experimental situation in which an answer would have to be pursued, if any answer were to be forthcoming, and we may be able to see that we cannot get to that situation, or that it is unlikely that we shall be able to do so. All of this must, inevitably, be speculative because, in not foreseeing future theory, we equally cannot foresee future experiment; perhaps less expensive ways of investigating nature on the micro-scale may come to be available which at present we cannot conceive. Certainly in these areas, our thoughts about what we do not know must be structured both by considerations of what experimental routes are or might become available to us, and also, as notably in the case of cosmology, by the question of the degree to which the most ambitious parts of the theory are, as I have put it, "cantilevered out" from the undisputed observational material; to such an extent that there is a possibility that under revision of some element in the structure, the theory might dramatically implode, and alter and change into something very different. This once again illustrates the point that it is a mistake for philosophers simply to discuss the status of theoretical science *as such*. Particle physics, cosmology, and indeed molecular biology are all theoretical sciences, but their relations to future experiment and refutation, and correspondingly their relations to our present ignorance, are very different from one another.

There is a very dramatic example of current ignorance the relations of which both to philosophy and to scientific enquiry are very different from what has so far been discussed. The main difference is that in this case it is a philosophical question how far our ignorance has anything to do with scientific enquiry at all. This is the problem of consciousness, the question of how we may explain, or even adequately describe, the difference between creatures *for* whom things exist or happen in certain ways, and creatures who lack any such experience. A great deal of work has been done in this area in recent years, and is now being done, and it can at least be said that we do possess more material, above all at the neurophysiological level, than we did before, which might prove relevant to a solution of this problem if a solution of this problem is possible. My extremely cautious formulation of this fact is dictated by the remarkably wide range of opinions that it is still possible to hold on this topic. At one extreme there are people, such as Daniel Dennett, who would claim at least in outline actually to have solved the problem. Then there are those, perhaps the majority, who think the problem has not been solved, but that some combination of physiological research, work in cognitive science, and philosophical clarification should or may eventually bring us the solution. Again, there are those, notably Thomas Nagel, who believe that at the present time we not only have no way of relating the facts of consciousness, the first-personal experiences of a conscious agent, to changes in the brain and the nervous system, but that we lack even any idea of what a theory that related those two things in a perspicuous and explanatory way might look like. Some who think this nevertheless suppose that this may be a situation such as that which has preceded other scientific advances, in which a step which has seemed incomprehensible to us has in fact been taken by means of a new conceptual invention.

At the furthest extreme of pessimism on the subject of consciousness is Colin McGinn, who suspects that the problem of giving a coherent and explanatory account of human consciousness is insoluble for a quite special reason, namely that the structure of the brain is such that it cannot possibly grasp this aspect of its own operations. This conclusion naturally, and perhaps healthily, attracts skepticism, because it sounds a great deal too much like previous claims about what might prove scientifically unintelligible: in particular the so-called problem of the nature of life, which gave rise to the pessimistic and obscurantist position of vitalism. However, this analogy does not necessarily lead one to discount McGinn's pessimism (which is in any case better argued than any vitalist position was): it also leads us to a further thought about what might happen to this problem. In a certain sense, the problem of the nature of life—the problem which vitalism declared insoluble—was never exactly solved: rather, we have learned so much about the operations of living things that the problem in that form has gone away. As things stand, it seems to us as though the problem of the nature of consciousness could not be like that, since consciousness seems so present and manifest a phenomenon we cannot understand how the question of its nature could, by an enormous elaboration of physiological and psychological understanding, seem ultimately to have evaporated. But perhaps that impression itself is a function of the present state of our understanding or rather of our lack of it.

Certainly the problem of consciousness is one that combines in the highest degree the various kinds of doubt that can constitute our admissions of our own ignorance. We are not agreed that there is a problem; or, if there is, whether it has been solved; or, if it has not, whether it is soluble; or, if it is soluble, whether the present obstacles to our solving it are technical, theoretical, or conceptual. In addition, we are not agreed whether the problem is of a kind which, even if it cannot directly be solved, might eventually turn out to have gone away. It is hard to think of any other problem-area in which so many impressions of the nature of our ignorance can coexist.

There is one last set of problems which, particularly perhaps as we discuss these matters under the auspices of UNESCO, should be mentioned as peculiarly defying our understanding and revealing our ignorance: the problems, that is to say, of how to live together. No-one is going to deny, presumably, that there is such a problem, in the sense that various groups constantly, repeatedly, all over the world, find it remarkably difficult to live with one another. In this sense, certainly, there is something we do not know—how to live together, except under a variety of fairly favorable circumstances. However, it is a different claim, and it might be thought on reflection rather an optimistic claim, that this represents an intellectual problem: the problem, as we might put it, that we do not know why we do not know how to live with each other. This suggests that there is something to be found out about the causes of conflict, something which is presently hidden from us and which, when it is found out, may enable us to negotiate and progressively eliminate those conflicts. Perhaps there is some such thing which is presently hidden from us, and certainly we should not relax our efforts in asking what it might be, seeking the help of psychology, anthropology, history and perhaps biology in so doing. However, we cannot be sure that there is an intellectual problem which takes the form of finding some central explanation which is hidden. Perhaps, rather, we already know most of what is to be known at a general level about the causes of human conflict, and there is nothing very deep or extensive, which we do not already recognize, to be learned about it. What we need to do is rather to organize the resources which, in general terms, we already know to be necessary to deal with such conflicts, in so far as they can be dealt with, understanding each in terms of its own circumstances. If we cannot mobilize the resources, or it is not the sort of conflict that will respond to any resources that we might mobilize, we shall not suppose that there is some further, potentially revealing thing we do not know. We shall have to reconcile ourselves to a perfectly obvious thing, that we do not know how to deal with the conflict.

This second, and bleaker, account, we do not necessarily have to accept. Perhaps the happier idea, that there is still some important thing to be learned about why human beings are so disposed to hate and kill one another, has some promise. If it has, we would certainly like to know that it has. If the bleaker story is true, however, perhaps we do not want to know that it is. With this, the most pressing of all our questions, the position is as it often is with matters that come close to our interests: we cannot know whether we really want to overcome our ignorance until we have done so.

SIXTEEN

Philosophy as a Humanistic Discipline[1]

1

In the formula 'humanistic discipline' both the elements are meant to carry weight. This is not a lecture about academic organisation: in speaking of philosophy as a 'humanistic' enterprise, I am not making the point that philosophy belongs with the humanities or arts subjects. The question is: what models or ideals or analogies should we look to in thinking about the ways in which philosophy should be done? It is an application to our present circumstances of a more general and traditional question, which is notoriously itself a philosophical question: how should philosophy understand itself?

Similarly with the other term in the phrase. It is not just a question of *a* discipline, as a field or area of enquiry. 'Discipline' is supposed to imply discipline. In philosophy, there had better be something that counts as getting it right, or doing it right, and I believe that this must still be associated with the aims of philosophy of offering arguments and expressing oneself clearly, aims that have been particularly emphasized by analytic philosophy, though sometimes in a perverse and one-sided manner. But offering arguments and expressing oneself clearly are not monopolies of philosophy. Other humanities subjects offer arguments and can express themselves clearly; or if they cannot, that is their problem. History, for instance, certainly has its disciplines, and they involve, among other things, both argument and clarity. I take history to be a central case of a humanistic study, and it makes no difference to this that history, or some aspects of history, are sometimes classified as a social science—that will only tell us something about how to understand the idea of a social science. History is central to my argument not just because history is central among humanistic disciplines, but because, I am going to argue, philosophy has some very special relations to it.

A certain limited relation between history and philosophy has been traditionally acknowledged to the extent that people who were going to learn some philosophy were expected to learn some history of philosophy. This

---

[1] Delivered as the Annual Lecture of the Royal Institute of Philosophy on 23 February 2000.

traditional idea is not accepted everywhere now, and I shall come back to that point. It must be said, too, that this traditional concession to history was often rather nominal: many of the exercises conducted in the name of the history of philosophy have borne a tenuous relation to anything that might independently be called history. The activity was identified as the 'history of philosophy' more by the names that occurred in it than by the ways in which it was conducted. Paul Grice used to say that we 'should treat great and dead philosophers as we treat great and living philosophers, as having something to say to *us*.' That is fine, so long as it is not assumed that what the dead have to say to us is much the same as what the living have to say to us. Unfortunately, this is probably what was being assumed by those who, in the heyday of confidence in what has been called the 'analytic history of philosophy', encouraged us to read something written by Plato 'as though it had come out in *Mind* last month'—an idea which, if it means anything at all, means something that destroys the main philosophical point of reading Plato at all.[2]

The point is not confined to the 'analytic' style. There is an enjoyable passage by Collingwood in which he describes how 'the old gang of Oxford realists', as he called them, notably Prichard and Joseph, would insist on translating some ancient Greek expression as 'moral obligation' and then point out that Aristotle, or whoever it was, had an inadequate theory of moral obligation. It was like a nightmare, Collingwood said, in which one met a man who insisted on translating the Greek word for a trireme as 'steamship' and then complained that the Greeks had a defective conception of a steamship. But, in any case, the points I want to make about philosophy's engagement with history go a long way beyond its concern with its own history, though that is certainly part of it.

I have already started to talk about philosophy being this or that, and such and such being central to philosophy, and this may already have aroused suspicions of essentialism, as though philosophy had some entirely distinct and timeless nature from which various consequences could be drawn. So let me say at once that I do not want to fall back on any such idea. Indeed, I shall claim later that some of the deepest insights of modern philosophy, notably in the work of Wittgenstein, remain undeveloped—indeed, at the limit, they are rendered unintelligible—precisely because of an assumption that philosophy is something quite peculiar, which should not be confused with any other kind of study, and which needs no

---

[2] The point, in particular, of making the familiar look strange, and conversely. I have said some more about this in 'Descartes and the Historiography of Philosophy', in John Cottingham (ed.), *Reason, Will and Sensation* (Oxford: Clarendon Press, 1994). [This is now reprinted in Bernard Williams, *The Sense of the Past: Essays in the History of Philosophy*, ed. Myles Burnyeat (Princeton: Princeton University Press, 2006).—Ed.] The reference to Collingwood is to *An Autobiography* (Oxford: Clarendon Press, 1939), p. 63 seq.

other kind of study in order to understand itself. Wittgenstein in his later work influentially rejected essentialism, and spoke of family resemblances and so on, but at the same time he was obsessed—I do not think that is too strong a word—by the identity of philosophy as an enterprise which was utterly peculiar compared with other enterprises; this is so on Wittgenstein's view, whether one reads him as thinking that the compulsion to engage in it is pathological, or is part of the human condition.[3] It does not seem to me as peculiar as all that, and, in addition, we should recall the point which Wittgenstein invites us to recall about other things, that it is very various. What I have to say applies, I hope, to most of what is standardly regarded as philosophy, and I shall try to explain why that is so, but I shall not try to deduce it from the nature of philosophy as compared with other disciplines, or indeed deduce it from anything else. What I have to say, since it is itself a piece of philosophy, is an example of what I take philosophy to be, part of a more general attempt to make the best sense of our life, and so of our intellectual activities, in the situation in which we find ourselves.

2

One definite contrast to a humanistic conception of philosophy is *scientism*. I do not mean by this simply an interest or involvement in science. Philosophy should certainly be interested in the sciences and some philosophers may well be involved in them, and nothing I say is meant to deny it. Scientism is, rather, a misunderstanding of the relations between philosophy and the natural sciences which tends to assimilate philosophy to the aims, or at least the manners, of the sciences. In line with the point I have just made about the variety of philosophy, there certainly is some work in philosophy which quite properly conducts itself as an extension of the natural or mathematical sciences, because that is what it is: work in the philosophy of quantum mechanics, for instance, or in the more technical aspects of logic. But in many other areas, the assimilation is a mistake.

I do not want to say very much about what might be called 'stylistic scientism', the pretence, for instance, that the philosophy of mind is the more theoretical and less experimentally encumbered end of neurophysiology. It may be suggested that this kind of assimilation, even if it is to some extent misguided, at least encourages a certain kind of rigour, which will help to fulfil philosophy's promise of embodying a discipline. But I doubt whether this is so. On the contrary: since the scientistic philosophy

---

[3] The former view was expressed, in a vulgarized form, in the literature of 'therapeutic positivism'. The latter is richly developed in the work of Stanley Cavell.

of mind cannot embody the rigour which is in the first instance appropriate to neurophysiology, that of experimental procedures, the contributions of philosophers in this style are actually more likely to resemble another well-known phenomenon of the scientific culture, the discourse of scientists when they are off duty, the slap-dash programmatic remarks that scientists sometimes present in informal talks. Those remarks are often very interesting, but that is because they are the remarks of scientists, standing back from what they ordinarily do. There is not much reason to expect as much interest in the remarks of philosophers who are not taking a holiday from anything, but whose business is identified simply as making such remarks.

A question that intrigues me and to which I do not know the answer is the relation between a scientistic view of philosophy, on the one hand, and, on the other, the well-known and highly typical style of many texts in analytic philosophy which seeks precision by total mind control, through issuing continuous and rigid interpretative directions. In a way that will be familiar to any reader of analytic philosophy, and is only too familiar to all of us who perpetrate it, this style tries to remove in advance every conceivable misunderstanding or misinterpretation or objection, including those that would occur only to the malicious or the clinically literal-minded. This activity itself is often rather mournfully equated with the boasted clarity and rigour of analytic philosophy. Now, it is perfectly reasonable that the author should consider the objections and possible misunderstandings, or at least quite a lot of them; the odd thing is that he or she should put them into the text. One might hope that the objections and possible misunderstandings could be considered and no doubt influence the text, and then, except for the most significant, they could be removed, like the scaffolding that shapes a building but does not require you after the building is finished to climb through it in order to gain access.

There is no doubt more than one force that tends to encourage this style. One is the teaching of philosophy by eristic argument, which tends to implant in philosophers an intimidatingly nit-picking superego, a blend of their most impressive teachers and their most competitive colleagues, which guides their writing by means of constant anticipations of guilt and shame. Another is the requirements of the PhD as an academic exercise, which involves the production of a quite peculiar text, which can be too easily mistaken for a book. There are demands of academic promotion, which can encourage one to make as many published pages as possible out of whatever modest idea one may have. Now none of these influences is necessarily connected with a scientistic view of philosophy, and many people who go in for this style would certainly and correctly reject any suggestion that they had that view. Indeed, an obvious example of this is a philosopher who perhaps did more than anyone else to encourage this style, G.E. Moore. However, for all that, I do not think that we should reject too quickly the thought that, when scientism is around, this style can be co-opted in the scientistic spirit. It can serve as a mimicry of scrupulous scientific procedures. People can perhaps persuade themselves that if they fuss around enough with qualifications and counter-examples, they are conducting the philosophical equivalent of a biochemical protocol.

3

But, as I said, stylistic scientism is not really the present question. There is a much more substantive issue here. Consider the following passage by Hilary Putnam from his book of Gifford Lectures, *Renewing Philosophy*:[4]

> Analytic philosophy has become increasingly dominated by the idea that science, and only science, describes the world as it is in itself, independent of perspective. To be sure, there are within analytic philosophy important figures who combat this scientism . . . Nevertheless, the idea that science leaves no room for an independent philosophical enterprise has reached the point at which leading practitioners sometimes suggest that all that is left for philosophy is to try to anticipate what the presumed scientific solutions to all metaphysical problems will eventually look like.

It is not hard to see that there is a large *non sequitur* in this. Why should the idea that science and only science describes the world as it is in itself, independent of perspective, mean that there is no independent philosophical enterprise? That would follow only on the assumption that if there is an independent philosophical enterprise, its aim is to describe the world as it is in itself, independent of perspective. And why should we accept that? I admit to being rather sensitive to this *non sequitur*, because, in the course of Putnam's book (which contains a chapter called 'Bernard Williams and the Absolute Conception of the World'), I myself am identified as someone who 'views physics as giving us the ultimate metaphysical truth . . .'.[5] Now I have never held any such view, and I agree entirely with Putnam in rejecting it. However, I have entertained the idea that science might describe the world 'as it is in itself', that is to say, give a representation of it which is to the largest possible extent independent of the local perspectives or idiosyncrasies of enquirers, a representation of the world, as I put it, 'as it is anyway'.[6] Such a representation I called in my jargon

---

[4] Cambridge MA: Harvard University Press, 1992: preface, p. x.
[5] Ibid., p. 108.
[6] *Descartes: The Project of Pure Enquiry* (Harmondsworth: Penguin, 1978), p. 64.

'the absolute conception of the world'. Whether it is attainable or not, whether the aspiration to it is even coherent, are of course highly disputable questions.

A sign that something must have gone wrong with Putnam's argument, or with mine, if not with both, is that he supposes that the idea of an absolute conception of the world must ultimately be motivated by the contradictory and incoherent aim of describing the world without describing it: as he puts it,[7] we cannot divide language into two parts, 'a part that describes the world "as it is anyway" and a part that describes our conceptual contribution.' (The ever tricky word 'our' is important, and we shall come back to it.) But my aim in introducing the notion of the absolute conception was precisely to get round the point that one cannot describe the world without describing it, and to accommodate the fundamentally Kantian insight that there simply is no conception of the world which is not conceptualized in some way or another. My idea was not that you could conceptualize the world without concepts. The idea was that when we reflect on our conceptualisation of the world, we might be able to recognize from inside it that some of our concepts and ways of representing the world are more dependent than others on our own perspective, our peculiar and local ways of apprehending things. In contrast, we might be able to identify some concepts and styles of representation which are minimally dependent on our own or any other creature's peculiar ways of apprehending the world: these would form a kind of representation that might be reached by any competent investigators of the world, even though they differed from us—that is to say, from human beings—in their sensory apparatus and, certainly, their cultural background. The objective of distinguishing such a representation of the world may possibly be incoherent, but it is certainly not motivated by the aim of transcending all description and conceptualisation

I do not want to go further today into the question whether the idea of an absolute conception is coherent.[8] I mention the matter because I think that Putnam's stick, although he has got the wrong end of it, may help us in locating a scientism in philosophy which he and I actually agree in rejecting. Putnam's basic argument against the idea of the absolute conception is that semantic relations are normative, and hence could not figure in any purely scientific conception. But describing the world involves deploying terms that have semantic relations to it: hence, it seems, Putnam's conclusion that the absolute conception is supposed to describe the world without describing it. Let us pass over the point that the argument

---

[7] *Renewing Philosophy*, p. 123.

[8] An outstanding discussion is A.W. Moore, *Points of View* (Oxford: Clarendon Press, 1997).

seems to run together two different things: on the one hand, *using* terms that have semantic relations to the world, and, on the other, *giving an account* of those semantic relations: I shall concentrate on the latter.[9] Let us also grant for the sake of the argument the principle, which is certainly disputable, that if semantic relations are normative, it follows that an account of them cannot itself figure in the absolute conception. It does not follow that the absolute conception is impossible. All that follows is that an account of semantic relations, in particular one given by the philosophy of language, would not be part of the absolute conception. But—going back for a moment to the purely *ad hominem* aspect of the argument—I never claimed that it would be; and in a related point, I said that, even if the absolute conception were attainable and it constituted knowledge of how the world was 'anyway', it was extremely doubtful that we could know that this was so.[10]

So why does Putnam assume, as he obviously does, that if there were to be an absolute conception of the world, philosophy would have to be part of it? I doubt that he was simply thrown by the Hegelian associations of the word 'absolute', with their implication that if there is absolute knowledge, then philosophy possesses it. What perhaps he does think is the conjunction of two things: first, that philosophy is as good as it gets, and is in no way inferior to science, and, second, that if there were an absolute conception of the world, a representation of it which was maximally independent of perspective, that would be better than more perspectival or locally conditioned representations of the world. Now the first of these assumptions is, as it were, half true: although philosophy is worse than natural science at some things, such as discovering the nature of the galaxies (or, if I was right about the absolute conception, representing the world as it is in itself), it is better than natural science at other things, for instance making sense of what we are trying to do in our intellectual activities. But the second assumption I have ascribed to Putnam, that if there were an absolute conception, it would somehow be better than more perspectival representations—that is simply false. Even if it were possible to give an account of the world that was minimally perspectival, it would not be particularly serviceable to us for many of our purposes, such as making sense of our intellectual or other activities, or indeed getting on with most of those activities. For those purposes—in particular, in seeking to understand ourselves—we need concepts and explanations which are rooted in

---

[9] This is the point that should be relevant to the question whether philosophy would form part of the content of the absolute conception. Moreover, if Putnam wanted to say that any statement which merely contained terms governed by normative semantic relations was itself normative, he would have to say that every statement was normative.

[10] *Descartes*, pp. 300–303.

our more local practices, our culture, and our history, and these cannot be replaced by concepts which we might share with very different investigators of the world. The slippery word 'we' here means not the inclusive 'we' which brings together as a purely abstract gathering any beings with whom human beings might conceivably communicate about the nature of the world. It means a contrastive 'we', that is to say, humans as contrasted with other possible beings; and, in the case of many human practices, it may of course mean groupings smaller than humanity as a whole.

To summarize this part of the argument, there are two mistakes to hand here. One is to suppose that just because there is an uncontentious sense in which all our conceptions are ours, it simply follows from this that they are all equally local or perspectival, and that no contrast in this respect could conceivably be drawn from inside our thought between, for instance, the concepts of physics and the concepts of politics or ethics. The other mistake is to suppose that if there is such a contrast, and one set of these concepts, those of physical science, are potentially universal in their uptake and usefulness, then it follows from this that they are somehow intrinsically superior to more local conceptions which are humanly and perhaps historically grounded. The latter is a scientistic error, and it will remain one even if it is denied that the contrast can conceivably be drawn. People who deny the contrast but hold on to the error—who believe, that is to say, that there can be no absolute conception, but that if there were, it would be better than any other representation of the world—these people are counterfactually scientistic: rather as an atheist is really religious if he thinks that since God does not exist everything is permitted.

Because Putnam assumes that if there were such a thing as an absolute conception of the world, the account of semantic relations would itself have to be part of it, he also regards as scientistic the philosophical programme, which has taken various forms, of trying to give an account of semantic relations such as reference in non-normative, scientific, terms. It might be thought there was a question whether such a programme would necessarily be scientistic, independently of Putnam's particular reasons for thinking that it would; but in fact this question seems to me to be badly posed. The issue is not whether the programme is scientistic, but whether the motivations for it are, and this itself is a less than clear question. I take it as obvious that any attempt to *reduce* semantic relations to concepts of physics is doomed. If, in reaction to that, the question simply becomes whether our account of semantic relations is to be consistent with physics, the answer had better be 'yes'. So any interesting question in this area seems to be something like this: to what extent could the behaviour of a creature be identified as linguistic behaviour, for instance that of referring to something, without that creature's belonging to a group which had something like a culture, a general set of rules which

governed itself and other creatures with which it lived? Related questions
are: is language a specifically human activity, so far as terrestrial species
are concerned, in the sense that it is necessarily tied up with the full human
range of self-conscious cultural activities? Again, at what stage of hominid
evolution might we conceive of genuine linguistic behaviour emerging?
These questions seem to me perfectly interesting questions and neither
they, nor their motivation, is scientistic. What would be scientistic would
be an *a priori* assumption that they had to have a certain kind of answer,
namely one that identified linguistic behaviour as independent of human
cultural activities in general, or, alternatively, took the differently reductive line, that cultural activities are all or mostly to be explained in terms
of natural selection. I shall not try to say any more about this aspect of
the subject here, except to repeat yet again the platitude that it is not, in
general, human cultural practices that are explained by natural selection,
but rather the universal human characteristic of having cultural practices,
and human beings' capacity to do so. It is precisely the fact that variations
and developments in cultural practices are *not* determined at an evolutionary level that makes the human characteristic of living under culture such
an extraordinary evolutionary success.

4

What are the temptations to scientism? They are various, and many of
them can be left to the sociology of academic life, but I take it that the
most basic motivations to it are tied up with a question of the intellectual
authority of philosophy. Science seems to possess intellectual authority,
and philosophy, conscious that as it is usually done it does not have scientific authority, may decide to try to share in it. Now it is a real question
whether the intellectual authority of science is not tied up with its hopes
of offering an absolute conception of the world as it is independently of
any local or peculiar perspective on it. Many scientists think so. Some
people think that this is the only intellectual authority there is. They
include, counterfactually speaking, those defenders of the humanities,
misguided in my view, who think that they have to show that nobody has
any hope of offering such a conception, including scientists: that natural
science constitutes just another part of the human conversation, so that,
leaving aside the small difference that the sciences deliver refrigerators,
weapons, medicines and so on, they are in the same boat as the humanities are.[11]

---

[11] A rather similar line was taken by some defenders of religion at the beginning of the
scientific revolution.

This way of defending the humanities seems to me doubly misguided. It is politically misguided, for if the authority of the sciences is divorced from any pretensions to offer an absolute conception, their authority will merely shift to the manifest fact of their predictive and technological successes, unmediated by any issue of where those successes come from, and the humanities will once again, in that measure, be disadvantaged. The style of defence is also intellectually misguided, for the same kind of reason that we have already met, that it assumes that offering an absolute conception is the real thing, what really matters in the direction of intellectual authority. But there is simply no reason to accept that—once again, we are left with the issue of how to make the best sense of ourselves and our activities, and that issue includes the question, indeed it focuses on the question, of how the humanities can help us in doing so.

One particular question, of course, is how to make best sense of the activity of science itself. Here the issue of history begins to come to the fore. The pursuit of science does not give any great part to its own history, and that it is a significant feature of its practice. (It is no surprise that scientistic philosophers want philosophy to follow it in this: that they think, as one philosopher I know has put it, that the history of philosophy is no more part of philosophy than the history of science is part of science.) Of course, scientific concepts have a history: but on the standard view, though the history of physics may be interesting, it has no effect on the understanding of physics itself. It is merely part of the history of discovery.

There is of course a real question of what it is for a history to be a history of discovery. One condition of its being so lies in a familiar idea, which I would put like this: the later theory, or (more generally) outlook, makes sense of itself, and of the earlier outlook, and of the transition from the earlier to the later, in such terms that both parties (the holders of the earlier outlook, and the holders of the later) have reason to recognize the transition as an improvement. I shall call an explanation which satisfies this condition *vindicatory*. In the particular case of the natural sciences, the later theory typically explains in its own terms the appearances which supported the earlier theory, and, furthermore, the earlier theory can be understood as a special or limited case of the later. But—and this is an important point—the idea that the explanation of a transition from one outlook to another is 'vindicatory' is not defined in such a way that it applies only to scientific enquiries.

Those who are sceptical about the claims of science to be moving towards an absolute conception of the world often base their doubts on the history of science. They deny that the history is really vindicatory, or, to the extent that it is, they deny that this is as significant as the standard view supposes. I shall not try to take these arguments further, though it is perhaps worth noting that those who sympathize with this scepticism need to be careful about how they express their historical conclusions. Whatever view you take of the scientific enterprise, you should resist saying, as one historian of science has incautiously said, 'the reality of quarks was the upshot of particle physicists' practice' (the 1970's is rather late for the beginning of the universe).[12]

5

Philosophy, at any rate, is thoroughly familiar with ideas which indeed, like all other ideas, have a history, but have a history which is not notably vindicatory. I shall concentrate for this part of the discussion on ethical and political concepts, though many of the considerations go wider. If we ask why we use some concepts of this kind rather than others—rather than, say, those current in an earlier time—we may deploy arguments which claim to justify our ideas against those others: ideas of equality and equal rights, for instance, against ideas of hierarchy. Alternatively, we may reflect on an historical story, of how these concepts rather than the others came to be ours: a story (simply to give it a label) of how the modern world and its special expectations came to replace the *ancien régime*. But then we reflect on the relation of this story to the arguments that we deploy against the earlier conceptions, and we realize that the story is the history of those forms of argument themselves: the forms of argument, call them liberal forms of argument, are a central part of the outlook that we accept.

If we consider how these forms of argument came to prevail, we can indeed see them as having won, but not necessarily as having won an argument. For liberal ideas to have won an argument, the representatives of the *ancien régime* would have had to have shared with the nascent liberals a conception of something that the argument was about, and not just in the obvious sense that it was about the way to live or the way to order society. They would have had to agree that there was some aim, of reason or freedom or whatever, which liberal ideas served better or of which they were a better expression, and there is not much reason, with a change as radical as this, to think that they did agree about this, at least until late in the process. The relevant ideas of freedom, reason, and so on were themselves involved in the change. If in this sense the liberals did not win an argument, then the explanations of how liberalism came to

---

[12] Andrew Pickering, *Constructing Quarks* (Edinburgh University Press, 1984). It should be said that Pickering's history does raise important questions about interpreting the 'discovery' of quarks.

prevail—that is to say, among other things, how these came to be our ideas—are not vindicatory.

The point can also be put like this. In the case of scientific change, it may occur through there being a crisis. If there is a crisis, it is agreed by all parties to be a crisis of explanation, and while they may indeed disagree over what will count as an explanation, to a considerable extent there has come to be agreement, at least within the limits of science since the eighteenth century, and this makes an important contribution to the history being vindicatory. But in the geographically extended and long-lasting and various processes by which the old political and ethical order has changed into modernity, while it was propelled by many crises, they were not in the first instance crises of explanation. They were crises of confidence or of legitimacy, and the story of how one conception rather than another came to provide the basis of a new legitimacy is not on the face of it vindicatory.

There are indeed, or have been, stories that try to vindicate historically one or another modern conception, in terms of the unfolding of reason, or a growth in enlightenment, or a fuller realization of freedom and autonomy which is a constant human objective; and there are others. Such stories are unpopular at the moment, particularly in the wide-screen versions offered by Hegel and Marx. With philosophers in our local tradition the stories are unpopular not so much in the sense that they deny them, as that they do not mention them. They do not mention them, no doubt, in part because they do not believe them, but also because it is not part of a philosophical undertaking, as locally understood, to attend to any such history. But—and this is the point I want to stress—we *must* attend to it, if we are to know what reflective attitude to take to our own conceptions. For one thing, the answer to the question whether there is a history of our conceptions that is vindicatory (if only modestly so) makes a difference to what we are doing in saying, if we do say, that the earlier conceptions were wrong. In the absence of vindicatory explanations, while you can of course say that they were wrong—who is to stop you?—the content of this is likely to be pretty thin: it conveys only the message that the earlier outlook fails by arguments the point of which is that such outlooks should fail by them. It is a good question whether a tune as thin as this is worth whistling at all.

However, this issue (the issue roughly of relativism) is not the main point. The real question concerns our philosophical attitude towards *our own* views. Even apart from questions of vindication and the consequences that this may have for comparisons of our outlook with others, philosophers cannot altogether ignore history if they are going to understand our ethical concepts at all. One reason for this is that in many cases the content of our concepts is a contingent historical phenomenon. This

is for more than one reason. To take a case on which I am presently working, the virtues associated with truthfulness, I think it is clear that while
there is a universal human need for qualities such as accuracy (the disposition to acquire true beliefs) and sincerity (the disposition to say, if anything, what one believes to be true), the forms of these dispositions and
of the motivations that they embody are culturally and historically various. If one is to understand our own view of such things, and to do so in
terms that are on anyone's view philosophical—for instance, in order to
relieve puzzlement about the basis of these values and their implications—
one must try to understand why they take certain forms here rather than
others, and one can only do that with the help of history. Moreover, there
are some such virtues, such as authenticity or integrity of a certain kind,
which are as a whole a manifestly contingent cultural development; they
would not have evolved at all if Western history had not taken a certain
course. For both these reasons, the reflective understanding of our ideas
and motivations, which I take to be by general agreement a philosophical
aim, is going to involve historical understanding. Here history helps philosophical understanding, or is part of it. Philosophy has to learn the lesson
that conceptual description (or, more specifically, analysis) is not self-suf-
ficient; and that such projects as deriving our concepts *a priori* from universal conditions of human life, though they indeed have a place (a greater
place in some areas of philosophy than others), are likely to leave unexplained many features that provoke philosophical enquiry.

6

There are other respects, however, in which historical understanding can
seem not to help the philosophical enterprise, but to get in the way of it.
If we thought that our outlook had a history which was vindicatory, we
might to that extent ignore it, precisely as scientists ignore the history of
science. (One can glimpse here the enormous and implausible assumptions made by those who think that philosophy can ignore its own history.) But if we do not believe that the history of our outlook is vindicatory, then understanding the history of our outlook may seem to interfere
with our commitment to it, and in particular with a philosophical attempt
to work within it and develop its arguments. If it is a contingent development that happens to obtain here and now, can we fully identify with it?
Is it really *ours* except in the sense that we and it happen to be in the same
place at the same time?

To some extent, this is one version of a problem that has recurred in
European thought since historical self-consciousness struck deep roots
in the early nineteenth century: a problem of reflection and commitment,

or of an external view of one's beliefs as opposed to an internal involvement with them—a problem, as it might be called, of historicist weariness and alienation. It may be a testimony to the power of this problem that so many liberal philosophers want to avoid any question of the history of their own views. It may also be significant in this connection that so much robust and influential political philosophy comes from the United States, which has no history of emerging from the *ancien régime*, since (very roughly speaking) it emerged from it by the mere act of coming into existence.

One philosopher, and indeed an American philosopher, who has raised the question within the local tradition is Richard Rorty, and he has suggested that the answer to it lies in irony:[13] that *qua* political actors we are involved in the outlook, but *qua* reflective people (for instance, as philosophers) we stand back and in a detached and rather quizzical spirit see ourselves as happening to have that attachment. The fact that '*qua*' should come so naturally into formulating this outlook shows, as almost always in philosophy, that someone is trying to separate the inseparable: in this case, the ethically inseparable, and probably the psychologically inseparable as well, unless the ironist joins the others (the outlook that Rorty calls 'common sense') and forgets about historical self-understanding altogether, in which case he can forget his irony as well, and indeed does not need it.

In fact, as it seems to me, once one goes *far enough* in recognizing contingency, the problem to which irony is supposed to provide the answer does not arise at all. What we have here is very like something that we have already met in this discussion, the phenomenon of counterfactual scientism. The supposed problem comes from the idea that a vindicatory history of our outlook is what we would really like to have, and the discovery that liberalism, in particular (but the same is true of any outlook), has the kind of contingent history that it does have is a disappointment, which leaves us with at best a second best. But, once again, why should we think that? Precisely because we are not unencumbered intelligences selecting in principle among all possible outlooks, we can accept that this outlook is ours just because of the history that has made it ours; or, more precisely, has both made us, and made the outlook as something that is ours. We are no less contingently formed than the outlook is, and the formation is significantly the same. We and our outlook are not simply in the same place at the same time. If we really understand this, deeply understand it, we can be free of what is indeed another scientistic illusion, that it is our job as rational agents to search for, or at least move as best

---

[13] *Contingency, Irony and Solidarity* (Cambridge University Press, 1989), especially chapters 3 and 4.

we can towards, a system of political and ethical ideas which would be the best from an absolute point of view, a point of view that was free of contingent historical perspective.

If we can get rid of that illusion, we shall see that there is no inherent conflict among three activities: first, the first-order activity of acting and arguing within the framework of our ideas; second, the philosophical activity of reflecting on those ideas at a more general level and trying to make better sense of them; and third, the historical activity of understanding where they came from. The activities are in various ways continuous with one another. This helps to define both intelligence in political action (because of the connection of the first with the second and the third), and also realism in political philosophy (because of the connection of the second with the first and the third). If there is a difficulty in combining the third of these activities with the first two, it is the difficulty of thinking about two things at once, not a problem in consistently taking both of them seriously.

7

In fact, we are very unlikely to be able to make complete sense of our outlook. It will be in various ways incoherent. The history may help us to understand why this should be so: for instance, the difficulties that liberalism has at the present time with ideas of autonomy can be traced in part to Enlightenment conceptions of the individual which do not fully make sense to us now. In these circumstances, we may indeed be alienated from parts of our own outlook. If the incoherence is severe enough, it will present itself to us, who hold this outlook, as a crisis of explanation: we need to have reasons for rearranging and developing our ideas in one way rather than another. At the same time, we may perhaps see the situation as a crisis of legitimation—that there is a real question whether these ideas will survive and continue to serve us. Others who do not share the outlook can see the crisis of legitimation, too, but they cannot see it as a crisis of explanation for themselves, since they did not think that our outlook made sense of things in the first place. We, however, need reasons internal to our outlook not just to solve explanatory problems, but in relation to the crisis of legitimation as well. We need them, for one thing, to explain ourselves to people who are divided between our present outlook and some contemporary active rival. If things are bad enough, those people may include ourselves.

There may be no crisis. Or if there is, there will be some elements in our outlook which are fixed points within it. We believe, for instance, that in some sense every citizen, indeed every human being—some people, more extravagantly, would say every sentient being—deserves equal consideration. Perhaps this is less a propositional belief than the schema of various arguments. But in either case it can seem, at least in its most central and unspecific form, *unhintergehbar*: there is nothing more basic in terms of which to justify it. We know that most people in the past have not shared it; we know that there are others in the world who do not share it now. But for us, it is simply there. This does not mean that we have the thought: 'for us, it is simply there.' It means that we have the thought: 'it is simply there.' (That is what it is for it to be, for us, simply there.)

With regard to these elements of our outlook, at least, a philosopher may say: the contingent history has no effect in the space of reasons (to use a fashionable phrase), so why bother about it?[14] Let us just get on with our business of making best sense of our outlook from inside it. There are several answers to this, some implicit in what I have already said. One is that philosophers reflecting on these beliefs or modes of argument may turn back to those old devices of cognitive reassurance such as 'intuition'. But if the epistemic claims implicit in such terms are to be taken seriously, then there are implications for history—they imply a *different* history. Again, what we think about these things affects our view of people who have different outlooks in the present, outlooks that present themselves as rivals to ours. To say simply that these people are wrong in our terms is to revert to the thin tune that we have already heard in the case of disapproval over the centuries. It matters why these people believe what they do; for instance, whether we can reasonably regard their outlook as simply archaic, an expression of an order which happens to have survived into an international environment in which it cannot last, socially or intellectually. This matters both for the persuasion of uncommitted parties, as I have already said, but also for making sense of the others in relation to ourselves—and hence of ourselves in relation to them. Even with regard to those elements of our outlook for which there are no further justifications, there can still be explanations which help to locate them in relation to their rivals.

Above all, historical understanding—perhaps I may now say, more broadly, social understanding—can help with the business, which is quite certainly a philosophical business, of distinguishing between different ways in which various of our ideas and procedures can seem to be such that we cannot get beyond them, that there is no conceivable alternative.

---

[14] This is (in effect) a central claim of Thomas Nagel's book *The Last Word* (Oxford University Press, 1997). His arguments bear closely on the present discussion. I have commented on them in a review of the book, *New York Review of Books* XLV, 18 (November 19, 1998).

This brings us back to Wittgenstein. Wittgenstein influentally and correctly insisted that there was an end to justifications, that at various points we run into the fact that 'this is the way we go on'. But, if I may say again something that I have said rather often before,[15] it makes a great difference who 'we' are supposed to be, and it may mean different groups in different philosophical connections. It may mean maximally, as I mentioned earlier, any creature that you and I could conceive of understanding. Or it may mean any human beings, and here universal conditions of human life, including very general psychological capacities, may be relevant. Or it may mean just those with whom you and I share much more, such as outlooks typical of modernity. Wittgenstein himself inherited from Kant a concern with the limits of understanding, from Frege and Russell an interest in the conditions of linguistic meaning, and from himself a sense of philosophy as a quite peculiar and possibly pathological enterprise. These influences guided him towards the most general questions of philosophy, and, with that, to a wide understanding of 'we', but they also conspired to make him think that philosophy had nothing to do with explanations—not merely scientific explanations (he was certainly the least scientistic of philosophers), but any explanations at all, except philosophical explanations: and they were not like other explanations, but rather like elucidations or reminders. In this sense, his ways of doing philosophy, and indeed his doubts about it, still focussed on a conception of philosophy's subject matter as being exclusively *a priori*. That is a conception which we have good reason to question, and so, indeed, did he.

Once we give up that assumption, we can take a legitimate philosophical interest in what is agreed to be a more local 'us'. But it may be said that when it is specifically this more restricted group that is in question, it cannot be that there are no conceivable alternatives. Surely the history I have been going on about is a history of alternatives? But that is a misunderstanding of what, in this context, is being said to be inconceivable. History presents alternatives only in terms of a wider 'us': it presents alternative ways, that is to say various ways, in which human beings have lived and hence can live. Indeed, in those terms we may be able to conceive, if only schematically and with difficulty, other ways in which human beings might live in the future. But that is not the point. What in this connection seem to be simply there, to carry no alternative with them, are elements of our ethical and political outlook, and in those terms there are no alternatives for us. Those elements are indeed *unhintergehbar*, in a sense that indeed involves time, but in a way special to this kind of case. We can

---

[15] See e.g. 'Wittgenstein and Idealism', reprinted in *Moral Luck* (Cambridge University Press, 1981). [This is now also reprinted in *The Sense of the Past.*—Ed.] The question of idealism is not relevant in the present context.

explore them on this side, in relation to their past, and explain them, and (if, as I have already said, we abandon scientistic illusions) we can identify with the process that led to our outlook because we can identify with its outcome. But we cannot in our thought go beyond our outlook into the future and remain identified with the result: that is to say, we cannot overcome our outlook. If a possible future that figures in those shadowy speculations does not embody some interpretation of these central elements of our outlook, then it may make empirical sense to us—we can see how someone could get there—but it makes no ethical sense to us, except as a scene of retrogression, or desolation, or loss.

It is connected with this that modern ethical and political conceptions typically do not allow for a future beyond themselves. Marxism predicted a future which was supposed to make ethical sense, but it notoriously came to an end in a static Utopia. Many liberals in their own way follow the same pattern; they go on, in this respect as with respect to the past, as though liberalism were timeless.[16] It is not a reproach to these liberals that they cannot see beyond the outer limits of what they find acceptable: no-one can do that. But it is more of a reproach that they are not interested enough in why this is so, in why their most basic convictions should seem to be, as I put it, simply there. It is part and parcel of a philosophical attitude that makes them equally uninterested in how those convictions got there.

8

I have argued that philosophy should get rid of scientistic illusions, that it should not try to behave like an extension of the natural sciences (except in the special cases where that is what it is), that it should think of itself as part of a wider humanistic enterprise of making sense of ourselves and of our activities, and that in order to answer many of its questions it needs to attend to other parts of that enterprise, in particular to history.

But someone, perhaps a young philosopher, may say: that is all very well, but even if I accept it all, doesn't it mean that there is too much that we need to know, that one can only do philosophy by being an amateur of altogether too much? Can't we just get on with it?

To him or her I can only say: I entirely see your, that is to say our, problem. I accept that analytic philosophy owes many of its successes to the principle that small and good is better than broad and bad. I accept that this involves a division of labour. I accept that you want to get on

---

[16] This needs qualification with regard to the more recent work of Rawls, which displays a stronger sense of historical contingency than was present in *A Theory of Justice*.

with it. I also admit something else, that it is typically senior philosophers who, like senior scientists, tend to muse in these expansive ways about the nature of their subject. As Nietzsche says in a marvellous passage about the philosopher and age:[17]

> It quite often happens that the old man is subject to the delusion of a great moral renewal and rebirth, and from this experience he passes judgments on the work and course of his life, as if he had only now become clear-sighted; and yet the inspiration behind this feeling of well-being and these confident judgements is not wisdom, but *weariness*.

However, there are things to be said about how one might accept the view of philosophy that I am offering, and yet get on with it. Let me end by mentioning very briefly one or two of them. One thing we need to do is not to abandon the division of labour but to reconsider it. It tends to be modelled too easily on that of the sciences, as dividing one field or area of theorising from another, but we can divide the subject up in other ways—by thinking of one given ethical idea, for instance, and the various considerations that might help one to understand it. Again, while it is certainly true that we all need to know more than we can hope to know—and that is true of philosophers who work near the sciences, or indeed in them, as well—it makes a difference what it is that you know you do not know. One may not see very far outside one's own house, but it can be very important which direction one is looking in.

Moreover, it is not only a matter of research or philosophical writing. There is the question of what impression one gives of the subject in teaching it. Most students have no interest in becoming professional philosophers. They often take away an image of philosophy as a self-contained technical subject, and this can admittedly have its own charm as something complicated which can be well or badly done, and that is not to be despised. It also in some ways makes the subject easier to teach, since it less involves trying to find out how much or how little the students know about anything else. But if we believe that philosophy might play an important part in making people think about what they are doing, then philosophy should acknowledge its connections with other ways of understanding ourselves, and if it insists on not doing so, it may seem to the student in every sense quite peculiar.

We run the risk, in fact, that the whole humanistic enterprise of trying to understand ourselves is coming to seem peculiar. For various reasons, education is being driven towards an increasing concentration on the tech-

[17] *Daybreak*, sec. 542.

nical and the commercial, to a point at which any more reflective enquiry may come to seem unnecessary and archaic, something that at best is preserved as part of the heritage industry. If that is how it is preserved, it will not be the passionate and intelligent activity that it needs to be. We all have an interest in the life of that activity—not just a shared interest, but an interest in a shared activity.

SEVENTEEN

What Might Philosophy Become?

1

If we are going to have labels in philosophy, this is a good time to have a new one, and "post-analytic philosophy" is an attractive label.[1] However, it immediately raises one or two points of intellectual policy.

First, I am sure that no time should be spent on trying to define the "analytic" that post-analytic philosophy is post-. That could lead one back to sterile controversies reminiscent of Supplementary Volumes of the *Proceedings of the Aristotelian Society* in the 1930s, with titles such as "Is Philosophy the Analysis of Commonsense?", and this would be all the more inappropriate when the analytic/synthetic distinction, on which the notion of analysis presumably rested, is less well regarded. Moreover, concentration on that particular notion will conceal powerful resources which have been deployed by analytic philosophy itself, in any ordinary understanding of what that is. An example, which explicitly illustrates the point, is Edward Craig's book *Knowledge and the State of Nature*,[2] which is pointedly subtitled *An Essay in Conceptual Synthesis*. Craig's method is to deploy a fictional (indeed, counter-possible) developmental story, rather like stories deployed in traditional political philosophy about the "origin" of the state. Fictional genealogies, as I would call them, can be very illuminating, and, as in Craig's case, they can belong to what is unequivocally analytic philosophy, while offering what is deliberately intended as an alternative to traditional analysis. I shall not try to say any more here about fictional genealogies and what they can offer, though I shall come back later to a role for real genealogies, genuine history.

Second, we do not want "post-analytic" to become the name of one style as opposed to others. The category of "our style" merely as opposed to "the other styles" is not going to do any useful work, however it is deployed; and it is equally being deployed, whether we simply defend our own style and attack theirs, or try to work terms of eirenic co-existence with them on a more or less diplomatic basis. If there is a real question for us *about* them, then—except in circumstances where it has literally

---

[1] This paper is based on an Inaugural Lecture given at the Centre for Post-Analytic Philosophy, Southampton University, in November 1997.

[2] Oxford: Clarendon Press, 1990.

and unfortunately become a matter of academic politics—it is a question raised for us *by* them, and that is a question, which we should be able to recognize anyway, of how we should understand what we are doing.

Last among these preliminary remarks, it is particularly important that "post-analytic" should not be understood in terms of the supposed distinction between analytic and continental philosophy.[3] I say this as one who is, both deniably and undeniably, an analytic philosopher: deniably, because I am disposed to deny it, and undeniably, because I suspect that few who have anything to say on the subject will accept that denial. What I do want to deny is the helpfulness of the distinction itself, and I shall mark that in particular by saying very little about it. But it is worth emphasizing that what is unhelpful in this contrast goes beyond the matter of the unfortunate labels it uses.

The labels are doubly unfortunate. First, they involve a cross-classification between the methodological and the geographical: it is like classifying cars as Japanese and front-wheel drive. But in addition, as Michael Dummett has reminded us, the geographical considerations are anyway wrong, since some of the most important original influences on analytic philosophy came from the German-speaking world.[4] But we should not suppose that the distinction would be all right if it were merely relabelled. For it is simply unclear what is supposed to be at issue between these different ways of going on in (something that may be called) philosophy: it is not obvious what it is that you would be relabelling, or to what point.

With some contemporary writers, the question is not so much whether they should be read, but where—whether in a philosophy department or in a department of literature (though of course one party or another may think some writers not worth reading at all). There are, of course, clear cases of writers who will appear on one list and not the other. But such lists are not self-explanatory. Moreover, they can be distractingly unhelpful, by the associations they impose (for instance for someone who would like to appropriate a good deal from Nietzsche, but not in ways that have much to do with Heidegger). When one tries to think of some principle or general account supposedly implicit in these lists, this raises a question of the professional identity of philosophy.

[3] David Wood, now of Vanderbilt University, has coined the helpful slogan "Post-Analytic = Post-Continental."

[4] *Origins of Analytical Philosophy* (London: Duckworth, 1993). Dummett himself, though his book claims only to discuss "Origins" of analytical philosophy, not "The Origins," does very much tend to identify the analytical style with the "linguistic turn," the method of treating language as explanatorily prior to thought. It is surely a problem for this account that the question of the priority between language and thought has itself been a central issue in analytical philosophy.

2

If people in a philosophy department are challenged about this, or challenge themselves, they will encounter and probably consult the professional self-image of philosophy. Assume that we are in a situation where our image of philosophy is one encouraged by analytic philosophy. We reflect on the virtues—the undoubted virtues—of such a philosophy: clarity, precision, checkability (or something like that), the possibilities of careful discussion and co-operation between different people. (Part of the joke about *Limited inc*[5]—a part not intended by Derrida—was Derrida's incomprehension of the very idea that people should do such a thing.) There is a concept of professional integrity—which includes all this, but also the idea that what philosophy does in this spirit it specially does (does, one may equally say, as a specialism).

Now why are these the virtues, or at least the basic and central virtues, of philosophy? One thing that will be said is that there has to be such a thing in philosophy as *getting it right*. That is certainly true, and centrally important. I have some sympathy with Richard Rorty's attempts to call in question the self-images of philosophy, and to broaden its range of reference. But he throws it all away when he ends in the position, as it seems to me that he does, in which nothing counts as getting it right.

He makes a bad inference: from the claim that there is no interesting definition of truth (which is true), via the claim that the concept of truth is not a very interesting concept (which is at least arguable), to the conclusion that trying to say something true is not as interesting as trying to say something interesting, which is false: in particular, because about most interesting things, what is interesting is that they are true.

Rorty favours a model of *conversation*[6] for the future of what used to be called philosophy; he intends it equally as a model for the future of activities which used to be called other things, such as literary criticism. (In fact, it seems to be the model for almost everything, including natural science.) But the model is not encouraging. Unless a conversation is very relentless—for instance, one between philosophers—it will not be held together by "so" or "therefore" or "but," but rather by "well then" and "that reminds me" and "come to think of it," and it is simply unclear who will stay around for conversations that supposedly inherit the role

---

[5] *Limited Inc*, ed. G. Graff (Evanston: Northwestern University Press, 1988). [It is likely that Williams specifically had in mind "Limited inc a b c . . . ," reprinted therein. (The German translation of this essay does not include this footnote, so there is no corroboration there.)—Ed.]

[6] See in particular *Contingency, Irony and Solidarity* (Cambridge: Cambridge University Press, 1989).

of philosophy, or why. In fact, it is tempting to think that the conversation model is secretly an ally of professionalization: the only people who will take part in such a conversation are those who are paid to do so. Relatedly, the model cannot possibly provide any basis for defending philosophy or more generally the humanities from those who want to exclude them from *their* conversation.

Getting it right has to be in place, and the same thing goes, indisputably, for clarity and precision. But there is more than one kind of all these things—for instance, more than one thing that can count as getting it right: it depends on what *it* is. So what is it about this particular interpretation of "getting it right" that means that writings in the analytical style end up in the philosophy syllabus, while writings in some other philosophical styles end up in the literature department?

I am not denying that there can be an answer to that question. It is part of my point that there can be more than one answer to it, and in some cases the answer may be justified. But what I want to call in question is the idea that there is a style which defines fairly clearly and uniformly across the range of philosophy what counts as clarity and precision and getting it right, and that this style has been defined by the typical procedures of analytic philosophy. People certainly have this idea. But what is the content of the notion of getting it right that goes with this idea, and where does it come from? It is hard to deny that over too much of the subject, the idea of getting it right which has gone into the self-image of analytic philosophy, and which has supported some of its exclusions, is one drawn from the natural sciences; and that the effects of this can be unhappy.

3

There are areas of philosophy very close to the sciences—philosophy of quantum mechanics, linguistics, philosophy of mathematics, probability, some philosophy of psychology (but probably less than some workers in that field suppose). In any science, there is a continuity between conceptual problems on the one hand, and empirical work and theory building on the other. In these particular fields, moreover, there are continuities between the more abstract, philosophical, aspects of conceptual problems, and the aspects that are closer to empirical work and scientific theory. So there is room for responsible philosophical theory here: something closer to scientific theory, a proposal for a reorganization of the concepts, which could be seriously discussed with someone employed in scientific work.

Philosophy has given birth to several sciences and may do so again. But in much of philosophy these relationships are not possible, and even in areas where its practices are most relevant, science can be a bad model for philosophy. We can leave aside the phenomenon of philosophy pretending to be science when it is not—the mannerisms of "e-mail philosophy," as it might be called, the familiar self-conscious and busily professional activity which plays a game of being at the cutting edge of empirical scientific progress. More seriously, there is a much more pervasive and unobtrusive scientism of style and procedure.

There are several features of natural science which, when the model is applied to philosophy, may have a baleful effect on it. One is that science does not really need to know about its own history. It is no doubt desirable that scientists should know something about their science's history, but it is not essential to their enquiries. A parallel conclusion has been drawn by some philosophers: in one prestigious American department a senior figure had a notice on his door that read, "JUST SAY NO TO THE HISTORY OF PHILOSOPHY." In one or two areas philosophy may be near enough to science for this attitude to be justified. But if so, they are an exception. In general, one must take extremely seriously Santayana's warning, that those who are ignorant of the history of philosophy are doomed to recapitulate it (not just reinventing the wheel, but reinventing the square wheel).

A second point is that science really does have an effective division of labour. It is of course true that great breakthroughs have been achieved by the transfer of skills between scientific fields: for instance, by John Maynard Smith, trained as an engineer, turning his attention to biology. But in everyday practice there are perfectly well established methods of getting local results, and even if the results are not very exciting, they are results. It follows from this that exercises involved in professional training, however run-of-the-mill, make a contribution not just to educating people in the subject, but to the subject itself.

This is not necessarily true in philosophy. It would be a bad friend of philosophy who did not admit that there is quite a lot of philosophical work that is unrewarding by any standard: unhelpful, boring, sterile. The awful fact is that some of it hardly tries to be anything else. It consists of exercises that are necessary for the structure of philosophy as providing an academic career. The professionalization of philosophy has been going on for more than a century (or longer, if you count the Middle Ages), but it is now at an unprecedented level. It undeniably brings its own deformations, and the question that Stravinsky used to ask disobligingly about much contemporary music—"Who needs it?"—can be pressed against many products of academic philosophy.

Last, there is a question of written style. Science of course displays imagination,[7] but when it does so, it tends to be creative rather than expressive. It leads to the discovery or the theory, and does not necessarily emerge in the way in which the result is expressed. Scientific writing should be clear and effective, and it can be stylish, but the question whether scientists have got it right or not is not much affected by the expressive powers of their writing. It is not necessarily so with philosophy. The traditions of the plain style that are familiar in analytic philosophy have much to be said for them, but they can become a dead weight under the influence of the scientific model. One should not approach philosophical writing in the spirit of the analytic philosopher who (in actual fact) said to another when they were trying to write a book together, "Let's get it right first and you can put the style in afterwards."

Why should we assume that it should be like this? When we turn, in particular, to moral and political philosophy, and we look at the canon of past philosophy that even analytic philosophy agrees on, does it look like this? Plato, Hobbes, Hume, Rousseau, indeed John Stuart Mill, not to go into more disputed territory: do we really suppose that their contributions to the subject are independent of the imaginative and expressive powers of their work? There is indeed the extraordinary and unparalleled case of Aristotle, who has had an immense influence on the analytic tradition's conception of what it is to get it right. But why should we even assume that these affectless treatises represent his own voice? To the extent that they do, what does the tone mean? The pictures that Aristotle gives or implies of the society he lived in are to a notable degree fictional: perhaps we should recognize the colourlessness, the lack of history, the technicality, as themselves an evasion? In any case, why should we want to sound like that? Most philosophers do not deserve their historical legacy: Plato did not deserve most sorts of Platonist, and even Hegel did not deserve many Hegelians, but Aristotle, perhaps uniquely, deserved what he got—he invented scholasticism.

As those other authors (and many others) remind us, moral and political philosophy (at least) demand more than such a style. A philosopher may need to give us a picture of life and society and the individual, and to give it in a way that integrates it with what he or she cares about. If a philosophical writer does not solve the problems of how to express those concerns adequately, or, as in many cases, does not even face those problems, he or she will have failed to carry reflection far enough. So the demand that moral and political philosophy should sound right, should

---

[7] "Of course": but cf. Lorraine Daston's excellent article. [Daston is a prolific writer and there is no way of being sure to which article Williams was referring. (The German translation of this essay does not include this footnote, so it affords no help with this problem.)—Ed.]

speak in a real voice, is not something arbitrarily imposed by those with a taste for literature, or for history, or for excitement. It follows from philosophy's ideal of reflectiveness, an ideal acknowledged in the subject's most central traditions.

Of course, there is another question about the compelling quality of the scientific model where it *is* more appropriate—and about the compelling quality of science itself. The accounts that some philosophers give of science do not adequately explain its moral power as a paradigm of the ideal of truthfulness—an ideal which they often, and passionately, evoke in vindicating the application of that paradigm to philosophical work in the analytic style. As Nietzsche said, the motive underlying this is not *I shall not be deceived* but *I will not deceive, not even myself*—"and with that we stand on moral ground."[8]

Philosophy's aims, I have suggested, require that the work sound right, and so they demand an attention to one's own words. In some dimensions, at least, this is an acknowledged ideal of the philosophical tradition, above all of analytic philosophy. Yet this attention has often been one-sided—one-eared, perhaps one might say. We encourage, rightly, a concern with whether it *is* true (and accurate, and so on), but less with whether it *rings* true. A good question, at least to start from, is whether what one has written is something that a grown-up, concerned, intelligent person might say to another about these subjects. Of course it is not the only question, and it does not always apply, since philosophy is not just ordinary conversation. Philosophy is, rather, in these fields, the extension of our most serious concerns by other means, but at least it should introduce our ordinary concerns in a humanly recognizable form. Of much philosophy purportedly about ethical or political subjects (and other kinds as well) one may reasonably ask: what if someone speaking to me actually sounded like that?

Some moral philosophy can take a different, more formal, tone for the special reason that it is directed to possible regulations. It is a commonplace that in modern societies many matters which used to be private concerns, or were conducted in private circumstances by professionals, such as medical practitioners, are now conducted in public institutions, where those involved should be publicly answerable. This can require that these decisions should be governed by statable principles. Those who discuss areas such as medical ethics are often addressing the question of what would be

---

[8] *The Gay Science*, ed. Bernard Williams, trans. Josefine Nauckhoff (Cambridge: Cambridge University Press, 2001), p. 344. I am not in the least suggesting (nor was Nietzsche) that the idea of truthfulness, in science or in philosophy, is unreal. The point is that the ideal, which plays an important part in controversies about the analytic as opposed to other styles in philosophy, is notably unexamined.

a fair, appropriate, and workable public regulation. Then *that* is what they are doing, and the style should be recognized as one possibility for philosophy, but only one among others, one that appropriately employs a legal, regulative, or political tone, as implying a change in the public order.

4

The demand on philosophy that it should listen to what it says leads to the concerns of Wittgenstein—particularly, perhaps, as interpreted by Stanley Cavell.[9] The position of Wittgenstein in relation to analytic philosophy— and, by implication, to post-analytic philosophy—is anomalous. On the one hand, he was entirely opposed to the assimilation of philosophy to science and to the very conception of philosophical theory (this is as true of the *Tractatus*, of course, as of the later work). On the other hand, he is surely, in terms of the canon, a leading figure of analytic philosophy.

This ought to be an embarrassment; and the use that is made of his presence in the canon shows that it is an embarrassment. For the most part now, Wittgenstein is assimilated to the theoretical enterprise, in philosophy of language or philosophy of mind. This is all right at the level at which any philosopher's ideas can become, in a rather indeterminate form, part of the intellectual resources of the subject. But it does not do much for those treating him as part of the canon, which involves reading some of the books, since the books (whatever historical or authorial status you attach to these writings) repeatedly make it clear that this was not what was supposed to happen to these ideas. Most of what Wittgenstein says about the nature of philosophy—its impossibility, in effect—has to be laid aside as an eccentricity.

Wittgenstein's work is not well protected against this use of it. In part, this is because the questions he worried about are indeed among central questions of analytic philosophy, and his reactions were to concerns of Frege and Russell, among others. Partly it is because practically none of the later writings is a book by him, and the reader is not helped to give the right place to the fact that he was talking to himself. And just because he was talking to himself, he did not think much about what people might do with these thoughts, and so did not prepare them against what he would have regarded as misuse.

In all these respects, it is worth saying, he differs from Nietzsche, with whom the strenuous attempts that have been made to assimilate him to the standard forms of philosophy, in any style, have been a continuous

[9] See in particular *The Claim of Reason* (Oxford: Clarendon Press, 1979), and *In Quest of the Ordinary* (Chicago: University of Chicago Press, 1988).

and salutary failure. But Nietzsche wrote his books himself (except for one which does not exist); his subject matter overlaps less with the concerns of analytic philosophy; and he had a powerful sense both of the importance and originality of what he was saying, and of the banality of those thinkers to whom he might be assimilated, and he mined or booby-trapped his works against being assimilated, so that it is only now (as he predicted) that we are beginning to have some idea of how best to read him.

There is of course a current of opinion in analytic philosophy which resists this assimilation of Wittgenstein to the theoretical enterprise. But this, typically, reveals the embarrassment in other ways. It has nothing very interesting to say about the point of such a philosophy, or why this canon is worth reading. The therapeutic model of philosophy which is recovered from some of Wittgenstein's texts does not carry conviction, above all because, granted his interests, the disease is represented as the interests of analytic philosophy itself, to which the course is otherwise inviting people; one is bound to recall Karl Kraus's famous remark about psychoanalysis being the disease for which it is itself the cure. Moreover, the idea is that philosophy is alienated from everyday consciousness, its speech from what someone would say outside philosophy: and the question must be, what this itself is taken to be. What it should not be taken to be—and this is the most important point—is merely banal conversation.

The idea that it should be understood in terms of banal conversation was a mistake made by some "ordinary language" philosophy, which identified ordinary language as the language of a life rendered ordinary by the subtraction of the imagination; and this has been carried on by some who, now, defend Wittgenstein against the assimilation of his work to theoretical philosophy. This is partly—indeed, I think, substantially—Wittgenstein's own fault. The everyday and pre-philosophical, from which philosophy is supposedly alienated, is poorly located by him. In a well-known passage[10] he writes:

> And you really get such a queer connexion when the philosopher tries to bring out the relation between name and thing by staring at an object in front of him and repeating a name (even the word "this") innumerable times. For philosophical problems arise when language *goes on holiday.*

[W]enn die Sprache feiert: there is a question about the translation. *Feiern* can mean "to celebrate," "to hold a festival," indeed "to enjoy oneself."[11]

---

[10] *Philosophical Investigations*, trans. G.E.M. Anscombe, rev. ed. (Oxford: Blackwell, 1974), emphasis in original.

[11] Cf. *Feierstag*, a public holiday. As I understand it, *feiern* does not standardly refer just to going on an ordinary holiday, or to taking a break; the central idea is perhaps that of the usual rules or expectations being relaxed.

It can also mean something like "to take it easy." So what is language supposedly doing? The contrast that Wittgenstein seems to evoke is reminiscent of the opening lines of Shakespeare's *Julius Caesar*:

> Hence! Home you idle creatures, get you home.
> Is this a holiday? What, know you not,
> Being mechanical, you ought not walk
> Upon a labouring day without the sign
> Of your profession?

But it cannot be simply that in the philosopher's strange performance language is not pursuing its ordinary profession. The philosopher's performance is alienated from ordinary life, but a public holiday, after all, is part of ordinary life. It cannot mean that for language there is no legitimate play (it is, after all, Wittgenstein who characterizes the ordinary use of language in terms of language games).

It might mean that language is doing one thing (something not very serious) when it should be doing something else. But what "should" is that? (How do we know that the words are mechanical, and that it is a labouring day?) After all, it would be possible for someone to do very much what the philosopher is doing, and it be to some recognizable and unalienated human purpose—if, perhaps, it were Petrarch saying the name "Laura" many times before a statue of Laura. If activity such as that were ruled out as an irresponsible use of language, we would be using a canon of the ordinary which would return us to the philistine banality of "ordinary language philosophy." Rather, we shall have to say: the philosopher's performance is alienated from the world (a world of which Petrarch's imagined activity, for instance, could be a part) because the purpose it supposedly has—to find the essence of the name relation—is one to which we are introduced most effectively through a use of language which has no independently recognizable human purpose or significance at all.

The famous phrase is misleading because it is not true that observing a holiday, or celebrating, or having a good time, fails to embody human purposes. Still less is it true that language is labelled in advance with the signs of its profession, that we can list what uses of language are unalienated and in that sense serious, and then recognize philosophy by contrast to those. Rather, of any use we can ask "What is language doing here?" and sometimes we shall get a good answer which is at the same time one that we would not have thought of. The philosopher's answer, when it is of the sort illustrated by Wittgenstein's example, is not a good answer, because (as Wittgenstein supposes) the best expression of the philosopher's puzzlement is to be found in uses of language which again raise the question "What is language doing here?" and receive no good answer.

This leads to an important point. In the case that Wittgenstein mentions, as with most—perhaps all—of the cases that concerned him, the uses of language that best express the philosopher's puzzlement are alienated from *every* human purpose and so can reasonably be called meaningless.[12] They are, so to speak, timelessly out of place, because they fit no conceivable human purpose, except the misguided philosophical impulse which they are supposed to illustrate. It is because philosophical compulsions of this sort are expressed through language which is alienated from *everything* that this line of thought in Wittgenstein is interpreted by Cavell in metaphysical terms. In discussing Wittgenstein, Cavell emphasizes what he takes to be ever-present possibilities of scepticism, implicit in the human condition, and the relations of those possibilities to what, misguidedly, we tend to think lies beyond the limits of our life. This indeed defines the philosophically alienated as in some way unintelligible. This is a Kantian definition, and it retains philosophy's connection with the timeless and the universal. But there are other ways in which philosophy can be alienated from human speech, and one is not helped to see this by Wittgenstein, who in his later work was struggling against just the kind of philosophy that he had created earlier, philosophy which aspired to the utmost generality.

Language which comes from philosophers, and which strikes us as offensive or inappropriate when we properly listen to it, may well not be *unintelligible*. It may rather be phony, mechanical, unengaged, or kitsch. These, significantly, are terms of appraisal for imaginative writing or the other arts, not terms of semantic diagnosis.

It is true that Cavell's own project, unlike Wittgenstein's, does often seek to engage with history or our present cultural situation, particularly through its involvement with modernism. But, granted its general presuppositions, in some part derived from the practice of Wittgenstein, this engagement is itself conducted in metaphysical terms, and this leaves room for not much more than the thought that there is something specially about the modern world that is metaphysically alienating. This then tends to impose an image of a fall from primal unity, and at this stage, it is not surprising that Heideggerian resonances are to be heard.

5

But why should we not, in urging attention to what philosophy sounds like, introduce *genuine* categories of history? What we can honestly and

---

[12] Under a broad conception of meaning, closely related to use. It is consistent with this approach to philosophy to accept (though followers of Wittgenstein tend not to do so) that there are narrower applications of "meaningless," relating to syntactic or semantic incoherence, in which the language in question here is not meaningless.

helpfully say, what can ring true, is in part a function of our time, and demands an imaginative grasp of what is alive and what is dying in our time. If this is in part a matter of history (of real history, rather than a mythical story of severance), it is even more likely that it can be conveyed only by methods that demand more imaginative and expressive resources than the standard story of analytic philosophy permits or encourages.

We should accept the idea that some of what has concerned philosophy, and does undoubtedly concern it, is the business of what is unequivocally some kind of history—an idea which in the culture of British philosophy has been taken seriously only by Collingwood and by Berlin. The so-called essence of a certain value (to take particularly the case of values) may be so schematic or indeterminate that it can be understood only by reference to particular historical formations. Nothing that has a history can be defined, as Nietzsche rightly said, and our virtues and our values certainly have a history.[13]

In a recent book, Mary Warnock argued that there could not be such a thing as feminist philosophy because philosophy was concerned only with the humanly universal.[14] There is a rather rapid reply to this argument in more or less its own terms—that among things which are humanly universal are the sorts of practices and attitudes that are the concern of feminist philosophy. But the important point is that the principle of Mary Warnock's argument must just be wrong. We know already the kinds of things that concern us when we are seized by questions in moral and political philosophy, and how can we know the ways in which those things relate to the humanly universal until we look and see?

I want to emphasize that the picture I am trying to sketch is not derived from outside philosophy. I very much prefer that we should retain the category of philosophy and situate ourselves within it, rather than pretend that an enquiry which addresses these issues with a richer and more imaginative range of resources represents "the end of philosophy." The traditions of philosophy demand that we reflect on the presuppositions of what we think and feel. The claim which I am making, from here, from inside

---

[13] *Zur Genealogie der Moral*, 2.13: "definierbar ist nur das, was keine Geschichte hat." (The context is a discussion of punishment.)

[14] *Women Philosophers* (London: Dent, 1996), pp. xxxiii–xxxiv. She also claims that to deny this (or, at least, to deny it in certain styles) is not to do philosophy: "Those who . . . argue, as postmodernists, . . . that there is no common shared world, but that we each construct our own world . . . are engaged . . . not in philosophy, but in a species of anthropology." This raises the same type of problem as the position mentioned at n. 4 above: how do we identify a philosophical question? It can hardly be that a question is philosophical if it gets an affirmative answer, and not if it gets a negative answer. (It is ironical, in relation to Mary Warnock's position, that one philosopher, perhaps the only one, to have explicitly considered this difficulty is Collingwood, with his thoroughly historicist theory of absolute presuppositions which are, precisely, not answers to questions.)

the subject, is that in certain areas, at least, this demand itself cannot be adequately met unless we go beyond the conceptions of getting it right that are too closely associated with the inexpressive models drawn, perhaps unconsciously, from the sciences.

I have suggested that this is so for at least two reasons. The very structure of our values, first, may be such as to require an historical understanding, which will involve an imaginative grasp of the past. Second, philosophy will not speak to our concerns unless it sounds right, unless the manner of the work itself expresses what the writer feels is living or alternatively derivative and phony, and that is likely to be an imaginative achievement. A failure to achieve what is required—required by the traditional aims of philosophy itself—may well show itself in failings which attract the kinds of criticism applicable to imaginative literature, not only those familiar from the standard range of philosophical criticisms.

Someone may indeed, as things are, say that a piece of philosophy is unimaginative, but usually this means that there is some line of argument that has not been explored, some theory that might have been applied, some objection that might have been turned away. But we should remember that work may be unimaginative not because it is badly argued but because it is arguing with the wrong people; not because it has missed an argument, but because it misses the historical and psychological point; not because it fails to be clever, but because it is stupid.

We can dream of a philosophy that would be thoroughly truthful and honestly helpful. This, of course, implies an impossible combination of characteristics.

It would be argumentatively well-ordered—that would be part of what made it philosophy—but it would retain the possibility, both in its content and in its manner, of being unsettling rather than reassuring. It would speak to a grown-up reader in terms that that person could recognize as worth listening to. It would need resources of expressive imagination to do almost any of the things it needed to do, but it would be likely to compel assent more of the time by the rhetoric of plain statement rather than by that of manifest imaginative association. This is not because philosophy is not literature. Some philosophy needs virtues of literature and should fear failing in ways that literature can fail. Sometimes it may even be literature, but there are only some kinds of literature it can be.

It would have to be true to the history of philosophy, or at least to some of it. It is not an empty platitude that philosophy is what the history of philosophy is the history of. It means that philosophy is an enterprise that has achieved certain things, and that there is a state of the subject. Philosophy needs to remain true to the practice of the subject, or at least be clear why it is rejecting parts of it. There are indeed professional deformations, and they are indeed severe, but distrust of them should itself be professional distrust—as one might say, Stravinskyan.

Philosophy must stand firmly by the idea that in confronting our discontents its strength lies in what it can specially bring to them, and what it can bring involves its unavoidable difficulty. Its special powers imply that what it says is always unobvious. There is more than one way of being that, and only some of them are technical (think of later Wittgenstein, or of Nietzsche). There are many true and obvious things to be said in the face of the world's horrors, and many kinds of writing can and should say those things in an obvious way—but these are not usually the things that philosophy, if it is to be helpful in its special ways, has reason to say; or if it does on occasion have reason to say those obvious things, it will be its reason for saying them that will not be obvious.

This emphasis is not just the product of a modernist prejudice on my part. Granted all the things that philosophy has to accommodate, such as its use of argument, the recognition that it must be unobvious only registers the consequence for philosophy of the general requirement that writing, if it is going to be truthful, should listen to what it is saying.

Bernard Williams:
Complete Philosophical Publications

Williams also wrote many essays on opera and many pieces of occasional journalism. The former will be published together as a book in due course. The latter, several of which are of a philosophical cast, are included in a select bibliography entitled "Bernard Williams: Writings of Political Interest" in *In the Beginning Was the Deed*, referenced below.

BOOKS

Morality: An Introduction to Ethics. New York: Harper & Row, 1972. Harmondsworth: Penguin, 1973. Cambridge: Cambridge University Press, 1976; Canto edition, with new introduction, 1993.

> German translation: *Der Begriff der Moral*. Leipzig: Reclam, 1978.
> Romanian translation: *Introducere in etica*. Bucharest: Editura Alternative, 1993.
> French translation: see *La fortune morale* (1994).
> Italian translation (of the Canto edition): *La moralità: un'introduzione all'etica*. Rome: Einaudi, 2000.
> Polish translation: *Moralność: Wprowadzenie do etyki*. Warsaw: Fundacia Aletheia, 2000.

Problems of the Self: Philosophical Papers 1956–1972. Cambridge: Cambridge University Press, 1973.

> German translation: *Probleme des Selbst*. Leipzig: Reclam, 1978.
> Spanish translation: *Problemas del yo*. Mexico City: Universidad Nacional Autónoma de México, 1986.
> Italian translation: *Problemi dell'io*. Milan: Il Saggiatore, 1990.

A Critique of Utilitarianism. In *Utilitarianism: For and Against*, by J.J.C. Smart and Bernard Williams. Cambridge: Cambridge University Press, 1973.

> German translation: *Kritik des Utilitarismus*. Frankfurt am Main: Klostermann, 1979.
> Spanish translation: *Utilitarismo: pro y contra*. Madrid: Tecnos, 1981.
> Italian translation: *Utilitarismo: un confronto*. Naples: Bibliopolis, 1985.
> French translation: *Utilitarisme: le pour et le contre*. Le Champ Ethique. Geneva: Labor et Fides, 1997.

Descartes: The Project of Pure Enquiry. Harmondsworth: Penguin; Hassocks: Harvester Press, 1978. Reprinted with a new introduction by John Cottingham, London: Routledge, 2005.

> German translation: *Descartes: Das Vorhaben der reinen philosophischen Untersuchung*. Frankfurt am Main: Athenaeum, 1981.

Spanish translation: *Descartes: el proyecto de la investigacion pura.* Mexico City: Universidad Nacional Autónoma de México, 1995.

Moral Luck: Philosophical Papers 1973–1980. Cambridge: Cambridge University Press, 1981.

German translation: *Moralischer Zufall.* Königstein: Hain, 1984.

Italian translation: *Sorte morale.* Milan: Il Saggiatore-Mondadori, 1987.

Spanish translation: *La fortuna moral.* Mexico City: Universidad Nacional Autónoma de México, 1993.

Ethics and the Limits of Philosophy. London: Fontana Books; Cambridge: Harvard University Press, 1985.

Italian translation: *L'etica e i limiti della filosofia.* Bari: Laterza, 1987.

French translation: *L'éthique et les limites de la philosophie.* Paris: Editions Gallimard, 1990.

Japanese translation: *Ikikata ni tsuite Tetsugaku wa Nani ga Ieru ka.* Tokyo: Sangyoutosho K.K., 1993.

Spanish translation: *La etica y los limites de la filosofia.* Caracas: Monte Avila Editores, 1997.

German translation: *Ethik und die Grenzen der Philosophie.* Hamburg: Rotbuch Verlag, 1999.

Shame and Necessity. Sather Classical Lectures, vol. 57. Berkeley and Los Angeles: University of California Press, 1993.

French translation: *La honte et la nécessité.* Presses Universitaires de France, 1997.

German translation: *Scham, Schuld und Notwendigkeit.* Polis, vol. 1. Berlin: Akademie Verlag, 2000.

La fortune morale. Paris: Presses Universitaires de France, 1994. (= *Morality* + selections from *Problems of the Self, Moral Luck,* and *Making Sense of Humanity.*)

Making Sense of Humanity and Other Philosophical Papers 1982–1993. Cambridge: Cambridge University Press, 1995.

Der Wert der Wahrheit. Translated by Joachim Schulte. Vienna: Passagen Verlag, 1998.

Plato: The Invention of Philosophy. London: Phoenix/Orion, 1998. Reprinted in *The Sense of the Past* (2006), details below.

Ile wolności powinna mieć wola? Warsaw: Fundacia Aletheia, 1999. (= Polish translation of selected papers.)

Truth and Truthfulness: An Essay in Genealogy. Princeton: Princeton University Press, 2002.

German translation: *Wahrheit und Wahrhaftigeit.* Frankfurt am Main: Surhrkamp, 2003.

Italian translation: *Genealogia della verità: storia e virtù del dire il vero.* Rome: Fazi Editore, 2005.

French translation: Title still unknown. Paris: Editions Gallimard, 2005.

In the Beginning Was the Deed: Realism and Moralism in Political Argument. Edited by Geoffrey Hawthorn. Princeton: Princeton University Press, 2005.

The Sense of the Past: Essays in the History of Philosophy. Edited by Myles Burnyeat. Princeton: Princeton University Press, 2006.

Philosophy as a Humanistic Discipline. Edited by A. W. Moore. Princeton: Princeton University Press, 2006.

BOOKS EDITED

(With A.C. Montefiore.) *British Analytical Philosophy*. London: Routledge, 1966.
  Italian translation: *Filosofia analitica inglese*. Rome: Lerici 1967.
(With A. K. Sen.) *Utilitarianism and Beyond*. Cambridge: Cambridge University Press, 1982.
  Italian translation: *Utilitarismo e oltre*. Milan: Il Saggiatore, 1984.

ARTICLES

In general, does not include references to reprints of articles, except in

[PS]: *Problems of the Self*
[ML]: *Moral Luck*
[MSH]: *Making Sense of Humanity*
[IBD]: *In the Beginning Was the Deed*
[SP]: *The Sense of the Past*
[PHD]: *Philosophy as a Humanistic Discipline*

"Tertullian's Paradox." In *New Essays in Philosophical Theology*, edited by Anthony Flew and Alasdair Macintyre. London: SCM Press, 1955. [PHD]
"Personal Identity and Individuation." *Proceedings of the Aristotelian Society* 57 (1956–57). [PS]
"Metaphysical Arguments." In *The Nature of Metaphysics*, edited by D. F. Pears. London: Macmillan, 1957. [PHD]
"Pleasure and Belief." *Proceedings of the Aristotelian Society*, suppl. vol. 33 (1959). [PHD]
"Descartes." In *A Dictionary of Philosophy and Philosophers*, edited by J. O. Urmson. London: Hutchinson, 1960.
"Personal Identity and Bodily Continuity—a Reply." *Analysis* 21 (1960). [PS]
"Mr Strawson on Individuals." *Philosophy* 36 (1961). [PS]
"The Individual Reason." *The Listener*, November 16, 1961.
"Democracy and Ideology." *Political Quarterly* 32 (1961).
"The Idea of Equality." In *Politics, Philosophy and Society*, edited by Peter Laslett and W. G. Runciman. Oxford: Blackwell, 1962. [PS and IBD]
"Aristotle on the Good: A Formal Sketch." *Philosophical Quarterly* 12 (1962). [SP]
"La certitude du *cogito*." In *Cahiers du Royaumont*, vol. 4. Paris: Editions de Minuit, 1962.
  English text: "The Certainty of the *Cogito*." In *Descartes: A Collection of Critical Essays*, edited by W. Doney. New York: Doubleday, 1967.

"Freedom and the Will," with a Postscript. In *Freedom and the Will*, edited by D. F. Pears. London: Macmillan, 1963.

"Imperative Inference." *Analysis*, suppl. vol. 23 (1963). [*PS*]

"Hume on Religion." In *David Hume: A Symposium*, edited by D. F. Pears. London: Macmillan, 1963. [*SP*]

"Ethical Consistency." *Proceedings of the Aristotelian Society*, suppl. vol. 39 (1965). [*PS*]

"Morality and the Emotions." Inaugural Lecture, Bedford College, London, 1965. Reprinted in *Morality and Moral Reasoning: Five Essays in Ethics*, edited by J. Casey. London: Methuen, 1971. [*PS*]

"Imagination and the Self." British Academy Annual Philosophical Lecture, 1966. [*PS*]

"Consistency and Realism." *Proceedings of the Aristotelian Society*, suppl. vol. 40 (1966). [*PS*]

"Descartes." In *The Encyclopedia of Philosophy*, edited by P. Edwards. New York: Macmillan and Free Press; London: Collier-Macmillan, 1967.

"Hampshire, S. N." In ibid.

"Rationalism." In ibid.

"Knowledge and Meaning in the Philosophy of Mind." *Philosophical Review* 79 (1968). [*PS*]

"Has 'God' a Meaning?" *Question* 1 (1968).
> German translation: "Der unverzichtbare Gehalt des christlichen Glaubens." In *Glaube und Vernunft*, edited by N. Hoerster. Munich: Deutsche Taschenbuch Verlag, 1979. Leipzig: Reclam, 1985.

"Descartes' Ontological Argument: A Comment." In *Fact and Existence*, edited by J. Margolis. Oxford: Blackwell, 1969.

"Existence-Assumptions in Practical Thinking: Reply to Körner." In ibid.

"Philosophy." In *General Education: A Symposium on the Teaching of Non-Specialists*, edited by Michael Yudkin. Harmondsworth: Penguin, 1969.

"The Self and the Future." *Philosophical Review* 79 (1970). [*PS*]

"Are Persons Bodies?" In *The Philosophy of the Body: Rejections of Cartesian Dualism*, edited by S. Spicker. Chicago: Quadrangle Books, 1970. [*PS*]

"Genetics and Moral Responsibility." In *Morals and Medicine*. London: BBC Publications, 1970.

"Deciding to Believe." In *Language, Belief, and Metaphysics*, edited by H. E. Kiefer and M. K. Munitz. Albany: State University of New York Press, 1970. [*PS*]

"The Temporal Ordering of Perceptions and Reactions: Reply to O'Shaughnessy." In *Perception: A Philosophical Symposium*, edited by F. Sibley. London: Methuen, 1971.

"Conversation on Moral Philosophy." In *Modern British Philosophy*, edited by B. Magee. London: Secker and Warburg, 1971.

"Knowledge and Reasons." In *Problems in the Theory of Knowledge*, edited by G. H. von Wright. The Hague: Martinus Nijhoff, 1972. [*PHD*]

"The Analogy of City and Soul in Plato's *Republic*." In *Exegesis and Argument: Studies in Greek Philosophy. Essays Presented to Gregory Vlastos*, edited by

E. N. Lee, A.P.D. Mourelatos, and R. M. Rorty. The Hague: Martinus Nijhoff, 1973. [*SP*]

"The Makropoulos Case: Reflections on the Tedium of Immortality." [*PS*]

"Egoism and Altruism." [*PS*]

Remarks in *The Law and Ethics of AIDS and Embryo Transfer*. CIBA Foundation Symposium 17. Amsterdam: Elsevier/North-Holland, 1973.

"Wittgenstein and Idealism." In *Understanding Wittgenstein*, edited by Godfrey Vesey. Royal Institute of Philosophy Lectures 7. London: Macmillan, 1974. [*ML* and *SP*]

"The Truth in Relativism." *Proceedings of the Aristotelian Society* 75 (1974–75). [*ML*]

"Rawls and Pascal's Wager." *Cambridge Review*, February 28, 1975. [*ML*]

"Persons, Character and Morality." In *The Identities of Persons*, edited by A. Rorty. Berkeley and Los Angeles: University of California Press, 1976. [*ML*]

"Utilitarianism and Moral Self-Indulgence." In *Contemporary British Philosophy*, edited by H. D. Lewis. Ser. 4. London: Allen & Unwin, 1976. [*ML*]

"Moral Luck." *Proceedings of the Aristotelian Society*, suppl. vol. 59 (1976). [*ML*]

"The Moral View of Politics." *The Listener*, June 3, 1976.

"Thinking about Abortion." *The Listener*, September 1, 1977.

"Linguistic Philosophy." In *Men of Ideas*, edited by B. Magee. London: BBC Publications, 1978.

"Politics and Moral Character." In *Public and Private Morality*, edited by Stuart Hampshire. Cambridge: Cambridge University Press, 1978. [*ML*]

Introduction to Isaiah Berlin, *Concepts and Categories: Philosophical Essays*. London: Hogarth Press, 1978.

Conclusion to *Morality as a Biological Phenomenon*, edited by Gunther Stent. Berlin: Dahlem Konferenzen, 1978. Berkeley and Los Angeles: University of California Press, 1980.

[With David Wiggins.] Introduction to *Ethics, Value and Reality: Selected Papers of Aurel Kolnai*. London: Athlone, 1978.

"Another Time, Another Place, Another Person." In *Perception and Identity: Essays Presented to A. J. Ayer, with His Replies to Them*, edited by G. Macdonald. London: Macmillan, 1979. [*ML*]

"Conflicts of Values." In *The Idea of Freedom: Essays in Honour of Isaiah Berlin*, edited by A. Ryan. Oxford: Oxford University Press, 1979. [*ML*]

"Internal and External Reasons." In *Rational Action: Studies in Philosophy and Social Science*, edited by T. R. Harrison. Cambridge: Cambridge University Press, 1979. [*ML*]

"Political Philosophy and the Analytical Tradition." In *Political Theory and Political Education*, edited by M. Richter. Princeton: Princeton University Press, 1980. [*PHD*]

"Moral Obligation and the Semantics of 'Ought'." *Proceedings of the Fifth Kirchberg Wittgenstein Conference*, 1980.
    Revised version: " 'Ought' and Moral Obligation." [*ML*]

"L'éthique et la philosophie analytique." *Critique* (Paris), August–September 1980.

"Philosophy." In *The Legacy of Greece: A New Appraisal*, edited by M. Finley. Oxford: Oxford University Press, 1981. [*SP*]

"Justice as a Virtue." In *Essays on Aristotle's Ethics*, edited by A. Rorty. Berkeley and Los Angeles: University of California Press, 1981. [*ML* and *SP*]

"Practical Necessity." In *Philosophical Frontiers of Christian Theology: Essays Presented to Donald Mackinnon*, edited by S. Sutherland and B. Hebblethwaite. Cambridge: Cambridge University Press, 1982. [*ML*]

"Cratylus' Theory of Names and Its Refutation." In *Language and Logos: Studies in Ancient Greek Philosophy Presented to G.E.L. Owen*, edited by M. Schofield and M. Nussbaum. Cambridge: Cambridge University Press, 1982. [*SP*]

"The Point of View of the Universe: Sidgwick and the Ambitions of Ethics." Henry Sidgwick Memorial Lecture, 1982. *Cambridge Review*, May 7, 1982. [*MSH* and *SP*]

"Evolution, Ethics, and the Representation Problem." In *Evolution from Molecules to Men*, edited by D. S. Bendall. Cambridge: Cambridge University Press, 1983. [*MSH*]

"Space Talk: The Conversation Continued." (Comment on B. Ackerman's *Social Justice in the Liberal State*.) *Ethics* 93 (1983).

"Descartes' Use of Skepticism." In *The Skeptical Tradition*, edited by Myles Burnyeat. Berkeley and Los Angeles: University of California Press, 1983. [*SP*]

"Professional Morality and Its Dispositions." In *The Good Lawyer: Lawyers' Roles and Lawyers' Ethics*, edited by David Luban. Maryland Studies in Public Philosophy. Totowa, NJ: Rowman and Allenheld, 1983. [*MSH*]

"Präsuppositionen der Moralität." In *Bedingungen der Möglichkeit: "Transcendental Arguments" und Transcendentales Denken*, edited by E. Schaper and W. Vossenkuhl. Stuttgart: Klett-Cotta, 1984.

"The Scientific and the Ethical." In *Objectivity and Cultural Divergence*, edited by S. Brown. Royal Institute of Philosophy Lectures 17. Cambridge: Cambridge University Press, 1984. [Shortened version of chapter 8 of *Ethics and the Limits of Philosophy*.]

"Morality, Scepticism and the Nuclear Arms Race." In *Objections to Nuclear Defence: Philosophers on Deterrence*, edited by N. Blake and K. Pole. London: Routledge, 1984.

"Formal and Substantial Individualism." *Proceedings of the Aristotelian Society* 85 (1984–85) [*MSH*].

"Theories of Social Justice—Where Next?" In *Equality and Discrimination: Essays in Freedom and Justice*, edited by S. Guest and A. Milne. Archiv für Rechts- und Sozialphilosophie 21. Stuttgart: F. Steiner, 1985.

"Ethics and the Fabric of the World." In *Morality and Objectivity: A Tribute to J. L. Mackie*, edited by T. Honderich. London: Routledge, 1985. [*MSH*]

"What Slopes Are Slippery?" In *Moral Dilemmas in Modern Medicine*, edited by M. Lockwood. Oxford: Oxford University Press, 1985. [*MSH*]

How Free Does the Will Need to Be? The Lindley Lecture, 1985. Lawrence: University of Kansas Press, 1986. [*MSH*]

"L'intervista di *Politeia*: Bernard Williams." *Politeia* (Milan) (Winter 1986).

"Formalism and Natural Language in Moral Philosophy." In *Mérites et limites des méthodes logiques en philosophie*, edited by Jules Vuilleman. Paris: J. Vrin, for Fondation Singer-Polignac, 1986.

"Types of Moral Argument against Embryo Research." In *Human Embryo Research: Yes or No?* London: Tavistock Publications, for the CIBA Foundation, 1986. Reprinted in *BioEssays* 6 (1987).

"Hylomorphism." *Oxford Studies in Ancient Philosophy* 4 (1986). *Festschrift* for J. L. Ackrill, edited by Michael Woods. [*SP*]

Introduction to René Descartes, *Meditations on First Philosophy with Selections from the Objections and Replies*, edited by J. Cottingham. Cambridge: Cambridge University Press, 1986. [*SP*]

"Reply to Simon Blackburn" (review of *Ethics and the Limits of Philosophy*). *Philosophical Books* 27 (1986).

Comments on Amartya Sen's Tanner Lectures, 1985, in Amartya Sen, *The Standard of Living*. Cambridge: Cambridge University Press, 1987.

"The Primacy of Dispositions." In *Education and Values: The Richard Peters Lectures*, edited by Graham Haydon. London: University of London Institute of Education, 1987. [*PHD*]

"Descartes." In *The Great Philosophers: An Introduction to Western Philosophy*, edited by B. Magee. London: BBC Publications, 1987.

"The Structure of Hare's Theory." In *Hare and Critics: Essays in Moral Thinking*, edited by Douglas Seanor and N. Fotion. *Festschrift* for R. M. Hare. Oxford: Oxford University Press, 1988. [*PHD*]

"Formal Structures and Social Reality." In *Trust: Making and Breaking Co-operative Relations*, edited by Diego Gambetta. Oxford: Blackwell, 1988. [*MSH*]

"What Does Intuitionism Imply?" In *Human Agency: Language, Duty, and Value. Philosophical Essays in Honor of J. O. Urmson*, edited by J. Moravscik and C.C.W. Taylor. Stanford: Stanford University Press, 1988. [*MSH*]

"Evolutionary Theory: Epistemology and Ethics." In *Evolution and Its Influence*, edited by Alan Grafen. Herbert Spencer Lectures, 1986. Oxford: Oxford University Press, 1989. [*MSH*]

"Dworkin on Community and Critical Interests." *California Law Review* 77 (1989).

"Modernita e vita etica." In *Etica e vita quotidiana*. Bologna: Biblioteca del Mulino, 1989.
    English text: "Modernity and the Substance of Ethical Life." [*IBD*]

"Voluntary Acts and Responsible Agents." Hart Lecture, Oxford, 1987. *Oxford Journal of Legal Studies* 10 (1989). [*MSH*]

"Social Justice: The Agenda in Social Philosophy for the Nineties." *Journal of Social Philosophy* 20 (1989).

"Internal Reasons and the Obscurity of Blame." *Logos* 10 (1989). [*MSH*]

Reply to the President. *Proceedings of the Aristotelian Society* 90 (1989–90).

"Who Might I Have Been?" In *Human Genetic Information: Science, Law and Ethics*. CIBA Foundation Symposium 149. Chichester: John Wiley & Sons, 1990.
    Revised version: "Resenting One's Own Existence." [*MSH*]

"Notre vie éthique." (Extract from the preface to the French translation of *Ethics and the Limits of Philosophy*.) *Esprit*, November 11, 1990.

"The Need to Be Sceptical." *Times Literary Supplement*, February 16, 1990.

"Making Sense of Humanity." In *The Boundaries of Humanity: Humans, Animals, Machines*, edited by James Sheenan and Morton Sosna. Proceedings of Stanford University Centennial Conference, 1987. Berkeley and Los Angeles: University of California Press, 1991. [*MSH*]

"Saint-Just's Illusion: Interpretation and the Powers of Philosophy." *London Review of Books*, August 29, 1991. [*MSH*]

"Subjectivism and Toleration." In *A. J. Ayer: Memorial Essays*, edited by A. Phillips Griffiths. Berkeley and Los Angeles: University of California Press, 1992. [*PHD*]

"Must a Concern for the Environment Be Centred on Human Beings?" In *Ethics and the Environment*, edited by C.C.W. Taylor. Oxford: Corpus Christi College, 1992. [*MSH*]

"Pluralism, Community and Left Wittgensteinianism." *Common Knowledge* 1 (1992). [*IBD*]

Introduction to Plato's *Theaetetus*, translated by M. J. Levett, revised by Myles Burnyeat. Indianapolis: Hackett, 1992. [*SP*]

"Moral Incapacity." *Proceedings of the Aristotelian Society* 92 (1992–93). [*MSH*]

"Nietzsche's Minimalist Moral Psychology." *European Journal of Philosophy* 1 (1993). [*MSH and SP*]

"Who Needs Ethical Knowledge?" In *Ethics*, edited by A. P. Griffiths. Royal Institute of Philosophy Lectures, 1992. Cambridge: Cambridge University Press, 1993. [*MSH*]

"Moral Luck: A Postscript." In *Moral Luck*, edited by Daniel Statman. Albany: State University of New York Press, 1993. [*MSH*]

"Les vertus de la vérité." In *Le respect*, edited by C. Audard. Paris: Editions Autrement, 1993.

"Pagan Justice and Christian Love." In *Virtue, Love and Form: Essays in Memory of Gregory Vlastos*, edited by Terence Irwin and Martha C. Nussbaum. Edmonton: Academic Printing and Publishing, 1994. [*SP*]

"Descartes and the Historiography of Philosophy." In *Reason, Will and Sensation: Studies in Descartes's Metaphysics*, edited by John Cottingham. Oxford: Oxford University Press, 1994. [*SP*]

"The Actus Reus of Dr Caligari." *Pennsylvania Law Review* 142 (May 1994). [*PHD*]

"Replies." In *World, Mind and Ethics: Essays on the Ethical Philosophy of Bernard Williams*, edited by J.E.J. Altham and Ross Harrison. Cambridge: Cambridge University Press, 1995.

"Ethics." In *Philosophy: A Guide through the Subject*, edited by A. C. Grayling, Oxford: Oxford University Press, 1995.

"Identity and Identities." In *Identity: Essays Based on Herbert Spencer Lectures Given in the University of Oxford*, edited by Henry Harris. Oxford: Oxford University Press, 1995. [*PHD*]

"Acts and Omissions, Doing and Not Doing." In *Virtues and Reasons: Philippa Foot and Moral Theory. Essays in Honour of Philippa Foot*, edited by Rosalind

Hursthouse, Gavin Lawrence, and Warren Quinn. Oxford: Oxford University Press, 1995. [*MSH*]

"La philosophie devant l'ignorance." *Diogène* 169 (Paris: Editions Gallimard, 1995).

> English text: "Philosophy and the Understanding of Ignorance," in the corresponding English edition of *Diogenes* (Oxford: Berghahn Books). [*PHD*]

"Acting as the Virtuous Person Acts." In *Aristotle and Moral Realism*, edited by Robert Heinaman. Keeling Colloquium 1, 1994. London: UCL, 1995. [*SP*]

"A Further Introduction." In *The Blackwell Companion to Philosophy*, edited by N. Bunnin and E. P. Tsui-James. Oxford: Blackwell, 1996.

"Truth in Ethics." In *Truth in Ethics*, edited by Brad Hooker. Oxford: Blackwell, 1996.

"Censorship in a Borderless World." Faculty Lecture 16, Faculty of Arts and Social Sciences. Singapore: National University of Singapore, 1996.

"Values, Reasons, and the Theory of Persuasion." In *Ethics, Rationality and Economic Behaviour*, edited by Francesco Farina, Frank Hahn, and Stefano Vannucci. Oxford: Oxford University Press, 1996. [*PHD*]

"The Politics of Trust." In *The Geography of Identity*, edited by Patricia Yaeger. Ann Arbor: University of Michigan Press, 1996.

"Toleration: An Impossible Virtue?" In *Toleration: An Elusive Virtue*, edited by David Heyd. Princeton: Princeton University Press, 1996.

"History, Morality and the Test of Reflection." In Christine Korsgaard with others, *The Sources of Normativity*, edited by Onora O'Neill. Cambridge: Cambridge University Press, 1996.

"Truth, Politics and Self-Deception." *Social Research* 63 (1996). [*IBD*]

"*The Women of Trachis*: Fictions, Pessimism, Ethics." In *The Greeks and Us: Essays in Honor of Arthur W. H. Adkins*, edited by R. B. Louden and P. Schollmeier. Chicago: University of Chicago Press, 1996. [*SP*]

"La tolérance: question politique ou morale?" *Diogène* 176 (Paris: Editions Gallimard, 1996).

> English text: "Toleration: A Political or Moral Question?," in the corresponding English edition of *Diogenes* (Oxford: Berghahn Books) [*IBD*].

"Dallo stato di natura alla genealogia." *Studi Perugini* 2 (1996).

"Shame, Guilt and the Structure of Punishment." *Festschrift* for the Margrit Egner-Stiftung Prize. Zürich, 1997.

"Stoic Philosophy and the Emotions: Reply to Richard Sorabji." In *Aristotle and After*, edited by R. Sorabji. Bulletin of the Institute of Classical Studies, Supplement 68. London: Institute of Classical Studies, School of Advanced Study, University of London, 1997.

"Forward to Basics." In *Equality*, edited by Jane Franklin. (Discussions of the Report of the Commission on Social Justice, 1997.) London: IPPR, 1997.

"Plato against the Immoralist." In *Platons Politeia*, edited by Otfried Höffe. Berlin: Akademie Verlag, 1997. [*SP*]

"Moral Responsibility and Political Freedom." *Cambridge Law Journal* 56 (1997). [*PHD*]

"Berlin, Isaiah." In *Routledge Encyclopedia of Philosophy*, edited by Edward Craig. London: Routledge, 1998.

"Virtues and Vices." In ibid.

"Did Thucydides Invent Historical Time?" Jahrbuch 1996–97, Wissenschaftskolleg zu Berlin. Berlin: Nicolaische Verlagsbuchhandlung, 1998.
Revised version: *Representations* 19 (2001).

Foreword to Angelika Krebs, *Ethics of Nature*. Berlin: Walter de Gruyter, 1999.

"Tolerating the Intolerable." In *The Politics of Toleration in Modern Life*, edited by Susan Mendus. Edinburgh: Edinburgh University Press, 1999. Durham: Duke University Press, 2000. [*PHD*]

"In the Beginning Was the Deed." In *Deliberative Democracy and Human Rights*, edited by Harold Hongju Koh and Ronald C. Slye. New Haven: Yale University Press, 1999. [*IBD*]

"Naturalism and Genealogy." In *Morality, Reflection, and Ideology*, edited by E. Harcourt. Oxford: Oxford University Press, 2000.

"Philosophy as a Humanistic Discipline." Third Annual Royal Institute of Philosophy Lecture, 2000. *Philosophy* 75 (2000). [*PHD*]

"Die Zukunft der Philosophie." *Deutsche Zeitschrift für Philosophie* 48 (2000).
English text: "What Might Philosophy Become?" [*PHD*]

"Understanding Homer: Literature, History and Ideal Anthropology." In *Being Human: Anthropological Universality in Transdisciplinary Perspectives*, edited by Neil Roughley. Berlin: Walter de Gruyter, 2000. [*SP*]

"Liberalism and Loss." In *The Legacy of Isaiah Berlin*, edited by Mark Lilla, Ronald Dworkin, and Robert Silvers. New York: New York Review of Books, 2001.

"Some Further Notes on Internal and External Reasons." In *Varieties of Practical Reasoning*, edited by Elijah Millgram. Cambridge: MIT Press, 2001.

"Foreword: Some Philosophical Recollections." In *Wittgensteinian Themes: Essays in Honour of David Pears*, edited by David Charles and William Child. Oxford: Oxford University Press, 2001.

"From Freedom to Liberty: The Construction of a Political Value." *Philosophy and Public Affairs* 30 (2001). [*IBD*]

Introduction to Friedrich Nietzsche, *The Gay Science*, edited by Bernard Williams, translated by Josefine Nauckhoff. Cambridge: Cambridge University Press, 2001. [*SP*]

"Why Philosophy Needs History." *London Review of Books*, October 17, 2002.

"Plato's Construction of Intrinsic Goodness." In *Perspectives on Greek Philosophy: S. V. Keeling Memorial Lectures in Ancient Philosophy 1991–2002*, edited by R. W. Sharples. London: Ashgate, 2003. [*SP*]

"Relativism, History, and the Existence of Values." In Joseph Raz et al., *The Practice of Value*, edited by R. Jay Wallace. Oxford: Oxford University Press, 2003.

"Unerträgliches Leiden." In *Zum Glück*, edited by Susan Neiman and Matthias Kroß. Berlin: Akademie Verlag, 2004.
English text: "Unbearable Suffering." [*SP*]

"Realism and Moralism in Political Theory." [*IBD*]

"The Liberalism of Fear." [*IBD*]

"Human Rights and Relativism." [*IBD*]

"Conflicts of Liberty and Equality." [*IBD*]

"Censorship." [*IBD*]
"Humanitarianism and the Right to Intervene." [*IBD*]
"Three Reasons for Talking about Collingwood." [SP]
"The Human Prejudice." [*PHD*]

SELECTED REVIEWS

Moral Judgement, by D. Daiches Raphael. *Mind* (1957).

The Contemplative Activity, by Pepita Haezrahi. *Mind* (1957).

Language and the Pursuit of Truth, by John Wilson. *Times Literary Supplement*, January 11, 1957 (published anonymously).

The Revolution in Philosophy, by A. J. Ayer et al., edited by G. Ryle. *Philosophy* (1958).

Aesthetics and Criticism, by H. Osborne. *Mind* (1958).

Plato Today, by R.H.S. Crossman. *Spectator*, July 11, 1959.

English Philosophy since 1900, by G. J. Warnock. *Philosophy* (1959).

The Four Loves, by C. S. Lewis. *Spectator*, April 1, 1960.

The Forms of Things Unknown, by Herbert Read. *Spectator*, July 29, 1960.

Descartes, *Discourse on Method*, translated by A. Wollaston. *Spectator*, August 26, 1960.

The Liberal Hour, by J. K. Galbraith; *Kennedy or Nixon?*, by Arthur Schlesinger, Jr. *Spectator*, November 4, 1960.

Thought and Action, by Stuart Hampshire. *Encounter* (1960).

Ethics since 1900, by Mary Warnock. *Philosophical Books* (1960).

Sketch for a Theory of the Emotions. by J.-P. Sartre. *Spectator*, August 3, 1962.

Sense and Sensibilia: Philosophical Essays, by J. L. Austin. *Oxford Magazine*, December 6, 1962.

The Concept of a Person, by A. J. Ayer. *New Statesman*, September 27, 1963.

Morals and Markets, by H. B. Acton. *Guardian*, April 1, 1971.

Responsibility, by Jonathan Glover. *Mental Health* (1971).

Education and the Development of Reason, edited by R. F. Deardon, P. H. Hirst, and R. S. Peters. *Times Literary Supplement*, April 1972.

A Theory of Justice, by John Rawls. *Spectator*, June 22, 1972.

Beyond Freedom and Justice, by B. F. Skinner. *Observer*, March 1972.

Essays on Austin, edited by G. J. Warnock and J. O. Urmson. *New Statesman*, August 31, 1973.

What Computers Cannot Do, by Hubert Dreyfus. *New York Review*, October 1973.

Essays on Wisdom, edited by Renford Bambrough. *Times Literary Supplement*, August 31, 1974.

The Socialist Idea, edited by Stuart Hampshire and L. Kolakowski. *Observer*, January 5, 1975.

Anarchy, State, and Utopia, by R. Nozick. *Times Literary Supplement*, January 17, 1975.

The Life of Bertrand Russell, by R. W. Clark; *The Tamarisk Tree: My Quest for Liberty and Love*, by Dora Russell; *My Father Bertrand Russell*, by Katharine Tait; and *Bertrand Russell*, by A. J. Ayer. *New York Review*, March 4, 1976.

Ethics of Fetal Research, by Paul Ramsey. *Times Literary Supplement*, September 5, 1975.

The Selfish Gene, by R. Dawkins. *New Scientist*, November 4, 1976.

"Where Chomsky Stands." *New York Review*, November 11, 1976.

The Fire and the Sun, by Iris Murdoch. *New Statesman*, August 5, 1977.

Moore: G. E. Moore and the Cambridge Apostles, by Paul Levy. *Observer*, October 28, 1979.

Thinking, by G. Ryle, edited by K. Kolenda. *London Review of Books*, October 1979.

Life Chances, by R. Dahrendorf. *Observer*, January 27, 1980.

Rubbish Theory, by Michael Thompson. *London Review of Books*, February 1980.

Lying, by Sissela Bok. *Political Quarterly* (1980).

Logic and Society and *Ulysses and the Sirens*, by Jon Elster. *London Review of Books*, May 1, 1980.

The Culture of Narcissism, by Christopher Lasch; *Nihilism and Culture*, by Johan Goudsblom. *London Review of Books*, July 17, 1980.

Religion and Public Doctrine in England, by M. Cowling. *London Review of Books*, April 2, 1981.

Nietzsche on Tragedy, by M. S. Silk; *Nietzsche: A Critical Life*, by Ronald Hayman; *Nietzsche, Volume I: The Will to Power as Art*, by Martin Heidegger, translated by David Farrell. *London Review of Books*, May 1981.

After Virtue, by A. MacIntyre. *Sunday Times*, November 22, 1981.

Philosophical Explanations, by R. Nozick. *New York Review of Books*, February 18, 1982.

The Miracle of Theism, by John Mackie. *Times Literary Supplement*, March 11, 1983.

Offensive Literature, by John Sutherland. *London Review of Books*, March 17, 1983.

Consequences of Pragmatism, by R. Rorty. *New York Review of Books*, April 28, 1983. Reprinted in *Reading Rorty*, edited by Alan Malachowski. Oxford: Blackwell, 1990.

Collected Papers of Bertrand Russell, vol. 1. *Observer*, January 22, 1984.

Reasons and Persons, by D. Parfit. *London Review of Books*, June 7, 1984.

Critical Philosophy and *Journal of Applied Philosophy*. *Times Higher Education Supplement*, June 15, 1984.

Wickedness, by Mary Midgley. *Observer*, October 7, 1984.

Secrets, by Sissela Bok; *The Secrets File*, by D. Wilson. *London Review of Books*, October 18, 1984.

Choice and Consequence, by Thomas Schelling. *Economics and Philosophy* (1985).

Privacy: Studies in Social and Cultural History, by Barrington Moore, Jr. *New York Review of Books*, April 25, 1985.

Ordinary Vices, by Judith Shklar; *Immorality*, by Ronald Milo. *London Review of Books*, June 6, 1985.

The Right to Know, by Clive Ponting; *The Price of Freedom*, by Judith Cook. *Times Literary Supplement*, October 4, 1985.

Taking Sides, by Michael Harrington. *New York Times Book Review* [mid-1980s?].

A Matter of Principle, by Ronald Dworkin. *London Review of Books*, April 17, 1986.

The View from Nowhere, by Thomas Nagel. *London Review of Books*, August 7, 1986.

The Society of Mind, by Marvin Minsky. *New York Review of Books*, 1987.

Whose Justice? Which Rationality? by Alasdair MacIntyre. *Los Angeles Tribune*, 1988.

Reprint: *London Review of Books*, January 5, 1989.

Intellectuals, by Paul Johnson. *New York Review of Books*, July 20, 1989.

Contingency, Irony, and Solidarity, by Richard Rorty. *London Review of Books*, November 1989.

Sources of the Self, by Charles Taylor. *New York Review of Books*, October 1990.

Realism with a Human Face, by Hilary Putnam. *London Review of Books*, February 7, 1991.

The Saturated Self, by Kenneth J. Gergen. *New York Times*, June 23, 1991.

Political Liberalism, by John Rawls. *London Review of Books*, May 13, 1993.

Inequality Reexamined, by Amartya Sen. *London Review of Books*, November 1993.

The Therapy of Desire, by Martha Nussbaum. *London Review of Books*, October 1994.

Several books by Umberto Eco. *New York Review of Books*, February 2, 1995.

The Last Word, by Thomas Nagel. *New York Review of Books*, November 19, 1998.